华东师范大学外语学院学术文库

赵刚　陈翔＿著

曲径通幽

汉语新词英译析辨百例

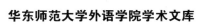

上海三联书店

前　言

　　2007 年 7 月，《辞书研究》编辑部的陆嘉琪老师致电于我，约我为该刊即将开设的"新词语新说"一栏撰写汉语新词英译的短文，要求是每篇千字余，集中讨论一个汉语新词的英译，内容包括该词的释义、现有译文及其问题，以及新译和如此翻译的理由。此后，从 2007 年第 3 期的"走光"一文开始，该刊陆续刊登了我所撰写的七八篇短文。这些，以及我近年来在《西安外国语学院学报》、《中国科技术语》、《东方翻译》、《双语词典新论》、《上海翻译》等刊物上发表的有关汉语新词英译的其他文章，最终催生了我撰写百篇短文，汇集成书的想法。

　　几乎同时，现任《英语世界》杂志社副社长兼副主编的魏令查学兄又约我为商务印书馆在国外出版发行的杂志《汉语世界》翻译一些稿子，而我负责翻译的那部分又恰好是该刊的"流行新词语解读"一栏，每期约有四到五个新词，不但有其释义，也有用例。两年下来，也积累了不少资料，同时更坚定了我写完该书的信心。

　　此外，关于《新世纪汉英大词典》（惠宇教授主编，外语教学与研究出版社 2003 年出版）的修订事宜也为该书的最终成稿奠定了基础。2006 年和 2008 年，外语教学与研究出版社辞书部经理姚红女士与我在上海两度会面，商讨《新世纪汉英大词典》的修订事宜。尽管该项目由于姚女士中途出国及其他种种原因，至今未能正式展开，但由于我们当时商定修订的一个重要方面就是增加新词新意，所以这几年来我一直非常重视汉语新词、新意、新译的收集、整理，收录了汉语新词共计 6000 余条,而本书所论及的新词大部分是从这 6000 余条中精选而出的。

　　啰啰嗦嗦讲了这么多,其实就是想说明一点:写作本书并非一时冲动,而是笔者近些年来所思所想的一个积累和总结。下面再简要谈谈该书的选词标准、短文框架、特色,以及适用的读者群体,权作导读。

　　1. 选词原则

　　本书共涉及汉语新词 100 条,这 100 条中既有尚未见诸汉语词典的"潮词"、"热词",也有虽然不"潮"不"热",但在一般读者眼中仍为新词的词汇,还有 2005 年版《现代汉语词典》已经收录,但诸汉英词典却漏收的新词。第一类如"型男"、"脑残"、"搞定"、"熟女"、"负翁"、"雷人"、"裸婚"等;第二类如"(耍)大牌"、"煲电话粥"、"充电"、"低调"、"信息化"、"艳遇"等;第三类如"傲人"、"惹火"、"代言"等。此外,本书还收录了个别虽算不上"新词",但却对新词翻译具有启发和指导的词,如"包公"、"休渔"、"黑车"等,以及一些法律方面的新词,如"亲子鉴定"、"单位犯罪"、"代位继承"等。

　　所有这些词汇几乎都有一个共同的特点,那就是其目前的英译均有不当甚至错误之处:有些译文完全错误,如"房奴"、"音乐电视"、"家庭影院"、"法治"、"城市病"、"艳遇"等;有些则值得商榷,如"宅男"、"蜗居"、"月光族"、"撞衫"、"面子工程"等;而另外一些译文则过于泛化,难以反映出原语词汇形象的外在和深刻的内涵,如"煲电话粥"、"晒工资"等;还有一些则译文不规范,如"署名权"、"买壳上市"、"无效婚姻"等。正是由于这些译文中所存在的这样或那样的问题,才构成了本书深入"探微"的基础。

　　另外,本书不收录那些已经具有公认的正确、规范译文的新词,如"博客"、"团购"、"星探"、"和谐社会"、"达人"、"司法救助"等;也不收录目前已经有大量学术讨论的新词,如"医托"、"山寨"、"擦边球"等;更不收录那些诸如"给力"之类虽使用广泛,但明显已呈现滥用态势的新词;但收录部分虽有正确译文,但还有其他种种现版汉英词典尚未"发掘"的地道英文表达的新词,如"AA 制"、"回头率"、"惹火"等。

　　2. 短文框架

　　本书由一篇自序和 100 篇短文构成。自序主要探讨汉语新词英译的现状、问题和出路,是笔者在汉语新词英译方面的一些心得。短文则辨析和论证这 100 个新词的英译状况。每篇短文基本上由新词释义、现有译文及其分析、新译文及其论证这三部分组成。新词释义一节是讨论该新词英译的基础,通常借鉴但不照抄《现代汉语词典》的释义,而是根据该词在语言中的实际使用情况对词典释义进行修正;对于那些汉语词典尚未收录的新词,则参考"百度百科"、"互动百科"或相关学术论文中的定义;对于那些网络百科和纸质词典均未收录的新词,则先列举其应用实例,再归纳总结出其具体含义。现有译文及其分析一节则列举目前各类汉英词典对该词的翻译,然后分析指出这些译文的问题所在,有些新词汉英词典尚未收录,则使用 *China Daily*"英语点津"栏目中的译文作为现有译文,然后在此基础上进行讨论;此外,还有一些新词的现有译文取自诸如 *China Daily* BBS 等上面网友所建议的译文。在新译文及其论证一节,笔者首先提出自己的译文,然后援引相关翻译理论或英美原版资料佐证译文的合理性。所引材料除少部分出自诸如 *China Daily*、*People's Daily Online*、*Shanghai Daily* 等国内权威英文媒体外,其他均来自英文报刊、杂志或书籍,以确保引文语言的权威性。此外,一者为了行文的简洁,二者考虑到读者只需输入引文,即可在网络上找到该引文的全文,本书中只有部分引文标注了来源网址和具体的出版年份及日期,大部分引文则只标明了来源媒体,未标注具体的网址及出版的年月日。还有一些地方则直接说明引文源于原版英文媒体和刊物,未标注其具体出处。

3. **本书的特色**

本书的特色可归纳为以下几点:

(1) 选词新颖:本书所收录的 100 个新词,绝大部分都是近些年来汉语中出现并广泛使用的最新词汇,如"群租"、"异性合租"、"霸王条款"、"私房菜"、"绝杀"、"色友"、"大牌"、"新锐"、"学区房"、"留守儿童"、"眼缘"、"上位"、"惹火"等等。

(2) 论述深入:本书对新词释义及其英译的讨论尤为详尽深入,从语言实例中对现有的释义进行分析、修正,以期文中所提供的释义能够更准确地体现该词的意义和用法;另外,笔者对现有的译文从翻译学(有时兼从词典学)的角度逐个进行批判性研究,指出其中的问题,并在此基础上提出新的译文,进行深入的论证。这种带着批判性眼光看待问题,不盲信、盲从权威的论述方式,对读者具有一定的启发性。

(3) 引证广泛:本书在释义、评论、论证的各个环节大量引证,既有引自国内权威英文媒体的例证,也有引自国外主流媒体的例证,还有引自学术论文及英文小说中的例证,从而使本书的各个环节具备严谨的科学性和学术性。另外,本书中的引证还注意体现所讨论的新词在不同语境下、不同搭配中的意义和表达,读者从中可以轻松地了解到这些新词在不同场合、不同语言环境中的应用情况。

(4) 拓展丰富:本书虽只收录讨论了 100 个汉语新词的英译,但事实上却包含了数倍于这个数量的汉语新词,读者在大多数短文的拓展部分都可以见到大量与该新词相关的其他新词的用法和译法。譬如,在"裸婚"一文中,读者还可以看到"裸奔"、"裸泳"、"裸替"、"裸捐"、"裸退"、"裸聊"、"裸检"、"裸官"等词的英译;在"色友"一文中,还可以看到"色驴"的英译;在"熟女"一文中,还可以看到"轻熟女"的英译;在"多军"一文中,还可以看到"空军"、"多方"、"空方"的英译;在"法治"一文中,还可看到"人治"的英译;在"型男"一文中,还可看到"索女"、"打女"、"没女"、"超女"、"俊男"、"靓女"、"酷男"、"浪女"的英译;在"闪孕"一文中,还可看到"闪婚"、"闪离"的英译;在"按揭"一文中,还可看到"转按揭"、"倒按揭"的英译等等。凡此种种,不一而足,大大丰富了本书的内容。

(5) 行文轻松:本书所收的词汇决定了该书兼具学术性和趣味性。本书行文轻松风趣,融严谨的学术性于轻松的阐述之中,融知识性于可读性之中。这也是本书有别于其他同类著作的一个重要方面。

4. 适用的读者群

正如本书的评审人上海交通大学外国语学院胡开宝教授在其评审意见中所说,"该著作的研究成果对于翻译学、词典学、术语学和语言接触研究均具有很强的理论意义和实际价值。"本书适用于广大对翻译感兴趣的大学生,尤其适用于翻译专业的本科生和研究生,同时也可以为广大的辞书编纂人员、术语研究人员及英语教学人员提供有益的参考。

希望本书能成为一本让读者感到开卷有益的"枕边书",在轻松愉快的阅读中获取语言学习和对比的无尽乐趣。

最后,特别值得指出的是,本书的最终完成和出版,得益于许多人的帮助。首先感谢原《辞书研究》的副主编陆嘉琪先生,没有他和他在《辞书研究》中所开设的"新词语新说"栏目,我不会萌发写作此书的初衷,而陆先生给我机会,让我的数篇短文能连续发表于《辞书研究》,无疑又大大增强了我的自信心。另外,感谢华东师范大学外语学院的领导们和他们所创设的学术专著出版基金,这使本书的最后出版成为可能。我深信,他们的远见卓识必将大大推动外语学院的教学和科研发展以及青年教师的培养工作。当然,我还要感谢我的朋友郭冉以及我的研究生李理、刘志刚、荣璐璐、朱怡华、谢士波、张丹、凌艳,他/她们不辞辛苦,帮我撰写了个别条目的初稿,并审校了全书的初稿,他/她们细致入微的工作,良好的双语语感,使本书避免了不少"愚蠢的错误"(stupid mistakes)的发生。最后,我要感谢我的家人,感谢我那任劳任怨的父母、妻子,以及我那不足三岁、可爱至极的儿子。没有他们的辛勤付出和支持,此书的最终成稿可能还会遥遥无期。

当然,由于新词所固有的一些特色,如词义的未完全确定化、用法的灵活性等,以及我本人学术水平的局限和目力所及之狭窄,本书中的论述难免有不当、不全、甚至不对之处,我将为所有这些不足或不当之处承担全责。

本书对汉语新词英译的讨论和辨析,可作为引玉之砖,希望能引起学界的关注和进一步讨论,最终促进汉语新词的英译工作及汉文化的对外传播事业。

作　者
2010 年 10 月 11 日凌晨写于上海

目 录

汉语新词的英译:现状、问题及出路

(代自序)

一个新词的出现,往往揭示了一种社会现象、反映了一种社会现实、彰显了一种生活方式、折射了一种生活态度。可以说,一个新词就展现了某个特定领域内的一个全新世界。而探讨新词的翻译,无论是从文化推介的角度,翻译实践的角度还是从辞书编纂的角度,都具有现实意义,非常必要。有鉴于此,本文简要阐述目前汉语新词英译的现状和问题,并在此基础上提出一些改进汉语新词英译的建议,权作本书的一个引子。

一、汉语新词英译的现状

总体而言,汉语新词英译的现状丝毫不容乐观,这从种种英译质量堪忧的汉英新词词典和汉英词典中便可管窥一斑,更遑论那些误译、错译、硬译、随心所欲译充斥的各种其他出版物了。尽管国内有不少学者(如杨全红,2003;张健,2001/2003;金其斌,2003/2004;邵斌,2006/2008;徐昌和,2009;王逢鑫,2009 等)均撰文指出了汉语新词英译实践中存在的种种问题,但此类零星的讨论和零敲碎打式的研究方式却依然很难彻底改观目前汉语新词英译的整体状况。

另外,还有一些学者试图从理论上探讨汉语新词的英译,提出了汉语新词英译的目的论(阎瑾,2009)、实用翻译论(金其斌,2008)、等效论(梁志坚,2007)、归化论和异化论(邹星,2009;王春,2006)、文化视角论(罗宁萍,2008)等等。这些理论尽管对新词译者具有一定的启发意义,但由于新词种类繁多,用法各异,单凭某一个理论,不要说全部,即使是部分的新词英译问题也难以解决。事实上,新词译者在确定译文之前,通常总会根据所译词语的不同性状,综合考虑各种理论、策略、方法和技巧。也唯如此,译文才能在达意的基础上兼顾传神,做到形神兼备。

二、汉语新词英译的问题

经过详细考察现版的汉英新词语词典和汉英词典,笔者认为,目前汉语新词的英译主要存在以下问题:

1. 译者不负责任,随意照抄网络词典中的译文。这个问题集中体现在商务印书馆出版的一本享有盛名的汉英新词词典之中。笔者曾做过一个简单的统计,该词典中共收录了法律新词 40 个,而其中的误译竟然达到了 32 个,错误率之高,令人触目惊心! 此后,笔者更为惊讶地发现,原来该词典中条目的英译有极大一部分是一字不漏地照抄网络在线词典"dict. cn 海词"(http://dict. cn/) 中的译文。这种对待翻译不负责任的态度本就危害甚大,而当这些译文出现在由权威出版社出版发行的权威词典中时,对读者的误导则更甚。

2. 译者偷懒释译。也就是说译者不愿动脑筋去思考,不愿动手去调查,只是一味采用释译的方式处理新词的英译,或干脆不顾译文的规范和地道而直接硬译。这种情况在一些学术性刊物中表现得尤为突出,例如,《辞书研究》2006 年第 2 期"新词新义荟萃"中就把"袋鼠族"释译为"young people resembling kangaroo babies"、把"负翁"释译为"young people with a big loan from a bank"、把"啃老族"释译为"young people relying on their parents"、把"月光族"释译为"young people who spend out all their monthly income"。而《新华新词语词典》在翻译法律术语时则采纳了大量不合规范的译文和不地道的译文,如把"婚内强奸"译为"rape committed by spouse",而非规范地道的译文"marital rape";把"非法取证"译为"obtain evidence in unlawful way",而非"obtain evidence illegally";把"家庭影院"译为 family cinema,而非"home theatre";把"买壳上市"译为"go public through buying a shell",而非"reverse merger"等等。

3. 译者一味采用归化法,丝毫不考虑再现原词中所包含的丰富、生动的形象。这种情况在最新出版的《汉英词典》(第3版)中表现尤为突出,譬如把"煲电话粥"简单归化为"chat for a long time on the telephone"和"long telephone chat";把"走红"归化为"popular"和"well-known";把"惹火"归化为"eye-catching";把"晒工资"归化为"make public one's salary";把"抖包袱"的"包袱"归化为"joke";把"爆料"归化为"report (sensational news)";把"暴利"归化为"sudden huge profit";把"充电"归化为"study to acquire more knowledge"等等。这些译文严格来说或不为错,但却让人感觉索然无味,汉语新词中所包含的生动的形象或动态意义丧失殆尽,译文味同嚼蜡。究其原因,这些译文的出现大概也是由于译者只图省事或一味追求"正确",而不求"准确"。这种翻译态度同样是要不得的。

4. 译者不顾译语的可接受性一味硬译。这种情况在翻译实践中最为常见,如把"拳头产品"译为"fist product";把"名片"译为"name card";把"黑车"译为"black taxi";把"低调"译为"low-key";把"领头羊"译为"leading sheep";把"法治"译为"rule by law";把"关键先生"译为"key player";把"城市病"译为"urban disease";把"票贩子"译为"ticket broker";把"双赢"译为"win-win";把"充电"译为"recharge one's batteries";把"房奴"译为"house slave";把婚姻中的"第三者"译为"the third party"等等。这些译者丝毫不考虑译语读者是否可以接受这些"字对字直译"的译文以及这些译文可能在译语中的固有含义。如此翻译,译者痛快省事了,读者却痛苦困惑了。

5. 译者对新词的含义不求甚解,想当然地翻译。譬如,把"吊膀子"译为"(of a man) act fresh with a woman",而不知道"吊膀子"既可用于男人"吊"女人,也可用于女人"吊"男人;把"艳遇"译为"encounter with a beautiful woman",而不知道"艳遇"不但是男人的权利,也是女人的渴望;把"负翁"译为"spend-more-than-earn",而不知道中国的大部分"负翁"们赚的钱远比花的多,只是在这个物价,尤其是房价,"一飞冲天"的时代,不小心沦为"负翁"而已;把"城市病"译为"urban diseases"或"diseases typical of cities",而不知道"城市病"根本就不是"身体上的疾病"，而是一个抽象的用法，指城市森林、城市噪音、失业、城市暴力等。

6. 译者对汉语词汇及其英译的文化意义把握不准，结果出现了文化上的误读。譬如，把"蜗居"一词译为 snail's house 就存在这个问题，因为 snail 在英美文化中常常表示"缓慢"、"懒散"，而非"狭小"。因此，把汉语中表示居所狭小的"蜗居"一词按照字面译为 snail's house 不但难以唤起英美读者的共鸣，而且极有可能令其产生误解，认为"蜗居"与居所主人的懒惰或不洁有关。有鉴于此，译者在确定新词的英译文之前应仔细调查译文中所包含的文化信息，一者看译文是否包含特殊的文化含义，二者看这种文化含义是否和原语词汇的文化含义一致，切忌不假思索，随意翻译。譬如，上海世博会期间，上海世博会宣传及媒体服务指挥部志愿者部办公室经常会就一些翻译问题向笔者咨询，其中有一次就问及"小白菜"和"小蓝莓"的英译，问者云，《环球时报》将上述二词分别译为了 little cabbage 和 little blueberry，但他们却不能确认这两个译文是否可用。在回答他们的问题之前，笔者首先翻查了几本英文词典，看 cabbage 和 blueberry 这两个词在英文中是否还有什么特别的文化含义，惟有如此，才能确保译文不会引起文化误读。

7. 译者对译文和原文在文体意义和情感意义上的一致认识不清。例如，有些地方将"色友"（摄影爱好者的幽默称呼）译为 cameraman、photographer 和 lensman，就没有考虑到原语非正式的、甚至常常带有戏虐口吻的文体风格。而 *China Daily* BBS"翻译点津"中"钉子户"的译文 die-hard house-owner 则没有注意到原词的情感意义，因为 die-hard 是指那些拒不接受变化和新观点的死硬派，是一个彻头彻尾的贬义词，而"钉子户"最起码在大多数中国老百姓眼中并无贬义，否则，大家也不会为某些"钉子户"大声喝彩了。

8. 译者缺乏翻译的基本常识。譬如，大凡新词译者应该都知道，如果某个新词为"舶来品"，那在翻译时就应该尽量还其"舶来品"的本来面目，而没有必要费劲心机，另起炉灶，进行"创造性"的翻译。但有些译者对此却是只知其一，不知其二，对以上原则生搬硬套。譬如《汉英大词典》（第三版）中对"宅男"、"宅女"的英译就是一个典型的例子。不错，"宅男"和"宅女"的确来自日语词 otaku，而"宅文化"也起源于日本，但"宅男"在英译时是否就应该直接使用 otaku 这个日语词,而"宅女"是否就是日语词 otaku 和英文词 girl 的简单相加呢? 肯定不是! 因为我们很难想象在日语翻译为英语时英文译文中突然出现一个原汁原味的日语单词,这和我们在进行汉译英时不可能把汉字直接搬到英文中去是一个道理,更何况原语词汇和 otaku 之间还有文体上的差异。事实上,英美国家也有"宅男"和"宅女",但人家没有借用日语的 otaku 一词,而是用 indoors man 和 indoors woman 来表达。这样看来,新词译者不但要通晓译事,而且在翻译实践中应根据具体情况灵活处理。

当然,以上 8 点只是汉语新词英译中具有代表性的一些问题,事实上,除此之外,还有其他不少细节上的问题,值得新词译者注意。譬如有些词典中提供的译文,纯粹是译者"梦游"时的翻译,读者根本看不懂是什么意思。如把"钟点房"误译为"cloak room"(衣帽间)、把"耍大牌"译为"put on airs of a megastar"、把"另类"乱译为"completely new of fashionable type or trend"等等。还有一些译者缺乏批判精神和调查研究的精神,盲信国内"权威"的刊物和译者,不加辨别地照搬别人别处的译文。他们不知道,汉语新词英译本来就是一个隐藏很深的宝石矿,你我均有权利在这里挖掘、探索、打磨。至于谁能最后挖掘到原矿,并打磨成闪闪发光的宝石,依赖的不是挖掘者的名气,而是他的努力、执着以及打磨原矿的能力。名人名刊或许具备高超的打磨能力,但却不一定有时间、有精力去努力执着地挖掘,所以他们/它们得到的宝石也就不一定是最为耀眼的那颗了。

三、汉语新词英译的出路

如此多的问题,如此揪心的局面,是否就意味着汉语新词英译就是一个不可能完成的任务(mission impossible)呢? 当然不是! 汉语新词英译是一个大有作为的事业,但译者要突破语言和文化的障碍,最终顺利到达翻译的彼岸,还需要注意以下四点:

1. 新词译者要有高度的责任心。如果说翻译是一个要求译者有高度责任心的工作的话,新词译者则更应如此。只有那些有责任心,对读者负责,对自己负责的译者,才会锲而不舍地挖掘更好的译文,孜孜不倦地打磨现有的译文,加倍努力地验证译文的生动性以及其在译语中的可接受性。惟有如此,才能使译文形神兼备,成为真正的精品。

2. 新词译者要精通译事,但又不为形而上的翻译理论所束缚。上面说过,新词的翻译从实质上而言是一个基于翻译实践的工作,没有哪种现成的理论能够解决所有的新词翻译问题。新词译者要通晓各种翻译理论,但在翻译实践中却不能机械地照搬这些理论,而应综合考虑所译新词的意义、形象、内涵,以及译文的地道性和在译语中的可接受性,能异化的时候异化,实在不能异化则归化,能体现原词"形"的时候就要体现"形",不能体现时则需考虑原词的功能是否能够在译语中得到充分的传达。在整个翻译过程中,既要考虑等效,又要考虑"形"的传递以及文化的传播。说白了,新词译者需要通晓翻译理论,但更要能够将这些理论融合到自己的翻译实践之中。

3. 新词译者在翻译过程中要能充分利用现有的资料和工具帮助自己进行翻译。这些资料和工具既包括书面的,也包括网络的,下面主要谈谈网络资料的使用。我们所处的时代无疑可以称为"网络时代",很多工作离开网络几乎已经无法进行,而新词的翻译亦是如此! 网络上大量的中文和原版英文资料就是一个海量的语料库,既可以帮助译者确定或修正现版词典中汉语新词的意义,还可以让译者通过超链接(superlinks)对新词词义及用法的发展追根溯源,对自己的译文进行验证。很多时候,译者会发现,结合网络内和网络外的知识可以使自己的译文更为地道、确切。譬如,笔者在翻译"煲电话粥"一词时,发现张健教授已经提供了一个译文:do marathon talk on the phone,但当笔者将该译文输入 *Google* 进行验证时,却找不到一条同样的原版英文表达,后来细细思考,觉得问题在动词 do 和 talk 的搭配上,受此启发,笔者暂时将 do 省略不查,把 talk on the phone 换为了 phone conversation,然后进行搜索,网络上随即出现了大量这样的表达,足见该译文为地道的英文。此外,既然是 conversation,那么与其搭配的应该是 have a converstaion 或 carry on a conversation,所以笔者再将 have/carry on a marathon phone conversation 加上双引号,进行网络定点搜索,结果也发现了大量这样的表达法。至此,"煲电话粥"的英译文基本确定,为 have/carry on a

marathon phone conversation。新译文既形象又地道,远胜于《汉英词典》(第三版)中的译文"chat for a long time on the telephone"和"long telephone chat"。网络的助译作用由此可见一斑！除此之外,新词译者还必须认识到"山外有山,人外有人",网络上有些网友的翻译能力不见得就比我们这些"专业人员"差,一些 BBS 上面出现的译文甚至堪称绝妙,或至少可以为译者提供一些继续深入调查的线索。新词译者如能充分利用这些网络资源,同时对其去粗存精,深入考察和研究,定能找到较为理想的译文。

4. 新词译者要用批判的眼光看待现有的译文,不能盲从"权威"。这一点其实是做学问的一个基本要求,很难想象一个人云亦云的人能在学术上有所建树。新词英译亦是如此。译者对国内那些权威刊物、权威辞书或权威人物所提供的译文不能简单盲从,因为人非圣贤,孰能无过。只有对这些权威的译文持批判性接受的态度,才能发现其不足之处,进而从中入手进行考察,最后就其英译取得质的突破。譬如《英汉大词典补编》中就把"ticket broker"译为了"票贩子",而这个译文由于出现在如此权威的词典中,所以广为流传。但经过笔者的细致调查,才发现"ticket broker"与我们汉语中的"票贩子"根本不是一回事,人家可是有营业执照、有营业场所,专门为购票者排忧解难的正式机构。

四、结语

本文简要探讨了汉语新词英译的现状、问题和出路。文章认为,目前汉语新词英译的现状不容乐观,问题较多,但如果新词译者具有高度的责任心,精通译事,而又不为理论所困,能熟练、充分地运用网络内外的资源协助自己进行翻译,不盲从"权威",就会在新词翻译的领域大有作为,而汉语新词的英译工作也才能取得更大的进展。

参考书目

曹兰萍,新词新义集粹:袋鼠族,《辞书研究》,2006(2)。

金其斌,实用翻译理论指导下的汉语新词翻译,《术语标准化与信息技术》,2008(2)。

金其斌,谈一些汉语新词语的英译问题——评《新华新词语词典》部分词条的译文,《中国翻译》,2003(6)。

金其斌,汉语新词语中法律、经贸术语的翻译问题——以《汉英最新特色词汇》和《新华新词语词典》为例,《中国翻译》,2004(4)。

梁志坚,汉语新词的衍生与等效翻译——以"下岗"的英译为例,《天津外国语学院学报》,2007(1)。

刘谨,新词新义荟萃:负翁,《辞书研究》,2006(2)。

刘谨,新词新义荟萃:啃老族,《辞书研究》,2006(2)。

刘谨,新词新义荟萃:月光族,《辞书研究》,2006(2)。

陆谷孙,《英汉大词典补编》,上海:上海译文出版社,1999。

罗宁萍,基于文化视角的汉语新词英译,《福建金融管理干部学院学报》,2008(4)。

商务印书馆辞书研究中心,《新华新词语词典》,北京:商务印书馆,2003。

邵斌,《漫话英语时尚新词》,大连:大连理工大学出版社,2006。

邵斌,《透过新词看文化——英语时尚超 IN 词》,杭州:浙江大学出版社,2008。

王春,异化翻译在汉语新词英译中的优化应用,《教学与管理》(理论版),2006(1)。

王逢鑫,《100 个热门话题汉译英》,北京:北京大学出版社,2009。

吴光华,《汉英大词典》(第 3 版),上海:上海译文出版社,2010。

徐昌和,《英语新词新语导论》,上海:上海交通出版社,2009。

阎瑾,从目的论看汉语新词的英译,《湖南医科大学学报》(社会科学版),2009(1)。

杨全红,《汉英词语翻译探微》,上海:汉语大词典出版社,2003。

姚小平,《汉英词典》(第 3 版),北京:外语教学与研究出版社,2010。

张健,汉语新词翻译中出现的失误,《北京第二外语学院学报》,2003(2)。

张健,《报刊新词英译纵横》,上海:上海科技教育出版社,2001。

邹星,具有中国特色新词的归化与异化翻译,《科技信息》,2009(6)。

Ａ　Ａ　制

"AA 制"指聚餐或其他消费结账时个人平摊出钱或个人算个人账的做法。关于其来源,说法不一。一是说它来源于英文中的"go Dutch",二是说它是英文"Acting Appointment"的缩写。在香港,人们认为"AA"是"All Apart"的缩写,意为"全部分开",很是形象。

大概是由于受到第一种说法的影响,一般词典中均把"AA 制"翻译为 go Dutch(《新华新词语词典》,2003)、have a Dutch treat(《新世纪汉英大词典》,2003)或 Dutch treat(《新时代汉英大词典》,2001)。

尽管这种说法没有问题,但"go Dutch"这个表达中明显包含对荷兰人的歧视(历史上,英国人认为荷兰人很吝啬,所谓的 Dutch treat 其实就是没有任何 treat。类似的歧视性表达还有 Dutch courage,意为酒后之勇;Dutch feast,意为客人尚未尽兴而主人却已酩酊大醉的宴席;Dutch concert,指极为嘈杂、喧闹或各唱各调的音乐会;Dutch bargain,指饮酒时达成的交易;Dutch defense,讽喻虚张声势的抵抗;Dutch auction,指先把价开得甚高然后逐步减价的拍卖;Dutch comfort,指不起作用的慰问。英国人甚至在赌咒发誓时都说"I'm a Dutchman, if..."表示"如果…,我就不是人",或表示"我才不干呢"之意。他们还用"The Dutch have taken Holland"来挖苦把众所周知的事情当作新闻来传,意为"少见多怪")。由于这个原因,"go Dutch"在英语国家的日常生活中,使用并不像我们想象中的那样频繁。因此,人们在不同语境中往往采用不同的说法,来表达"AA 制"这个概念。譬如,在餐厅,我们常说,Let's split the bill/payment（equally/evenly），而和别人共同打车则说 share the cab。所以在翻译实践中，英译该词要视情况而定，最好不要一概而论译为 go Dutch。下面的例子进一步说明了这种情况：

When I want to **go Dutch with** my Chinese friends, they seem unable to accept it.

When the bill came, we **went Dutch**.

The Friday dinner will be **a Dutch treat**.

We **went fifty-fifty on** the dinner check.

Let's **pay our own expenses**.

Let's **share our expenses**.

That was an expensive meal. Let's **go halves**.

"I need someone to **go in halves with** me. I can get the boat for five hundred dollars, but I only have two hundred and fifty," he confessed.

Let's **go halves in** buying the wine.

The two children had to **go halves on** the last piece of cake.

有趣的是，目前流行的男女初次约会时各自买单的情况在英文中称作 Dutch date，例如：Her parents agreed that she might date if it were a Dutch date.

此外，"AA 制"还没过时，最近在年轻人当中又出现了一个新词"AB 制"（AB treat）。请看相关报道：

In China, people tend to call "going Dutch" an "AA treat," meaning dividing the bill equally among all the diners. But now "AB treat" has become a fad among young people as some males now choose to pay a bigger slice of the bill, say 70 percent, while female friends dining with them pay the rest.

从上面这段报道我们可以看出，如果外出用餐时，由男性来支付账单的大头，比如 70%，剩下的部分由女性来支付，这就叫"AB 制"。再如：

The dinner party last night was on an AB treat, so the ladies didn't spend much on that.

按 揭

　　"按揭"一词是英文"mortgage"的粤语音译,最初起源于西方国家,大约于 10 年前从香港流入大陆。[1]《新词语大词典》(亢世勇等,2003)对该词的定义为:一种先从银行贷款购物(如汽车、房子等),然后分期归还银行本息的购物方式。

　　"按揭"在英文中的对应词为"mortgage",这是众所周知的。然而与"按揭"相关的一些表达却值得我们注意,譬如,

　　按揭成数:loan-to-value ratio

　　按揭转让:transfer/assignment of a mortgage

　　按揭期限:mortgage tenor

　　按揭贷款计算器:mortgage calculator

　　按揭尚欠余额:outstanding loan balance

　　按揭购房/车:buy a house/car on mortgage;mortgage a house/car

　　按揭利率:mortgage rate

　　按揭贷款:mortgage(loan)

　　按揭拖欠:mortgage delinquency

---

〔1〕关于"按揭"一词的来源,崔山佳(2010)先生在"'按揭'是外来词吗?"一文中提出了异议,认为"按揭"是地地道道的汉语方言词。崔先生的说法是有道理的,但由于本文主要关注的不是该词的来源,而是它的英译,所以在这里对其来源不加深究,仍按照《新词语大词典》(2003)的说法,将其归为外来词。

按揭保险：mortgage insurance

此外，近两年来在上海等大城市又出现了"倒按揭"的概念。例如，《第一财经日报》2006 年 3 月 10 日就刊登了题为"两会热提'以房养老'，上海调研'倒按揭'可行性"的文章，相关报道在《解放日报》等主流媒体中也屡见不鲜。那么，什么是"倒按揭"呢？

"倒按揭"又叫"住房反向抵押"，在国外兴起只有一二十年时间。人们在年轻时为买房按揭多年，到老了再把房产抵押，按月领钱用于养老，辞世后住房由金融或保险机构收回，用以还贷。"倒按揭"最早起源于荷兰，发展最为成熟的则是美国。

那么，"倒按揭"在英文中的对应词是什么呢？答案为 reverse mortgage。请看下面关于 reverse mortgage 的英文表述：

A "reverse" mortgage is a loan against your home that you do not have to pay back for as long as you live there. With a reverse mortgage, you can turn the value of your home into cash without having to move or to repay the loan each month. The cash you get from a reverse mortgage can be paid to you in several ways：

* all at once, in a single lump sum of cash；
* as a regular monthly cash advance；
* as a "creditline" account that lets you decide when and how much of your available cash is paid to you; or
* as a combination of these payment methods.

No matter how this loan is paid out to you, you typically don't have to pay anything back until you die, sell your home, or permanently move out of your home. To be eligible for most reverse mortgages, you must own your home and be 62 years of age or older.

另外，我们也可以用 conversion mortgage 或其全称 home equity conversion mortgage（HECM）来表达"倒按揭"的概念，因为"The Home Equity Conversion Mortgage program enables older homeowners to withdraw some of the equity in their home in the form of monthly payments for life or a fixed term, or in a lump sum, or through a line of credit."

HECM 与 reverse mortgage 在按揭的目的、条件、方式等方面完全同义。

最后,由于近些年来房地产市场发展还比较混乱,我们还时常听到诸如"零首付"(zero down payment)、"假按揭"、"转按揭"这些概念,这里谈谈与"按揭"有关的"假按揭"和"转按揭"的英译。例如,2009 年 10 月 30 日的《江西日报》上就刊载了题为"防范假按揭,堵截信贷资金进股市,银监会新规亮剑"的报道。所谓"假按揭"是指开发商为资金套现,将手中的存量住房以虚构的买房人(内部职工或开发商亲属或素不相识的人)的名字购买,从银行套取购房贷款的一种行为,实际上,"假按揭"是一个风险转嫁过程,开发商通过"假按揭",提前收回成本,变现利润,把包袱和风险悉数丢给银行,自己进退自如,完全占据主动。

"假按揭"通常译为 fake mortgage。下面的报道可以为证:

In reality, **fake mortgage** has long existed throughout the country. The practice of "zero down payment", which prevailed in many big cities, is indeed a form of fake mortgage. It is a tricky business. The agents make out fake invoices certifying down payments to enable a prospective house buyer to apply for a bank loan to meet the capital requirement over and above their own funds.

The China Daily, 2009 − 05 − 28

The exposure of **fake mortgages** reveals not just the sharp practices in the real estate sector but also serves as a warning of the risks the market is facing. The real estate agents are feeding their greed with such non-existent mortgages. When they are no longer in a position to honor the loans, they will simply stop paying the banks, who may end up carrying the can for the defaulting real estate agents.

The China Daily, 2009 − 05 − 28

与"假按揭"不同,"转按揭"有两层意思,第一层意思是指银行的利率发生变化后,按揭者可以要求银行根据新的利率重新进行按揭。在国外,按揭者既可以要求自己的贷款银行"转按揭",也可以另外找一家银行,由该银行负责和贷款银行结清贷款,然后在这家银行重新按照新的较低的利率进行贷款。这种"转按揭"的方式一般称为 mortgage refinancing。请看下列表述：

There are lots of reasons you might want to refinance. One of the main reasons homeowners refinance their mortgages is to take advantage of lower interest rates. If rates have lowered since the time of your original mortgage you may refinance your mortgage at a better rate and therefore reduce your monthly payments.

"转按揭"的第二层意思就是我们常见的该词的意思，即个人住房转按贷款，是指已在银行办理个人住房贷款的借款人，向原贷款银行要求将抵押给银行的个人住房出售或转让给第三人而申请办理个人住房贷款变更借款期限、变更借款人或变更抵押物的贷款。在英文中，这种"转按揭"一般叫 mortgage transfer。请看下面的定义：

Mortgage transfer is a transaction where either the borrower or lender assigns an existing mortgage (bank loan to purchase a residential property) from the current holder to another person or entity. Homeowners who are unable to keep current on their mortgage payments may seek a transfer so that they don't default and go into foreclosure.

原载《辞书研究》2008 年第 2 期，有改动

傲　人

　　"傲人"一词近年来使用频繁,常与身材、身姿、业绩、成绩、资本、学历等词语搭配使用,偶尔与票房、气质、记录等词联用,例如,

　　傲人的身材/曲线/身姿

　　傲人的家世/背景/资历/经历

　　天赋、悟性、爆发力,除此之外,她拥有最**傲人**的资本:青春。

　　在现有的六大产业中,集成电路产业一路高歌猛进,业绩**傲人**。

　　许晴全新英伦写真曝光,身材**傲人**掩面娇笑

　　戴娆《但愿人长久》本周称王,**傲人**成绩印证实力

　　其后,杨丞琳马甲装上阵,凭借小女人的好身材展露十足女性味,**傲人**上围惹关注。

　　《现代汉语词典》(第五版)已正式收录该词,释义为:(成绩等)值得骄傲、自豪。而该词的英译却未见于目前出版的各汉英词典或汉英新词词典。

　　基于汉语词典的释义,我们似乎可将该词译为:(of one's achievements, etc.) deserving pride; exceptional; brilliant; outstanding; impressive 等,但在不同的语境下则应区别翻译,例如:

　　傲人的身材:nice/perfect/great body shape

　　例如:Most people know that having great health and fitness is important. Many try to stay fit and healthy and to get a **great body shape** by exercising regularly and joining a gym.

傲人的曲线：impressive body shape/curve

例如：No doubt that there are many diet pills that work at a fast pace to provide you with an **impressive body shape**.

傲人的业绩：brilliant/outstanding achievements

傲人的家世：illustrious family background

（注：根据 *Macmillan English Dictionary for Advanced Learners*，an **illustrious family background** is well-known and respected because of what the family have achieved。这一点在下例中可以看出。）

例如：Despite Cooper's **illustrious family background** — his mother is socialite Gloria Vanderbilt and his father was the screen writer Wyatt Cooper, who died of a heart attack when Cooper was 10 — Cooper never chose to ride the tide of comfort. As a student at the Dalton School in New York City, he decided to begin amassing his own income by modeling — a short-lived career, but a career nonetheless.

Yale Daily News, 2005 - 09 - 25

当然，"傲人"的搭配可能不止以上种种，例如我们还可以看到诸如"傲人的双峰/胸部/乳房"（peerless/big/beautiful/impressive breasts）这样常见的说法。看来译者只能根据具体的语境，琢磨"傲人"的真实含义，再在英文中找出与该词外延和内涵都基本对等的说法了。

白 骨 精

世事变化飞快,昔日《西游记》中诡计多端的"白骨精"今天却被用来形容职场上的"白领"、"骨干"和"精英"!专门用来指代那些拥有高学历、高收入、高层次的"三高女性",她们通常被看作是职场的半边天。下面两例可以基本展现该词在汉语中的实际使用情况:

1. Nancy 是标准的"**白骨精**",也是矛盾的综合体。长得漂亮,但逻辑严谨;思维传统,又有留学背景;看起来年轻,但做事老到;在家相夫教子,在公司一呼百应。

2. 但在成为职场中独当一面的"**白骨精**"之前,"王珞丹版"的杜拉拉着实是被折腾得够呛。

然而,《西游记》中的"白骨精"可以直译为 white-bone demon,职场上的"白骨精"却显然难以套用此译。碰到这种情况,译者恐怕只能采用归化的策略,抛弃原文所含的形象,另辟蹊径进行翻译了。

这里提供两种译文,以供讨论:white-collar elite 和 office elite。

先看 white-collar elite。这个译文直译了"白领",缩译了"骨干"和"精英",因为这二者在本质上而言为同义词。这种表达在国内一些刊物和报纸上可以找见,在原版英文中也不罕见,而且与汉语的"白领"、"骨干"和"精英"基本契合,尽管该译文并不见得可以回译为汉语的"白骨精"。例如:

Since spa's first appearance in Beijing in 2000, it has been warmly received by the city's **white-collar elite** and its wealthier housewives.

Beijing This Month, 2006 - 01 - 27

As America's **white-collar elite** grows rich, must the poor and near-poor be left behind?

The New York Times, 1989 – 04 – 26

　　再看 office elite,首先,一般认为,所谓"白领",就是指那些出入高级写字楼、衣着光鲜、从事脑力劳动、收入较高的年轻人。这些人的办公地点大多在 office building(写字楼)中。此外,"骨干"和"精英"套用英文的 elite(a group of people who have a lot of power and influence because they have money, knowledge, or special skills)一词,也颇为恰当。

　　值得注意的是,white-collar elite 可以算是套用英文中本来就存在的表达来翻译意义相似的中文新词,而 office elite 则为建立在理解原文基础上的合理的再创造。孰优孰劣,其实难判。

原载《辞书研究》2009 年第 1 期

霸王条款

　　"霸王条款"这个词虽然还未出现在 2005 年出版的《现代汉语词典》(第五版)中,但对一般老百姓来说,可能已经不算太新了,因为我们在日常生活中仍然频频遭遇"霸王条款"的纷扰。这不,2010 年春节未到,已经出现了不少和"霸王条款"相关的新闻了:

　　年夜饭频添**"霸王条款"**还没开吃已成"年夜烦"(《联合早报》,2010 年 2 月 13 日)

　　酒楼**霸王条款**:年夜饭限时吃的是饭还是时间?(《高端财经》,2010 年 2 月 8 日)

　　饭店年夜饭设**霸王条款**最低消费　1000 元(《新华网》,2010 年 2 月 11 日)

　　那么,什么是"霸王条款"呢?就是一些经营者单方面制定的逃避法定义务、减免自身责任的不平等合同、通知、声明和店堂告示或者行业惯例等。它大量存在于消费领域内,已经成为束缚、阻止消费者依法维权的障碍之一,并引起了广大消费者的强烈不满。今年 315 晚会上揭晓的十大霸王条款中,"打折商品不退换"位列"霸王条款"之首。

　　"霸王条款"一词的译文不少,但核心是如何翻译"霸王"一词,有译做"overbearing"的,但考虑到 overbearing 的意思为:frequently trying to tell others what to do without regard for their ideas or feelings,似乎考虑的主要是听话人的感情,而且其中的"frequently"所传达的意思在"霸王条

款"中也没有体现,所以该词并不恰当。也有译为 unfair、imparity 或 inequality 的,但这三个词只强调"不公平",似乎难以译出"霸王条款"中的"霸气"和"霸道"。此外,还有译为 overlord 的,但 overlord 是"(昔日的)封建君主",该词强调的是对方对某个事情有权威性(a person who has general authority over others),并没有"霸王"、"霸道"的意思。另外,用该词来译"霸王"明显存在硬译,甚至"假朋友"(false friend)之嫌。

事实上,笔者认为,我们可以用两个词来试译"霸王条款"中的"霸王"一词。一个是 arbitrary,另一个是 high-handed。首先,请看朗文词典对 arbitrary 的释义:decided or arranged without any reason or plan, often unfairly,汉语译文为:专横的、霸道的。无论从那个意义上来讲,该词都可以表示出"霸王条款"中不公和霸道。再看 high-handed,其英文释义为:using one's power too forcefully and without considering the wishes of other people。"霸王条款"的制定者在制定这些条款时又何曾考虑过消费者的需求和愿望?

综上所述,"霸王条款"可以用 arbitrary/high-handed provision/clause 来表达。下面是两个来自原版英文的例子,以证明这两个译文是否合理。这两例中的黑体部分译为"霸王条款"似乎都没有什么问题。

(1) One of the most controversial aspects of the Directive is that database makers must be nationals of an EU Member State, or have their habitual residence in the Union, in order to obtain the benefit of the sui generis right. U. S. database producers lobbied the Commission unsuccessfully to remove this provision, and ironically adopted a similarly **high-handed provision** in the Semiconductor Chip Protection Action of 1984. In that law, the US protected mask works fixed in semiconductor chip products only if the owner of the mask work was a national or domiciliary of the US, or if the foreign country had adopted similar legislation protecting mask works.

(2) We continue to be concerned regarding the evidentiary provision (MAR 1. 9. 2CE) that any failure to provide adequate ongoing disclosure

of a disclosable short position will be considered market abuse by the FSA. We consider this to be an **arbitrary provision** which takes no account of the intent of the party involved or whether any other actions are involved showing an abusive purpose.

摆　平

　　"摆平"这个词被认为是"搞定"的孪生兄弟,近年来引起了不少讨论,譬如中国人民大学教授张鸣 2007 年 10 月 16 日在"国际在线"上撰文"中国人为何热衷摆平",认为"摆平是现今的流行语"、"但凡摆平,都是有事,这个事不是平常的吃喝拉撒,买车买房,往往涉及法纪,不是违法,就是违纪"、"摆平和摆平术存在的原因,主要在制度和文化"。而晓滨在"说'摆平'"一文中,则认为"在充满诱惑的现实社会里,人们,首先应该'摆平'自己的浮躁心态,'摆平'自己的'补偿'心理,'摆平'自己的'升官'欲望,'摆平'自己与群众的关系,尤其是有人直接或间接地用金钱、美色等来'摆平'你的时候,你还是把腰杆挺直为好。"另外,"中思网"于 2009 年 5 月 12 日发表了"心如大海"的文章"摆平现象",认为"'摆平'与'搞定'这两个词还没有被主流媒体和官方文书所采用,但其使用频率却很高,社会的各个阶层都有意无意地和这两个词有过接触,而且这两个词的使用往往在人和人,事和事之间来回穿梭"。此外,"'摆平'的结果是'摆平'了社会的公信度,'摆平'了社会的管理体系,'摆平'了人们的信念和信仰,'摆平'了本来就脆弱的赖以维系社会公平的那一丝期望,'摆平'了人们心中那一丝的真诚和友善,'摆平'把人和人之间的关系变成了赤裸裸的金钱关系,把社会的正常交往变成了钱与权的交往"。

　　然而,就是这样一个几乎人人都在使用的流行义项,2005 年出版的《现代汉语词典》(第五版)却也没有收录,而只收了该词的常用义:放平,比喻公平处理或使各方面平衡,以及其方言义:惩治、收拾。2010 年出版的《汉英词典》(第三版)同样依样画葫芦,只收录和翻译了上述的两个义项。而同时出版的《汉英大词典》(第三版)则只收译了该词的第一个义项。截至目前,似乎尚未有正式出版物讨论过该词该义的英译。

那么,如何用英语"摆平""摆平"这个词呢?笔者认为,该词尽管来源不明,但可以确定为口语体,而且隐约带有一种"痞子气",透过该词,读者往往可以看到一种"不屑一顾"的傲气、"信誓旦旦拍胸脯"的豪气或所谓"侠肝义胆"和"自告奋勇"的允诺。例如,"这件事我去摆平"、"你找人把他摆平不就完了吗?"或"黑道白道我都熟,这点小事还不好摆平?"等。当然,我们老百姓有时也用用该词,但却不含上面的含义,例如,"你可以不买房,除非你摆平丈母娘"、"摆平美丽问题,让你三十也能成花"等等。因此,用来翻译该词的英文必须首先在文体上与原词对应,像 solve、handle、dissolve、tackle 这些词虽然意思上相近,但从风格上而言都不太合适。其次,由于需要找人"摆平"的事应该都不是小事,如身家数亿的山西某煤炭局长"摆平纪委"、"七十码"事件胡斌父母企图用钱"摆平"受害者等均非小事,所以,英文中诸如 iron out 这样的词也应该排除在外,因为尽管该短语的意思为"解决"(to solve)或"消除"(get rid of),但目标都是一些"小问题或困难"(small problems or difficulties)。

有鉴于此,笔者认为,"摆平"一词可如下翻译:

1. 用 straighten (things) out/up 来译:这两个短语都有解决(settle or put right)的意思,而且语体上也较为适合。请看下列例证:

I'm just to **straighten things up** for you, man.

Just like the camera, if you let go of the controller, the automatic controls will take over and **straighten things up** for you anyway.

Adding CleanSweep to your computer is like getting a housekeeper for your PC. Just give it the word, and it'll **straighten things up** for you.

Everyone is really nice, and if you have any problems they will be there to try and **straighten things out** for you.

You'll either have to try to re-download or call Microsoft to **straighten**

things out for you.

2. 用 fix 或 take care of 来译。例如：

I will **fix** it for you regardless of whatever happens.

Don't worry; I'll **take care of** it.

3. 除了上述短语和词语外，有时依据语境，译者还可以灵活处理，如"没关系，我帮你摆平"一句，还可以译为：

Noting important, just **leave it to me**/I'll **help you out**.

Don't worry, **leave everything in my care**!

Take it easy, I'll **cope with** it.

Don't worry, I'll **see to** it.

It's nothing. I'll try to **sort things out** for you.

包 公

"包公"一词本算不得新词,但对其英译的讨论却牵涉到对汉语新词英译的一些基本策略和方法的认识,兹以为文。

《新世纪汉英大词典》对该词的英译为 Lord Bao,但有学者(赫迎红,2007)却认为,"该译文是随意搬用英语成语,造成误解,因为"尊称Lord"在英语中通常指'某某勋爵'(一般只用于英国)。赫先生于此发出感慨:包拯何时成了英国勋爵?"

"包公"一词到底能否译为 Lord Bao 呢? 我们可先从汉语的"公"谈起。

"公"为"封建五等爵位的第一等",一般认为,身居高位的天子重臣称公,如周公、召公、毕公等。包公名包拯(999—1062),宋朝重臣,曾任开封府知府(相当于现在北京市的市长),最高官居枢密副使,相当于副宰相。包拯去世后,朝廷追封他为礼部尚书,并赠谥号为"孝肃",即孝道和铁面无私。由于包公一生为官正直无私,百姓称他为包青天、包老爷,士大夫们则尊为包公。由此可见,包公的"公"既是尊称,又与其官职相称。

再看 Lord 一词,根据朗文英语词典,该词在英文中不但指爵位(a man of noble rank),而且是英国用以称呼法官、主教或某些男性贵族成员的用语,以示尊敬(the title of someone who has a particular type of official job),例如,Lord Mayor of London 即为"伦敦市长大人"。再如,我国的香港地区,在法庭上对法官的称呼,承袭了英国的传统,十分庄重和典雅。在高等法院,诉讼双方都会尊称法官为"My Lord","My Lady"或"Your Lordship"。

这样看来,把"包公"译为"Lord Bao",不但不错,而且相当恰当。从翻译学的角度来看,包公的"公"为词汇空缺(lexical blank),必须从英文中借用一词来翻译。从词语的选择来看,两相对比,Lord 实为最佳译文。从翻译实践来看,用"Lord Bao"来译"包公",译例比比皆是,例如,Foreign Languages Press 于 1997 出版的由 Ben Hu 所著的英文著作:*Exchanging a Leopard Cat for a Prince*:*Famous Trials by Lord Bao* 用的就是这个译文。此外,Dolphin Books 也于 1996 出版过名为 *Lord Bao Interrogates the Stone* 一书。更不用提合肥包公祠的译名 Memorial Temple of Lord Bao 了。

事实上,在翻译实践中,译者面临词汇空缺(lexical blank)的现象时常用此法,譬如,中国封建社会的"贵妃"、"妃子",在英文中基本上都译为"concubine",但该词在英文中的意思却是"妾"、"姨太太"(a woman who lives with and has sex with a man who already has a wife or wives, but who is socially less important),与"贵妃"的外延意义大致相同,但内涵却大相径庭。尽管如此,译界似乎也没有人提出异议。此外,汉语中的"龙"与英文中的"dragon"也差异较大,但尽管学界颇有争议,估计也很难因这些争议而不把"龙"译为"dragon"。再譬如,汉语中的"道万福"一词常用英文的 courtesy 一词来译,尽管二者在外延、内涵和用法上的区别不可谓不大。既然我们可以接受 concubine、dragon 和 courtesy,为什么就不能接受 Lord Bao 呢?

包　袱

　　我们这里所说的"包袱",可不是用来包裹物件的布面,也不是"累赘"、"负担"的意思,而是指相声或小品演员在表演过程中常常"抖"出来"逗"观众发笑的东西。例如,著名小品王赵本山小品《不差钱》中的一些经典对白,如"长得挺委婉的"、"人这一生可短暂了,有时候跟睡觉是一样的,眼睛一闭一睁一天过去了,哈嗷,眼睛一闭不睁,这辈子就过去了,哈嗷"、"人这一生最最痛苦的事情你知道是什么吗?就是人活着呢,钱没了!"等等。这些"包袱"常常出乎听众的意料,从而让他们捧腹大笑,达到很好的"笑果"。

　　那么,究竟什么是"包袱"呢?一般认为,相声的"包袱"就是相声的笑料。按照演员的说法,"包袱"是一个装满笑料的包裹。演员在观众不知不觉中将包袱皮打开,把笑料一件一件装在里面;然后又偷偷系牢包袱扣子,等待时机成熟时突然抖落。由于笑料是在观众不知不觉中装在里面的,因此当包袱抖落时,观众一定会出乎意料而失声大笑。同时又由于笑料是面对观众一件一件装在里面的,因此在大笑之余又觉得合理可信。

　　马季(1980)在其《相声艺术漫谈》中将组织包袱儿的手法分为二十二类:三翻四抖、先褒后贬、性格语言、违反常规、阴错阳差、故弄玄虚、词义错觉、荒诞夸张、自相矛盾、机智巧辩、逻辑混乱、颠倒岔说、运用谐音、吹捧奉承、误会曲解、乱用词语、引申发挥、强词夺理、歪讲歪唱、用俏皮话、借助形声、有意自嘲。这些手法一般是交错混合使用,以达到理想的效果。

　　这样看来,其实"包袱"就是笑料。所以应该译为诸如 joke 或

laughing-stock 之类的词。而所谓的"抖包袱"则首先可简单译为 reveal a joke/jokes、crack a joke/jokes。例如下面两个例子：

两位相声演员不时**抖包袱**，令现场观众捧腹大笑。

In the comic dialogue, the two performers revealed jokes from time to time, which made the audience convulse with laughter.

喜剧演员每次**抖包袱**，都让观众大笑不已。

Every time the comedian cracked a joke, his audience broke up laughing.

然而，"包袱"更为地道的英文说法则是 punch line。事实上，不但中国的相声演员喜欢抖包袱，西方人说话时有时候也"包袱"不断，让人忍俊不禁。而他们则把此种"包袱"形象地称作 punch line。下面请看 Wikipedia 对该词的释义：

A punch line is the final part of a joke or comedy sketch, usually the word, sentence or exchange of sentences which is intended to be funny and to provoke laughter from listeners. Punch lines generally derive their humor from being unexpected. （笑话中最后几句抛出笑料的部分，常常通过出其不意制造幽默）

此外，Wikipedia 还列出了一个经典的"包袱"(punch line)：

A man walks into a bar with a duck under his arm.

The bartender asks："Say, where did you find the pig?"

"It's not a pig, it's a duck," the man answers.

To which the barman replies："I was talking to the duck."

这样看来，"抖包袱"不但可以译为 reveal a joke/jokes、crack a joke/jokes，还可以译为 reveal/deliver a punch line，例如：

Only a true master knows how to tell an elaborate story and then **reveal a pun chline** without losing the audience along the way.

Public Speaking：How To **Deliver a Punch Line**：The punch line gets its name from the delivery technique used. You must punch the line out a little harder and with a slightly different voice than the rest of the joke.

煲电话粥

  "煲电话粥"的意思是长时间拿着电话和对方无聊地闲谈。原本"煲电话粥"来自广东话"煲粥"。"煲"字在广东话里是指烹饪方面的"长时间地煮",那么长时间地打电话,打个没完没了,就是"煲电话粥"了。

  《汉英词典》(第三版)中将"煲电话粥"译为了 chat for a long time on the telephone 和 long telephone chat。这样翻译在意思上倒是没有太大的问题,但原词中所包含的生动的形象已然丧失殆尽,所以并非佳译。

  事实上,英美人也"煲电话粥",而且强度一点也不比中国人差。笔者在加拿大和美国访学期间,曾入住所谓的 homestay family(寄宿家庭),那些女主人"煲电话粥"时"煲"得比中国人(通常是女人)更是有过之而无不及,让等着打电话的人心急如焚,据说这是因为英美国家电话费便宜的缘故。

  那么,英美人怎么表达"煲电话粥"这个概念呢?他们通常用 carry on/have a marathon phone conversation 或 be on a marathon conversation over telephone。请注意这里的 marathon(马拉松)一词,其形象程度一点也不亚于中国人"煲粥"这个概念。请看下面的实例:

  1. Gary Hart stayed up most of the night before the Selby rail crash in **a marathon phone conversation** with a woman he met over the internet.

  2. A riotous, stream-of-consciousness dialogue follows, in which Molly and Lily subject virtually every aspect of their lives to interrogation

and analysis. Over the course of several hours, the two friends **carry on a marathon phone conversation** from Connecticut to New York that touches on other unusual deaths suffered by friends and family they have known, their chance meetings with the famous, travels abroad, various loves lost, their children, and their pets.

3. We emailed back and forth the first week before **having a marathon phone conversation** that lasted over twelve hours long.

4. Most often, before love comes dating, and with it, the excitement and adventure of a first dinner, first **marathon phone conversation**, and (possibly) a first kiss.

5. One fine morning while he **was on a marathon conversation over telephone** in a phone booth, we alerted the police and managed to bundle him into our Scorpio and take him to the police station.

此外,笔者还注意到,有一些地方将"煲电话粥"译为 shoot/fan the breeze over the phone。Shoot the breeze 就是"闲聊"、"乱侃"的意思,通过电话 shoot the breeze 仿佛就是"煲电话粥"了。这个译法对吗?有点悬! 因为译者忽略了"煲电话粥"的另外一个重要特征,就是"长时间的聊"。Shoot the breeze over the phone 是在电话上聊天的意思,但却不一定是"长时间"的,所以和"煲电话粥"还是有区别的。譬如在下句中,shoot the breeze on the phone 最好不要译为"煲电话粥",而应译为"闲扯"或"侃大山":

Physicians do not have time to **shoot the breeze on the phone** with patients for sure, but they do get phone calls and make phone calls, they do get interrupted by their assistants, patients do call back, and some get dissatisfied with a curt call-back at an inopportune time.

爆　料

　　"爆料"一词在民间的使用已经极为广泛了,我们常听到新闻中出现如下的报道:

　　1. 世界杯惊天**爆料**,百度百科已经预定了西班牙为 2010 的冠军!

　　2. 有网友向苹果日报**爆料**,指出 24 岁的 XXX 以"天使 OL"为号召,从今年 4 月起开始当视讯女郎,每天上线 7 小时,底薪 2 万元台币(约合人民币 4 千)、奖金另计,每月收入约 4、5 万元(台币)。

　　3. 昨日又有网友**爆料**称,此前百度百科里还充斥着许多网民杜撰的词条,这些词条中有些是英文粗口和国骂的音译,有的则是对现实生活中某一现象的恶搞。

　　从这些例证中我们可以看出,所谓"爆料",其实是一种新闻炒做的字眼,就是一些人跟踪和偷拍一些个人行踪和隐私,还有一些真实的奇闻事件,给以曝光出去。将别人的隐私或者不愿意公开的事情通过媒体、报纸、杂志等平台说出来。

　　"爆料"有时候又简称"爆",例如,"×××是女 F4 团员中最具争议性的一个,前后**爆**出被陈姓男室友偷拍出浴裸照、和人妖 Pub 有财务纠纷,被挟持逼签本票,并坦承与人妖是"男女朋友",之后就没有新闻传出。"

　　目前,"爆料"和"爆"已经进入了《现代汉语词典》(第五版),文体标识为"方言",释义分别为"发表令人感到意外或吃惊的新闻、消息等"和"出人意料地出现;突然发生"。最新出版的《汉英词典》(第三版)和

《汉英大词典》(第三版)均收录了该词,下面是这两本词典对这个词的处理:

爆料:名词:report(sensational news):英国媒体~说,该俱乐部将买入一名中国球员。British media reported earlier that the club will buy a Chinese player.

《汉英词典》(第三版)

爆料:tip-off

《汉英大词典》(第三版)

《汉英词典》(第三版)所提供的该词的译文就是对《现代汉语词典》(第五版)释义的一个简单的翻译,可以看出,译者几乎没有动任何脑筋。此外,配例中的译文使用 report,实在让人看不出来"爆料"和"报道"有什么不同。最后,该配例的译文不但存在任意乱译之嫌(无中生有加了一个 earlier),而且语法有误(will 应该是 would)。《汉英大词典》(第三版)中的译文则更为简单,直接就是一个 tip-off,从下面的讨论我们可以知道,tip-off 的确可以翻译为"爆料",但这只是"爆料"作为名词的用法,而该词首先则是一个动词。

"爆料"真的如此难译吗?其实不然,译者只要多读一些英美报刊,就可以看到以下多种"爆料"的译法:

第一,用 disclose 来译。Disclose 的意思为:to make something publicly known,especially after it has been kept secret from the public,汉语通常译为"透露"、"揭露"、"公开"等,基本上就是"爆料"的意思。譬如,"The newspaper **disclosed** earlier that Barker also had been the subject of five child abuse complaints,including one substantiated case involving her biological child."该句中的 disclosed 完全可以翻译为汉语的"爆料"。

第二,用 expose、reveal、uncover、leak 或 unveil 来译。Expose 本身就是揭露、暴露隐私的意思,来译"爆料"再恰当不过。Reveal、uncover 和 unveil 的意思也是 to make known something that was previously secret or unknown,和 disclose 的意思差不多,用来翻译"爆料"也较为合适。譬如,下面句子中的 expose 和 reveal 等词均可译为"爆料"。

In 2004,it was **exposed** that USA Today correspondent and Pulitzer

Prize nominee Jack Kelley had been fabricating stories and sources.

When the media **revealed** that following his liver transplant George Best's alcoholism was continuing unabated, the number of organ donations dropped enormously.

The newspaper **uncovered** that Baghdad is waiting for answers from Tehran and Ankara, and will cancel the whole idea of the agreement in case Iran and Turkey provide such guarantees.

He **leaked** the scandal to the newspaper.

KGB **Unveiled** UFO Secrets（KGB 爆料不明飞行物之秘）

第三，用 tip off 来译。Tip off 就是"告密"、"揭露"的意思，而且在文体上与"爆料"更为相似。例如：

Bell says it was **tipped off** by an informant mid-January that its security had been breached.

第四，除了上面的译法外，在英文中还有一些习惯性的表达，它们间或也可以用来翻译"爆料"。这些表达包括：make（sth.）public、spill the beans 以及 blow the whistle 等。此外，有些本身不是"爆料"的词放在特定的语境下也可以表示"爆料"，例如下例中的 air 一词：

A shocking incident happened in the entertainment business lately. April Hou, sister of the current legislator Hou Kuan-chiung, repeatedly **aired** the family's dirty laundry in public. Not only did it stun people, but also embarrass and pain her older brother and mother a great deal.

影剧圈内最近发生了一件令人震撼的事情，现任议员侯冠群的妹妹，女星侯炳荧不断**爆料**家中多年的丑事，不但让大家看得傻眼，更让哥哥与妈妈非常难堪和伤心。

以上列举了"爆料"的不同译法，但主要还是该词作为动词时的翻译。然而，这些译法也给我们翻译作为名词的"爆料"提供了一些启示。那就是，名词"爆料"可以用 tip-off、disclosure、exposure、revelation、sensational leakage 等词来译。譬如下面句子中的各黑体词均可理解为"爆料"。

The paper's **disclosure** shocked the public.

This **exposure** shocked Korean people who believed that authoritarian rule was over with the inauguration of President Roh Tae-woo in 1989.

Many news media nowadays rely heavily on **tip-offs** from their stringers or street tipsters to scoop some exclusive news. They usually offer the tipsters a handsome reward in cash. Seeing this trend, some laid-off workers and migrants have turned tipping into a business to eke out a living.

最后,有趣的是,英文中还有一个表达叫"(explosive) tell-all book",在汉语中通常翻译为"爆料书",也就是出书爆料秘闻,因为 tell-all 就是和盘托出,一点也不保留的意思。譬如:

Hollywood superstar Jennifer Lopez sued her ex-husband Ojani Noa claiming he demanded five million dollars to keep him from publishing an **explosive tell-all book** about the entertainer.

珍妮弗·洛佩兹的第一任老公 Ojani Noa 扬言要出版一本爆炸性的**爆料书**来自爆内幕,这让她觉得很伤脑筋,就把他告上法院了。

John Mayer will not be writing a **tell-all book** about life with his former girlfriend Jennifer Aniston.

潮 人

我们这里所谈论的"潮人",可不是潮汕人或潮州人的简称,而是指那些在穿着打扮方面不随波逐流、总是引领流行风尚的年轻人。简单而言,潮人就是潮流人士,他们衣着时尚新颖,总是走在时尚的顶端。

"潮"这个字和前两年流行的"新锐"一样,都是"流行、时尚"的意思,如果非要说"潮"和时尚的不同,那可能就是潮是潮流的最前沿,比时尚更甚。潮人的标志往往是时尚发型、时尚人物、时尚生活、潮流品牌或潮流服饰。

根据"互动百科"的介绍,潮人一般指引领时尚、富有个性、思想超前的人。潮人的外表一般很时尚新颖,内在很注重内涵和创新。这样看来,"潮人"一词应为褒义词,这从和"潮人"相关的另外一个词"潮爆"也可以看出。"潮爆"一词 2001 年起源于香港的一个杂志,意思是"某一事件具有潮流味,同时在民间造成一窝蜂现象,具有"很有潮流感"和"很有爆炸性"两大特点,但该词一经出现便产生滥用现象,以至于香港一个名为"至硬的讨论区"的高登吹水论坛最终将其定义为贬义词:"有钱没文化"和思想守旧的人,正式将潮爆 = 傻瓜的意思公布天下,迅速颠覆了潮人思想。在这个背景下,就有刊物疾呼:要潮! 千万不要爆!

《中国日报》的"英语点津"栏目中将"潮人"具体化为"潮男"和"潮女",并提供了英文对应词 trendy guy 和 trendy girl。这种译法正确吗? 如果只考虑到 trendy 是"时尚"的意思,那么该译文是没有问题的,但如果我们对 trendy 一词进行深入的研究,就会发现该词在英文中其实是一个贬义词。请看 *Macmillan English Dictionary for Advanced Leanders* 对 trendy 的定义：extremely fashionable，but often silly or annoying。而《朗文当代英语词典》干脆就把 a trendy person 标识为贬义（*derog*）。我们的诸位潮人可是具有很高品位（taste）的时尚者，他/她们的确新潮，但却绝不 silly 或 annoying。

另外，还有些地方把"潮人"译为 fashion follower 和 faddish guy。这种译法其实也不对。首先，第一种译文与潮人的定义完全相反，"潮人"熟知 fashion，但却永远不会盲目地 follow a fashion，他/她们有自己的主见，有自己的品位。第二种译文中的 faddish 虽然也可以表示"时髦"、"时尚"的概念，但和 trendy 一样，该词在英文中也是贬义词，往往指一种短命的、没有多少内涵的时尚。

有鉴于此，我们认为"潮人"译为 trendy person 并不恰当，而比较合适的译文应该是 style/trend/fashion setter 或最起码是 a stylish guy。譬如，*Longman Dictionary of Contemporary English* 对 style/trend/fashion setter 的定义便为：someone who does things that other people admire and try to copy，这与褒义词"潮人"基本相符。另外，stylish 也可以表示"时髦的"、"时尚的"，而且是一个褒义词，是说着装、服饰搭配等不仅漂亮时尚，而且有自己的风格个性。相比"trendy"，"stylish"则更讲究细节、搭配等整体效果，以及个人的品味，即 showing good judgment about how to look attractive and fashionable。所以，该词与通常表示年轻人的 guy 一词连用，来翻译"潮人"也比较恰当。

炒鱿鱼

听到"炒鱿鱼",也许热爱美食的您会垂涎三尺,但我们这里所说的"炒鱿鱼"不仅不是一道美味佳肴,而且还让很多人避之惟恐不及。这里的"炒鱿鱼"是指被辞退、解雇,甚至开除。《现代汉语词典》(第五版)对该词的定义为:鱿鱼一炒就卷起来,像是卷铺盖。比喻解雇。

说到该词的来源,还相当有趣。它最初为广东的一个方言词,在旧社会,人们常用"卷铺盖"(或粤语中对应的说法"执包袱")来代替解雇或开除,例如,我们常听到"员工如不会上网就请卷铺盖走人"这样的说法。不知从何时起,人们忽然从"炒鱿鱼"这道菜中发现,在烹炒鱿鱼时,每块鱼片都由平直的形状慢慢卷起来成为圆筒状,这和卷起的铺盖外形差不多,而且卷的过程也极为相像。人们由此产生了联想,就用"炒鱿鱼"代替"卷铺盖",表示被解雇和开除的意思。

"炒鱿鱼"一词目前在诸汉英词典中常被译为 fire。乍一看,该译文堪称绝妙:二者均为动词,且均能表示被解雇、被开除的意义。但是,fire是否和"炒鱿鱼"完全对等呢?答案是否定的。这是因为,"炒鱿鱼"在汉语中是一个口语化的表达,而 fire 在英文中则较为正式,或至少不是非正式文体,所以,二者在文体上并不对应。可以说,fire 虽可传达出"炒鱿鱼"的本义"解雇",但却无法传达该词在读者头脑中所激发的形象性联想。因此,严格来说,用 fire 来译"炒鱿鱼"并不确切。

那么,英语中有没有哪个词能够形神兼顾地表达汉语"炒鱿鱼"的意思呢?答案是动词 sack 和其同根短语 get the sack。首先,sack 的文体为非正式，与"炒鱿鱼"一词的文体较为对应。例如，《朗文当代高级英语词典》(第三版)和《牛津高阶英汉双解词典》(第六版)均注明了 sack 为非正式用法，意思为 to dismiss someone from their job。此外，Charles Westmacott 于 1869 出版的 *Slang Dictionary* 中收录了 get the sack 一词，包括该短语的两个变体：get the bag (from the North of England) 和 get the empty (from London)。这说明 get the sack 在英文中是一个俚语，表示"解雇"，与"炒鱿鱼"在文体和意义上均较为对应。最后，有趣的是，作为名词的 sack 本身就是"铺盖"的意思，例如《牛津高阶英汉双解词典》(第六版)中 the sack 就有一个义项为 a bed。这样看来，用 sack 的动词和名词形式来译"炒鱿鱼"简直就是神来之笔！

综上所述，如果仅仅表达"解雇"的含义，fire、sack 及 get the sack 都可使用，但如考虑到文体特色和形象意义，"炒鱿鱼"则只能用 sack 和 get the sack 来译了。当然，如果是老板炒别人鱿鱼，不妨使用 give sb. the sack。例如，They've never actually given anyone the sack.

城 市 病

随着现代城市生活节奏的加快,城市白领的健康状况每况愈下,令人担忧。这不,大家刚刚熟悉了"亚健康"(sub-health),又出现了"过劳死"(die from overwork/overstrain)。不过,我们在这里谈的"城市病"和城市居民的身体健康没有太大关系,尽管,如果细究的话,"城市病"可能也会间接地导致"亚健康",甚至"过劳死"。另外,据《北京科技报》2009年10月27日报道:专家披露,未来五年我国"城市病"将进入高发期。

那么,什么是"城市病"呢? 根据《新华新词语词典》(2003),"城市病"是"现代大城市中普遍存在的人口过多、用水用电紧张、交通拥堵、环境恶化等社会问题"以及"由于上述原因使城市人容易患的身心疾病"。而"百度百科"则认为,国际上特大型城市的"城市病"主要表现在以下几个方面:人口膨胀、交通拥堵、环境污染、资源短缺、城市贫困。陈长德先生于2004年7月13日在《中国建设报》上撰文,非常形象地指出了新时期的12种"城市病"及其诊断与治疗。这些"城市病"包括:溃烂症(环境恶劣,脏、乱、差)、中风瘫痪(长期没有新发展)、难产(半截子工程)、流行性感冒(相互模仿、盲目照搬,城市缺少特色和个性)、高血压(城市用地和资金的浪费)、筋骨疼痛,四肢麻木(马路市场、占道经营,严重影响了交通和路网系统的活力)、牛皮癣(斑块状皮肤病,与城市环境不协调)、中暑(城市"热岛效应")、面黄肌瘦,形同枯槁(城市没有亮点,缺少现代气息等)、消化不良,胃酸(住宅开发量过大,

"空壳"现象严重)、鸡胸、缺钙(城市中除中心点较繁华外,其他地段环境条件明显较差,导致城市功能不能充分发挥)、气血凝滞,小腹胀痛(公交站点布点不匀,网络覆盖不均,导致繁华地段过于拥挤,其他地段则过于冷清)。

近几年,各种媒体中关于"城市病"的报道比比皆是,甚至有不少关于"城市病"的学术探讨,如张世银(2008)、邵景安(2002)等。然而,遍观国内出版的词典,除了《新华新词语词典》外,其他词典,包括《现代汉语词典》以及2010年刚刚出版的《汉英词典》(第三版)和《汉英大词典》,均未收录该词。

目前关于"城市病"的英译主要有四种:《中级翻译教程》(第二版)在第12单元"上海申办世界博览会"一文中将该词译为 diseases typical of cities;"百度百科"中将该词译为 urban/city disease;《新华新词语词典》中将该词译为 urban social problems;*The China Daily* BBS 上有人将其译为 urban malady。下面就这四种译文一一进行分析:

首先,把"城市病"译为 diseases typical of cities 实属无稽之谈,译者根本没有搞清楚"城市病"是什么意思,就贸然动笔了。Disease 的意思是 an illness or unhealthy condition in your body, especially one caused by infection([尤指感染而得的]身体疾病),大到心脏病、糖尿病,小到感冒、发烧、头疼、脑热,均可称作 disease,但这些 diseases 与我们这里所谈的"城市病"风马牛不相及。

其次,用 urban/city disease 用来翻译"城市病"也属于翻译研究中形似而神非的"假朋友"。的确,在《韦氏新大学词典》(第九版)中,我们可以找到 disease 的一个义项:a harmful development (as in a social institution),但该义项事实上也难以佐证用 disease 来译"城市病"中的"病"的合法性。原因有二,首先,该义项的意思是"社会制度等的弊病"。对照前文中"城市病"的定义,我们可以看出,"城市病"并非是指"社会制度的弊病"。其次,英文中的确有 urban disease 的说法,但一般还是指"在城市中发生的疾病、流行病"等,与"城市病"的含义大相径庭。譬如,Haaretz.com 这个英文网络杂志上就有一篇题为"A worrying urban disease: Reports of rabies cases are up"的报道[1]。很明显,这里的 urban disease 指的是诸如 rabies(狂犬病)这样的疾病,而非"城市病"。再如,下面一段摘自 *The New York Times* 上 2010 年 6 月 22 日的报道也可以说明 urban disease 是指"疾病",而非"城市病"。该报道的题目为"The Health of the Cities",作者为爱德华·L. 格莱瑟(Edward L. Glaeser)。文中第一句中的 urban disease 就和下文中的 cholera epidemics(霍乱)相对应,而霍乱并不属于所谓的"城市病"。

The conquest of **urban disease** in the developed world has been one of the great triumphs of the past two centuries. The chart below, which has adorned the Summary of Vital Statistics of the City of New York for decades, gives a sense of the magnitude of the achievement. In the 19th century, 2 percent of the population died in a normal year, and during extreme events, like the **cholera epidemics** of 1832 and 1849, 5 percent of the population might perish.

再次,urban social problems 这个译文更是有问题,这一点金其斌先生(2003)已经谈及,他认为,"social problems"与 terrorism(恐怖主义)、crime and violence(暴力与犯罪)、drug use(毒品)、sexually harassment(性骚扰)、gays and lesbians(男、女同性恋)、mental disorders(心理障碍)、ethnic minorities(少数民族)等相关,而非"城市病"的所指。在此基础上,金先生又根据词典的定义自己拟定了一个译文:problems arising from overpopulation in big cities such as pressure on electricity and water supply, heavy traffic and environmental deterioration, and consequently health problems。

金先生的译文怎么样呢? 首先,译文太长。与其说是翻译,不如说是解释。而由于译文太长,在翻译实践中便难以使用。譬如,上面《北京科技报》中的那句"专家披露,未来五年我国"城市病"将进入高发期"在翻译时就无法套用金先生的译文。其次,该译文内容不全面。从上面"城市病"的定义我们可以看出,"城市病"起码包含了五个方面,译者用

---

[1] 见 http://www.haaretz.com/print-edition/news/a-worrying-urban-disease-reports-of-rabies-cases-are-up-1.1797

such as 这样的结构来表示,注定在表达内容上不全面,譬如"城市贫困"一项就没有体现。当然,该词定义中所提及的只是五个主要方面,至于其他一些次要方面以及由这五个主要方面所引发的其他问题那就更多了。

最后,urban malady 这个译文其实也不正确。译者在提出该译文时,曾引用了下面一段话来佐证[2]:

Lying across the Hudson River in sight of Manhattan's towers, Newark is a grimy, sprawling industrial ghetto, heir in full measure to nearly every **urban malady** of modern America. Its rich are few, its poor numerous, its population of 405,000 nearly equally and often acrimoniously divided between black and white. The miasma of the oil refineries in the nearby Jersey meadows hangs over the city, and so, too, does the pervasive smog of crime and corruption.

但他很快就认识到,引文中的 urban malady 其实是指各种各样的 social problems,也非帖子中所争论的"城市病"。

当然,关于 urban malady 的谬误,我们还可以从 malady 一词本身的意义进行佐证。根据《朗文当代高级英语词典》,malady 一词有两个含义:(1) something that is wrong with a system or organization [制度或机构的]弊病,弊端;(2) *esp. old use* an illness [尤旧]疾病。这样看来,用该词来翻译"城市病"的"病"也不恰当。

那么,"城市病"应该如何英译呢?笔者认为,"城市病"不是中国城市独有的问题,国外城市也存在"城市病",所以英文中理应有该词的地道表达。在这个思路的指引下,经过调研,笔者发现,其实汉语中的"城市病"就是英文中的 urban problem。下面通过两个例子进行说明:

第一个例子是出自联合国计划署(United Nation Development Programme)的一份报告[3]。该报告的题目为 URBAN PROBLEMS REMAIN SIMILAR WORLDWIDE,其中列举了 14 种 urban problems 以及各市市长对其严重程度的看法。下面是节选的该文中的相关部分:

[2] 见 http://bbs. chinadaily. com. cn/viewthread. php? gid = 4&tid = 568699。

[3] 见 http://mirror. undp. org/magnet/icg97/SURVEY. HTM。

URBAN PROBLEMS REMAIN SIMILAR WORLDWIDE

NEW YORK, 28 JULY—The United Nations Development Programme announced today that unemployment remains the world's number one urban problem, according to a survey of mayors of cities from around the world. A similar 1994 survey also revealed unemployment as the world's foremost urban problem.

The UNDP survey of 14 categories of urban problems and the percentages of mayors identifying them as "severe" (they were permitted more than one choice), are as follows:

Ranking	Problem	Percent
1	unemployment	52.0
2	insufficient solid waste disposal	42.0
3	urban poverty	41.6
4	inadequate housing stock	33.8
5	insufficient solid waste collection	30.9
6	inadequate water/sanitation facilities	28.4
7	inadequate public transportation	26.2
8	traffic congestion	22.3
9	poor health services	21.5
10	insufficient civil society participation	20.9
11	inadequate education services	18.9
12	air pollution	17.4
13	urban violence/crime/personal safety	13.5
14	discrimination (women. ethnic, poor)	6.8

很明显,上面 14 项中包含了汉语"城市病"的所有表现,甚至还包括卫生健康问题(第 9 项),这与"城市病"的各项内容何等契合!

第二个例子是一篇报道香港的 urban problems 的文章[4],这篇文章

----

[4] 见 http://ihouse. hkedcity. net/ ~ hm1203/development/urb-problem. htm

非常详细地列举了香港的各种"病症"及相应的解决方案（如下），而这些"病症"基本上涵盖了"城市病"所包含的所有内容。

问　题	相关情况	主要解决方法
市区土地日少	地价及租金上升	发展市郊；向高空发展；移山填海
人口密度过高	使其他问题恶化	分散人口
居住环境挤迫	卫生差、易生意外	市区重建
房屋不足	寮屋、旧楼	增加建屋土地
交通挤塞	污染、意外	改善交通网；发展集体运输系统
城市蔓延	市容、意外、蚕食郊区	清拆重建；立法管制
市区破落	挤迫、意外、设施差	市区重建
污染	废气、垃圾、噪音、污水	提高认知；控制污染
生活指数高	居民及投资减少	社会保障；重订政策以吸引投资
生活紧张	容易生病	推广康乐活动
罪案多	生活紧张	加强警力
疾病多	降低生活素质	注意卫生；普及医疗
意外频生	人命及金钱损失	加强宣传；改善相关的设计
人口老化	加重社会负担	提高生产力；安排退休保障

　　这样看来，"城市病"的"病"只是国人的一个形象说法，事实上就是指"城市问题"。正如上面《北京科技报》中那篇文章所报道的那样："**所谓"城市病"，是对城市问题的一种形象说法**。它是存在于城市发展中比较突出的问题和矛盾，这种矛盾只有在城市化、工业化快速发展的阶段才会凸显出来。城市病主要包含城市的人口、环境、交通、住房、资源等社会问题。"有鉴于此，我们在英译该词时大可不必纠缠于具体的"病"应如何翻译，而应该通盘考虑该词的内涵和外延。"城市病"的英文就是 urban problems。

充　电

　　"充电"一词近年来颇为流行,《现代汉语词典》(第五版)对其的释义为:通过学习补充知识、提高技能等。并提供了一个例子:为适应新的形势,每个人都需要通过不断充电来提高自己。这个释义基本上是正确的,但在实际使用中,"充电"一词似乎不仅指"知识技能等的补充和学习",也指充分休息,让自己精力充沛。例如:

　　1. 秋困来袭,巧妙午睡**充电**

　　　　　　　　　　　　　　　　　　《新快报》,2010 年 9 月 14 日

　　2. 午睡为健康**充电**

　　　　　　　　　　　　　　　　　　搜狐网,2007 年 4 月 5 日

　　3. 休息是大脑的休整,好比是"**充电**",主要方式是睡眠。适度的睡眠能消除疲劳,恢复精力。睡眠时间的长短,应根据疲劳程度而定。

　　　　　　　　　　　　　　　　　　人民网,2007 年 1 月 8 日

　　4. 会休息的人才会工作,给心灵放假,等于给精气**充电**,要想不断地放电,平时就得不断地充电,做到磨刀不误砍柴工!

　　　　　　　　　　　　　　　　　　伊莎贝尔,《随笔小札》

　　5. 由于 10 月 1 号是中国国庆,当地快递将会放长假。而小店也会放假 10 天休息**充电**一番,以便应付即将进入的高峰期。

　　　　　　　　　　　　　　　　　　爱我时尚网站(25fashion.com)

这样看来,只把"充电"定义为"通过学习补充知识、提高技能"其实并不全面,或至少遗漏了该词"休息"的意思。所以,笔者认为,"互动百科"对该词的释义"该词现在多用于为企业、个人补充力量或知识,不断使自己得到进步与提高"或许更为全面、科学。

关于"充电"一词的英译,目前争议较多。杨全红先生(2003)及《英汉大词典补编》(1999)均认为可以译为 recharge one's batteries。而周邦友先生(2008)则认为"汉语'充电'强调的是'需努力学习',方能补缺补差,以适应新的工作或新的工作环境,而 recharge one's batteries 突出的却是'需要放松、休息,以恢复体能'。因此,汉语新词'充电'不能译为'recharge one's batteries'",而根据他的分析,"充电"应该译为 reskill 一词。另外,《汉英大词典》(第三版)则完全将该词意译为 study to acquire more knowledge、replenish(or extend)one's knowledge。该词典倒是用了 recharge one's batteries 这个译文,但却是用在了另外一个义项"休息、放松"之下,并将其置于 relax 和 spend one's leisure 之后。最后,《汉英大词典》(第三版)则用了 update one's knowledge 和 brush up 来译"充电"。

那么,上面的观点或译文如何呢?"充电"一词到底应该如何英译呢?下面一一进行分析:

首先,周邦友先生的观点是正确的。如果"充电"的意思为"通过学习补充知识、提高技能等",的确不能用 recharge one's batteries 来译,但另一方,如果"充电"的意思是"休息"或"养精蓄锐",则 recharge one's batteries 是一个形神兼备的译文。此外,表示"休息"的意思时,还可以直接用 recharge 来译。例如:

We all have too much to do, so take time out and **recharge yourself** by getting a good night's sleep.

Recharge yourself by getting plenty of rest, and stay comfortable in bed with a maternity pillow.

其次,reskill 一词的确是一个非常好的选择,该词的意思为:to train(workers)to acquire new or improved skills,是由 reskilling 逆生(back-formation)而成的。但该词一般用于失业人员的再培训。当然,在汉语中,"充电"既可以指从业人员通过"充电"提升自我,也可以指失业人员通过"充电"重新找到适合自己的岗位。所以用 reskill 来翻译"充电"是一个较好的选择。例如下面的引文:

Robert said: "You're never too old to **reskill** and start a new, exciting career."

It is an age where one needs to **reskill oneself**, or else one will surely perish.

Teachers in college obviously also have to **reskill themselves** to cope with the changing situation.

Lifelong learning with constant **reskilling** is thus imperative if workers are to keep pace with changes and remain relevant to the needs of the workplace.

Semi-skilled occupations will require **reskilling** and training to adapt to changes in the workplace.

第三, study to acquire more knowledge 虽然可以部分表达"充电"的意思,但该译过于直白,而且是纯粹的解释,并非"充电"一词的最佳译文。

第四,用 brush up 翻译"充电"并不合适,因为该词的意思是 to renew a skill,即"熟悉/温习某一个技巧",而这个技巧往往是以前已经掌握的,这与"充电"一词在意义上有所出入。

第五, replenish one's knowledge 和 update one's knowledge 是意译"充电"较为理想的译文。其中的 replenish 和 update 也较为形象地指出了"充电"的方式和目的。例如:

To keep up with times, we have to **update our knowledge.**

I know that to emulate them, I must constantly **replenish my knowledge.**

最后,"充电"除了以上译法之后,还可以用 upskill 来译。Upskill 的意思是: to improve the aptitude for work of (a person) by additional training,与"充电"一词较为契合。请看下面的引文:

1. If you're not earning as much money as you'd like to, get real

about it. Either **upskill yourself** by enrolling for extra training at work or by taking night classes so that you can apply for a better position or find a new way of making extra money, for example, by working on weekends.

2. Discover the Best Ways to Upskill Yourself and Boost Your Job Prospects!

值得一提的是,尽管笔者提出了"充电"的不同译法,但译者在翻译实践中不必拘泥于这些译文,其实,"充电"就是充实自我,提升自我,英文中表达这一意思的说法不在少数。例如:

我得多读些书,给自己充充电。

I need to read more books to **enrich** myself.

要想学好英语,不断给自己充电是很重要的.

Being persistent is a rather important rule if you want to learn English well.

传　销

　　传销是近年来传入我国的一种非法营销模式，《当代汉语新词词典》(曲伟等,2004)对该词的解释是："以传导的方式销售,在我国多属非法行为,其违法的主要表现有:骗人入盟、网罗下线、以次充好、哄抬价格、强买强卖、买空卖空。"简单地说,就是员工自己购买公司的产品,并把这种销售方式推广给下线。在整个传销网络中,真正受益的只是那些处在传销"金字塔"网络顶端的极少数人,绝大部分传销人员不仅没有挣到什么钱,到最后反而血本无归。

　　该词在《新华新词语字典》(2003)里被误译为 direct distribution,因为 direct distribution 在英文中的意思是:the method of marketing in which the manufacturer sells directly to customers without the use of retailers,这其实是"直销"的概念。根据第 443 号国务院令公布的《直销管理条例》,直销是指直销企业招募直销员,由直销员在固定营业场所之外直接向最终消费者推销产品的经销方式。"直销"的英文表达除了 direct distribution 外,常见的还有 direct selling/sales、door to door selling、people to people selling 等。"广告电话直销"规范的说法是 direct response advertising,"电话直销"则为 direct sales via/by telephone。

　　既然 direct distribution 不是"传销",那么"传销"这一概念如何英译呢?答案是 pyramid selling/sale 或 multi-level marketing。

　　下面这两段话不但揭示了 pyramid selling 的定义,而且明确认定其为非法或骗局:

Pyramid selling is an illegal type of network marketing in which recruits pay an admission fee to join the scheme to earn commissions on persuading other people to join the scheme, but little or no product of any real value is exchanged. Such schemes are banned in most countries.

Pyramid selling is a fraud. It is a mechanism by which promoters of so-called "investment" or "trading" schemes enrich themselves in a geometric progression through the payments made by recruits to such schemes.

"传销"之所以可以译为"multi-level marketing",是因为最早"传销"一词就是从英文"multi-level marketing"翻译过来的,意思是:多层次相关联的经营方式。下面对该词的定义可以帮助我们更好地理解这个概念:

Multi-level marketing is designed to create a marketing and sales force by compensating promoters of company products not only for sales they personally generate, but also for the sales of other promoters they introduce to the company, creating a downline of distributors and a hierarchy of multiple levels of compensation in the form of a pyramid.

最后,关于"传销"和"直销"的区别,我们也可以从 *Time* 中一篇介绍安利公司的文章管窥一斑:

Usually people with other jobs, they join Amway for extra income. They buy their wares from higher-level "direct distributors," who also sell door to door. Regular distributors are urged to become direct distributors themselves, and they do so by recruiting, training and supervising new salespeople. Though the direct distributor is not paid for signing up these recruits, he does make additional money by selling Amway products at a slight mark up to the distributors under him. ... Though the result is a many-layered sales organization, it differs significantly from unscrupulous pyramid sales schemes like Glenn ("Dare to Be Great") Turner's Florida-based cosmetics operation, in which participants earned money by signing up new distributors rather than by selling the company's products.

综上所述,direct distribution 并非"传销",而是"直销"。"传销"的正确译文应该是 pyramid selling/sales 或"multi-level marketing"。

大　牌

日常生活中,我们经常听到诸如"大牌明星"、"大牌产品"等说法,也听到"某某明星耍大牌"的种种报道。"大牌"到底是什么意思呢?"耍大牌"应该如何翻译呢?

《现代汉语词典》(第五版)正式收录了"大牌"一词,并释义如下:

大牌:(1)名词:指名气大、水平高、实力强的人(多指文艺界、体育界的)。(2)形容词:名气大、水平高、实力强的:~球星|歌星|俱乐部

《汉英词典》(第三版)没有收录"大牌"一词的形容词义项,只收了其名词义项,并给出了译文 famous or influential person。但令人感到奇怪的是,这个名词义项下的例证却是该词形容词的用法:大牌选手(famous player)。《新世纪汉英大词典》则收录了该词的名词和形容词义项,其处理如下:

大牌:(名)① (usu. of people in sports and arts circles) bigwig; celebrity ② famous, prestigious:~歌星 famous pop singer

《新世纪汉英大词典》对该词的处理也有不当之处,如词性标注错误:收了名词和形容词两个词性,但却只标注了名词一个词性。

从翻译的角度来看,这两本词典的译文均有问题。首先,《汉英词典》(第三版)忽略了该词的使用范围,译文 famous or influential person 并不一定就是"大牌",譬如现任美国总统奥巴马就是当今世界上最 famous or influential person,但我们能说奥巴马是一个"大牌"吗?《新世纪汉英大词典》使用了 bigwig 和 celebrity 这两个词,其实也不确切。

Bigwig 是重要人物,但影视和艺术圈的重要人物就叫"大牌"吗? 似乎也不是。譬如,我们很难把那些在影视或艺术圈里搞管理工作的人成为"大牌",尽管他们也是 bigwig。而 celebrity 为名人,译"大牌"就更不靠谱了。此外,《新世纪汉英大词典》中对该词形容词义项的译文 famous和 prestigious 也不甚确切。原词形象、生动,译文则过于平淡、平庸。当然,把"大牌歌星"翻译为 famous pop singer 也值得商榷,pop 一词明显多余,因为"大牌歌星"不一定只是"流行歌手",如著名歌唱家宋祖英肯定是"大牌歌星",但却并非"pop singer"。由此看来,辞书条目的翻译最忌想当然、随心所欲地翻译。

那么,"大牌"一词怎么翻译呢? 笔者认为,该词的形容词和名词义项均可用 big name 来译,区别仅仅在于:做形容词用时为 big-name,而做名词用是则为 big name。仅一个连字符的差别(有时甚至连连字符也不用)! 为何使用这个词呢? 请看朗文词典中 big name 的释义:

big name:*n.* a famous person or group, especially a musician, actor, etc.

这与"大牌"一词在外延和内涵上几乎完全对等,唯一一个有出入的地方是英文中的 big name 还可以指团体,汉语中的"大牌"一般只指个人。另外,big 和 name 用连字符连接,即可用作修饰语,翻译作为形容词的"大牌"再恰当不过了。例如,下面例证中 big-name 均可译为"大牌":

Although she, too, would be the first to downplay her accomplishments, some would say she is a **big name** in the small world of miniature art.

Playcast Media nabs support from **big-name publishers**, aiming to bring STB gaming to US.

It's a rare day when a **big-name film star** makes an appearance here.

When starting out in Internet Marketing, it can be hard to decide upon what product to promote. Do you want to go with a **big name product**, or a smaller less well known one? **Big name products** are established in the market place; however there are a lot of people promoting these and you are competing with them.

　　当然,翻译重在变通,譬如"大牌明星"也可以译为 megastar。而如果要翻译"大牌衣服/化妆品等",除了可以用 big-name,我们还可以用 big-brand,例如：

Big brand cosmetics aren't necessarily any better than those from small companies.

Shopping for **big brand clothes** has never been easier or more exciting.

　　弄明白"大牌"之后,让我们再来看看"耍大牌"这个词。该词是指明星人物自以为了不起,看不起别人,有高傲自大的意思。"耍大牌"的具体表现有：

　　1. 明星对待其他人态度傲慢无理；

　　2. 出席活动经常迟到；

　　3. 答应去的活动临时不出席,也不通知主办方,让人家无所适从；

　　4. 不愿接受采访而且态度十分恶劣。

　　关于该词,笔者目前见到的有三种译文,第一种为《汉英词典》(第三版)的译文：put on airs of a megastar,第二种为《中国日报》"英语点津"栏目中的译文：throw around a celebrity's hauteur,第三种为 *The China Daily* BBS 上一位网友的译文 snub,该网友还举了一个例子：Star snubs Oscar Awards。

　　事实上,这三种译文均有问题,第一种纯粹是乱译,估计是译者忘记了给 of a megastar 加上括号了,但即使是加括号,of a megastar 也应该放在 put on airs 的前面,而非后面。此外,"耍大牌"的不只是 megastar,君不见一些 lesser-known stars,甚至一些所谓的非 star 的"名人"也常常"耍大牌"吗？最后,把"耍大牌"这一形象、生动的汉语词汇译为 put on airs 似乎也有点江郎才尽,"捣浆糊"的味道。第二种译文从字面上看似乎没有问题,但笔者查遍手头的英文文献,似乎没有一个"a celebrity's hauteur"这样的说法。这最起码说明这种译文是不太地道的。能找到第三种译文 snub,的确说明了译者已经下了不少功夫,但 snub 的意思是：to treat someone rudely, especially by intentionally ignoring them when you meet,汉语常译为：冷落、怠慢,这与"耍大牌"还是有区别的,例如,我们不可能将"Mayor Koch snubbed the Giants and refused to offer them a victory parade."这个句子中的 snub 译为"耍大牌",而只能译为"冷落"或"不予理睬"。

"耍大牌"怎么译呢? 其实英文很简单: be self-important/pompous/self-aggrandizing。当然,我们也可以用动词 exaggerate/aggrandize one's importance/power/prestige 等来译。请看下面两段描述国际象棋冠军 Bobby Fischer 成名之后"耍大牌"的情景:

Born in Chicago but reared in Brooklyn, he first drew attention as an adolescent prodigy, able to hold his own with the strongest American players at the Marshall and Manhattan Chess Clubs in Manhattan. A national champion at 14 and a grandmaster at 15, he became an international celebrity in 1972 when, at the height of the cold war, he unseated the Russian world champion, Boris Spassky, in a match in Reykjavik, Iceland. That, however, was to be the last of Mr. Fischer's triumphs. A petulant, demanding man with a cruel unpredictable streak, by the time he became world champion he was already known for his outlandishly **self-aggrandizing behavior** (笔者按:耍大牌[的行为]). It was part of what made him a legend.

In "Searching for Bobby Fischer," the 1988 book about the chess world that is partly about Mr. **Fischer's status as an icon, the author, Fred Waitzkin, summed up Mr. Fischer's behavior in Reykjavik this way: "He drove the organizers of the tournament to despair. He argued about the choice of chess table, about his hotel room, about the noise in the auditorium, about the proximity of the audience to the players and about the lighting. He demanded that the organizers lend him a Mercedes with an automatic transmission and arrange for the private use of a swimming pool. He came late to each game and kept threatening to pull out of the match if his demands weren't met."**

看看 Bobby Fischer 所提出的这些无理要求,可不正是我们常说的"耍大牌"?

代　言

　　"代言"一词最初是指代天子草拟诏命,语出《书·说命上》:"恭默思道,梦帝赉予良弼,其代予言"。但该词现在却常用来指明星或名人为某产品代言,即利用名人、明星的平面肖像或录像,通过一系列的宣传载体让产品的终端受众广为知晓的一种营销工具。例如:

　　郭德纲涉嫌**代言**虚假广告,买者要其道歉

《竞报》,2006 年 7 月 17 日

　　成龙**代言**洗发水惹风波,"霸王"深陷致癌疑云

《辽沈晚报》,2010 年 7 月 15 日

　　全国人大代表秦希燕认为,我国现行《广告法》实行 14 年以来,已经暴露出明显的局限性和缺陷,应该尽快修改《广告法》,比如明确规定:名人、明星不得**代言**医疗服务、药品、医疗器械、保健食品等广告。

《中国青年报》,2009 年 3 月 6 日

　　"代言"一词目前使用极为广泛,但至今仍未为各汉语和汉英词典所收录。论及该词的英译,读者可能立刻会想到"代言人"一词的英文 spokesman,然后通过英语词典中该词的释义 someone who has been chosen to speak officially for a group, organization or government 而归纳出"代言"的英文为 speak for。

　　的确,"代言"可以用 speak for (a product, service, etc.)来译,请看下列引文:

　　1. In our celebrity-obsessed world, getting a celebrity to **speak for a**

product or service is seen as an effective advertising method. Using celebrities to hawk products has been used since the early days of radio.

2. When someone is getting millions of dollars to **speak for a product**, his personal life becomes everybody's business!

3. Celebrities **Speak for** Perfumes

The China Daily, 2007 - 05 - 17

然而,"代言"更为常见的一个译文则为 endorse(a product, service, etc),该词的意思是:to say in an advertisement that you use a particular product and like it,与我们常见的"代言"的意义完全吻合! 譬如,"找个名人为产品代言"就可以译为"get a celebrity to endorse the product",而我们常说的"代言费"则为"endorsement fee","名人代言"为 celebrity endorsement,"名人代言产品"则为 celebrity endorsed product。下面再看看 endorse 及其名词 endorsement 的具体用法用例:

1. Let us look at what a celebrity can do for a brand, and then see what qualities a celebrity must possess to successfully **endorse a brand**.

2. Now he is going to be paid money to **endorse a product** whose manufacturer wants to help him lose that extra "daddy weight".

3. The poll found that almost two in five US adults (37%) say business leaders are the most persuasive when they **endorse a product** in an ad.

4. I would never **endorse a service** I didn't actively use myself—it would not be honest.

5. **Celebrity endorsements** have proven very successful in China where, due to increasing consumerism, it is considered a status symbol to purchase an endorsed product.

6. Celebrities **endorsing a brand** can definitely help promote a product, but it is only a means to an end, and not an end in itself.

代孕妈妈

"代孕妈妈"这个词这些年来流传甚广,让很多人大开眼界:原来怀孕也可以"代"! 而"代孕妈妈"似乎也成了一个利润不菲的职业。请看下面各个新闻的报道:

网站招聘**代孕妈妈**,大学生靠代孕狂赚30万(《广州日报》,2009年12月7日)

3名未婚女子做**代孕妈妈**,成功生育可获利10万(《信息时报》,2009年3月4日)

代孕网公开招募**代孕妈妈**,按姿色学历标价(《半岛晨报》,2009年6月10日)

年轻女子为赚10万元做**代孕妈妈**(《广州日报》,2009年12月28日)

什么是"代孕妈妈"呢? 那首先要从"代孕"谈起。女性如接受他人委托,用人工辅助生育的方式为他人生育子女,则称为代孕。代孕分为体外受精和人工授精两种方式,没有身体接触。而代孕妈妈指的就是这些代人怀孕,借腹生子的女性。

代孕妈妈在有些国家,如俄罗斯、美国等,是合法的,而在另外一些国家,如德国、日本等,则是非法的。在我国,尽管还没有相关的法规出台,但是已经悄然流行。目前,网上有很多代孕机构为没有生育能力的夫妇和代孕妈妈牵线搭桥。反对者认为这种行为是对女性身体的践踏,而没有生育能力的夫妇则认为这是让自己婚姻幸福的一个好方法。

"代孕妈妈"如何用英文来表达呢？也许有人很快会想到 2008 年美国的一个同名电影"Baby Mama"。影片讲述的是一位 37 岁事业成功但没有生育能力的单身女性寻找"代孕妈妈"以完成自己做母亲的愿望的一个喜剧。然而，我们很容易会发现，这里的 Baby Mama 虽然在汉语中被翻译为了"代孕妈妈"，但这个译文只是译者基于电影剧情的翻译，baby mama 本身并非"代孕妈妈"。

事实上，代孕妈妈的正确英文表达为 surrogate mother。请看 *Columbia Encyclopedia* 对该词的定义：

Surrogate mother is a woman who agrees, usually by contract and for a fee, to bear a child for a couple who are childless because the wife is infertile or physically incapable of carrying a developing fetus.

这里的 surrogate 即可以作形容词，意思是"替代的"、"代用的"，也可以做名词，即"代替者"。该词的抽象名词形式 surrogacy，即为"代孕"的意思，请看下列相关的表达：

Surrogacy is defined as the use of a third party female to provide the eggs for a conception and to carry the pregnancy until delivery. A couple who decides to **use surrogacy** must make some large sacrifices. The female partner will not have any genetic contribution to the pregnancy and will not get to carry or deliver the pregnancy. **Potential candidates for surrogacy** are those women who are in need of BOTH viable eggs and a host uterus.

另外，"代孕妈妈"还有一个比较专业的说法：gestational carrier，它的意思是：a woman who agrees to carry a baby on behalf of someone else。

最后，代孕还分为"有偿代孕"和"无偿代孕"两种，前者是指代孕者接受雇主除医疗费和其他合理的费用之外的补偿费用，英文为 commercial surrogacy，后者指代孕者不接受上述的补偿费用，英文为 altruistic surrogacy。

代位继承

"代位继承"是和"本位继承"相对应的一种继承制度,是法定继承的一种特殊情况。它是指被继承人的子女先于被继承人死亡时,由被继承人子女的晚辈直系血亲代替先死亡的长辈直系血亲继承被继承人遗产的一项法定继承制度,又称间接继承、承租继承。

"代位继承"一词已为 2003 年商务印书馆出版的《新华新词语词典》所收录,该词典所给的英文对应词为 succession by deceased heir's descendants。而 2003 年年底出版的《新世纪汉英大词典》则将该词译为 suborganization succession。稍作考察,我们即会发现,《新华新词语词典》的译文其实是一种根据汉语释义的硬译,根本没有法律术语的严谨性和规范性,而《新世纪汉英大词典》的译文则更不可思议,因为词典编者不但把 suborganization 误拼为 suborganization(应为 subrogation,英文中没有 suborganization 这个词),而且 suborganization succession 在英文中并不存在。

那么,"代位继承"应如何翻译呢? 正确的译法应该是:inherit in subrogation 或 representation/succession by representation。首先来看 inherit in subrogation,《中华人民共和国继承法》第 11 条的汉语和英文版可为此译提供佐证:

第十一条 被继承人的子女先于被继承人死亡的,由被继承人的子女的晚辈直系血亲**代位继承**。代位继承人一般只能继承他的父亲或者母亲有权继承的遗产份额。

Article 11. Where a decedent survived his child, the direct lineal descendants of the predeceased child shall **inherit in subrogation**. Descendants who inherit in subrogation generally shall take only the share of the estate their father or mother is entitled to.

当然,从 inherit in subrogation,我们还可以推知"代位继承"英文的名词表达形式 subrogation inheritance。请看下面两个来自原版英文的段落:

(1) The result is that the right of subrogation varies from state to state in detail. In addition, because the right of subrogation is so old, there are separate rules as **subrogation inheritance**, mechanic liens, collateral, co-debtors, co-partners, mortgagees or government units.

(2) The term victim means a person who has incurred a pecuniary loss as a direct result of the commission of the offense underlying a forfeiture. A drug user is not considered a victim of a drug trafficking offense under this definition. A victim does not include one who acquires a right to sue the perpetrator of the criminal offense for any loss by assignment, **subrogation inheritance**, or otherwise form the actual victim, unless that person has acquired an actual ownership interest in the forfeited property.

再看 representation 和 succession by representation,在一篇讨论加拿大魁北克的继承法的文章中就有如下表述[1]:

Succession by representation takes place when a descendant becomes a successor in the place of an ascendant who has died or is declared unworthy of inheriting.

Example

Norman has two sons, George and Robert. George has a daughter, Mary.

George dies in 1990.

---

[1] 见 http://www. justice. gouv. qc. ca/english/publications/generale/success-a. htm。

Then Norman dies in 1995.

Norman's successors are his descendants George and Robert.

Since George is deceased, Norman's granddaughter Mary, as a representative of George, becomes a successor in the place of George.

Representation takes place ad infinitum in the direct-line descendants of the deceased: children, grandchildren, great-grandchildren, and so forth.

In the privileged collateral line, **representation** is permitted only in favour of the children of the deceased's brothers and sisters.

另外,陆谷孙先生所编纂的《英汉大词典》(第二版)中也收录了 representation 的这层意思。

最后,有些学术论文中还把"代位继承"翻译为 succession by subrogation,但这种说法在原版英文中并不存在,估计也是想当然的译法。

值得一提的是,用 subrogation 来译"代位"在英文中也比比皆是。譬如,subrogated right 或 right of subrogation 为"代位权", claim by subrogation 为"代位索赔"等等。

单位犯罪

　　"单位犯罪"是近年来出现的一个汉语新词,商务印书馆 2003 年出版的《新华新词语词典》中即收录该词,并提供了英文译文: crimes committed by organizations。很明显,这个译文一看就是解释性翻译,并非"单位犯罪"的英文对应词。想要弄清楚该词的英译,我们首先要搞清楚它的意义。

　　所谓"单位犯罪",在刑法理论上一般称为法人犯罪(corporation crime),是进入 20 世纪 80 年代以后在我国社会生活中新出现的一种犯罪现象。它是指公司、企业、事业单位、机关、团体实施的依照法律规定应当负刑事责任的危害社会的行为。"单位犯罪"是个人犯罪的对称,是指以单位为主体的犯罪。

　　"单位犯罪"的正确英文表述应该是 unit crime,有时为了行文需要可以翻译为 crime committed by a unit,而非《新华新词语词典》中所用的 organizations 一词。例如,《中华人民共和国刑法》英文版目录中第四节"单位犯罪"的表述即为 unit crime,而在法律文本中又变通译为 crime committed by a unit。

　　值得注意的是,法律术语的英译一定要注意译文的规范性,但遗憾的是,在《新华新词语词典》中,我们发现不少类似 crimes committed by organizations 这样不规范的英文,作为"标准书"的词典,在很大程度上可能会对读者产生误导作用,所以作为编者的译者一定要小心谨慎,在落笔之前多查查,多问问相关的专业人士,避免说外行话。下面是我们发现的该词典中法律条目英译中的一些问题、笔者修正后的译文以及相关的支持材料：

（1）侵犯商业秘密罪：crime of breaching business secrets，应该是 crime of encroachment upon commercial secrets。

例如：Whoever engages in one of the following activities which **encroaches upon commercial secrets** and brings significant losses to persons having the rights to the commercial secrets is to be sentenced to not more than three years of fixed-term imprisonment, criminal detention, and may in addition or exclusively be sentenced to a fine. ...

Criminal Law of the People's Republic of China （Provisions of Intellectual property Crime）

（2）婚内强奸：rape committed by spouse，应该是 marital rape、spousal rape、rape in marriage、rape by a spouse。

例如：**Marital rape**, also known as **spousal rape**, is non-consensual sex in which the perpetrator is the victim's spouse. As such, it as a form of **partner rape**, of **domestic violence**, and of **sexual abuse**. Once widely condoned or ignored by law, spousal rape is now repudiated by international conventions and increasingly criminalized. Still, in many countries, spousal rape either remains legal, or is illegal but widely tolerated and accepted as a husband's prerogative. （From Wikipedia）

Rape in marriage：Rape in marriage was criminalised as recently as 1982 in Scotland and 1991 in England. Before these dates a woman had no legal protection for the crime of rape perpetrated against her by her husband.

http://www.rapecrisis.org.uk/maritalrape2.php

Spousal rape, also known as **marital rape**, is non-consensual sex in which the perpetrator is the victim's spouse.

While rape by a stranger is highly traumatic, it is typically a one-time event and is clearly understood as rape. In the case of **rape by a spouse** or long term sexual partner, the history of the relationship affects the victim's reactions.

http://en. wikipedia. org/wiki/Spousal_rape

（3）缺席判决：make a judgment by default,应该是 default judgment/ have a default judgment。

例如：**Default judgment** is a binding judgment in favor of either party based on some failure to take action by the other party. Most often, it is a judgment in favor of a plaintiff when the defendant has not responded to a summons or has failed to appear before a court of law.

Wikipedia

（4）妨害公务罪：crime of interference with public functions,应该是 crime of interference with public administration 或 crime of interference with state functions。

例如：The Shanghai No. 2 Intermediate People's Court sentenced Zhang Hongfu, Liu Xiaohua and Ai Daiqing, major leaders of the two gangs to death for murder, drug dealing, illegally manufacturing firearms and ammunition, illegally possessing firearms, and **the crime of interference with public administration**, provocation and group fighting, according to a written statement issued by the court.

"How China looks after its homeless people", *China National News*, 2010 - 12 - 06

（5）非法拘禁罪：crime of illegal confinement,应该是 crime of unlawful detention。

例如：The authorities who order that a detainee be concealed and the agents who carry out that order or in any way violate these guarantees shall be guilty of the **crime of unlawful detention**.

Minors in Detention v. Honduras, Case 11. 491, Report No. 41/99, Inter-Am. C. H. R. , OEA/Ser. L/V/II. 95 Doc. 7 rev. at 573（1998）

（6）非法取证：obtain evidence in unlawful way,应该是 obtain evidence illegally。

例如：In most situations, police **obtain evidence illegally** by intimidating a suspect to confess, and then the prosecution uses the confession as evidence during trial.

（7）巨额财产来源不明罪：crime of possessing properties if unclear sources by public servants,应该是 crime of holding a huge amount of property with unidentified sources。

例如：The Amendment raised the legally-prescribed punishment of **crime of holding a huge amount of property with unidentified sources**.

（8）介绍贿赂罪：crime of introducing bribery,应该是 crime of introducing bribery to state functionaries。

例如：Before prosecution, if the person **introducing bribery to state functionaries** takes the initiative to admit his/her crime, he or she may receive a lighter punishment or be exempted from punishment.

（9）破坏选举罪：crime of interfering with election,应该是 crime of sabotaging elections/electoral sabotage。

例如：**ELECTORAL Sabotage** charges were filed by the Commission on Elections (Comelec) before the Regional Trial Court of Pasay City against an election officer for alleged "dagdag-bawas" in the senatorial race during the May 2007 elections.

"Canvasser sued for **sabotaging elections**",

The New York Times, 2011 – 02 – 16

（10）涉黄：deal with pornography,应该是 involved in dealing with pornography。

例如：But as I have suggested, one of the problems **involved in dealing with pornography** is that it is difficult to find a definition of pornography that everyone can agree upon. Pornography is, like many concepts, hard to pin down.

Media and society：*a critical perspective*,

by Arthur Asa Berger, Rowman & Littlefield

Publishers (October 7,2003)

低　调

　　几千年来,中国一直是一个崇尚礼教的国家,谦逊也自古就被视为贤士的美德之一。时至今日,在日常生活中,"低调做人,高效做事"仍是长辈嘱咐后辈的训语之一。《现代汉语词典》(第五版)上"低调"的释义有二:(1)指低的调门儿,比喻缓和或者比较消沉的论调;(2)形容和缓而不张扬。在日常生活中,第二层意思更为常见,如:十大处事**低调**气质透明女星;以色列总理来访美方**低调**;部分企业**低调**行善无人知等等。

　　《新华新词语词典》、《新时代汉英大词典》以及《新世纪汉英大词典》等各类具有较大影响的汉英词典均把"低调"的第二义译为"low key"或"low pitch/voice"。这种处理方法把"低调"的两层意思简单地混淆一起,比较混乱,而且由于读者不易弄懂这些译文之间的区别,使用时也容易出错。下面从以上词典中的译文出发,简单讨论一下"低调"一词第二层意义的各种译法。

　　首先,low pitch/voice 指的是"低调"一词的第一层意思,不能用来翻译其"和缓而不张扬"的意义。

　　其次,low key 既可用来指第一层意思,也可用来指第二层意思,但当它用来指第二层意思时,通常使用其形容词用法 low-key,后跟介词 on/toward 或名词。例如:

　　In fact, the two companies **remain low key on** the project at this stage because the details are not finalised and hence there is no certainty that they will eventually go ahead with the project.

While Tokyo has long opted to **remain low-key on** the Taiwan issue for fear of upsetting Beijing, Japan has taken a public interest in stability across the Taiwan Strait.

President Reagan was briefed of the military action but the White House maintained **a low-key attitude** on the developing conflict in the South Atlantic.

最后,"低调"更为常见的译文为"low profile",而它的反义词"高调"则为"high profile"。请看《牛津高阶英汉双解词典》对 a high/low profile 的解释:the amount of attention sb/sth has from the public。此外,该词典还提供了一个例证:I advised her to **keep a low profile** for the next few days.(我建议她接下来一些天能保持低调。)

事实上,low profile 这一成语的来源非常形象,profile 是指人的侧面轮廓,如果一个人不抬高自己的侧面轮廓,别人就很难看清你,比方说,去剧院欣赏歌剧的你匆匆来迟,为了不挡住其他观众的视线,你就得弯下身子(bent down, literally keep a low profile)到达你的座位上。在英语中,这种表达很是常见,例如:

I was late for work today. I should **keep a low profile** so the boss doesn't notice.

American film actress Vanessa Hudgens has revealed that she tries to **keep a low profile** whenever out in public so as to avoid any negative news.

Japan today simply stands too tall and too rich to **maintain a low profile.**

当然,如只注重意义的传达,"低调"一词似乎也可以译为 restrained 等词,如"反应低调"就可以译为:be restrained in his response.

综上所述,"低调"一词的可译为 low-key、low profile 或者 restrained,"保持低调"则为 keep/remain a low profile/low key。而文章开头的古训"低调做人,高效做事!"则可以译为:Be efficient while keeping a low profile。

地　王

　　最近 10 年来,中国老百姓感受最深的恐怕就是房价的飚涨了。据说中国的一线城市(first-tier city),如北京、上海的房价目前完全可以比肩甚至超过诸如纽约、东京这样的国际大都市了。而这一怨声载道的现象的成因之一,大概就是近年来"地王"频显,频频刷新各个城市的地价,最终导致房价快速上涨、居高不下。难怪财经评论家时寒冰先生在自己的博客中宣称"地王""是一个邪恶的魔咒"、"是畸形的房地产催生出来的一个怪胎"。

　　那么,什么是"地王"呢? 简而言之,"地王"是指在商品房用地拍卖中以极高价被拍得的建筑用地。譬如,据《第一财经日报》2010 年 2 月 8 日报道,国土部已经接连对外公开了九宗 2009 年地王的出让合同细节,最新的一宗来自上海,是 2008 年 12 月 23 日成交的上海市新江湾城 C6 地块,其 32484 元/平方米的楼面地价一度创下国内住宅地块最高单价。中国房市一直居高不下,因而地价随房价一起只涨不降,地价记录经常被刷新,这些创纪录的高价地便被称为"地王"。在"新华网"近期评出的年度热词中,"地王"一词赫然在列,其在 2009 年的"火爆"程度可见一斑。

　　"地王"应该如何翻译呢?《21 世纪英语报》中将其译为 imperial estate。该报认为,"在英语中,'高得出奇的价格'(天价)可以用 at an imperial price 来表示,而 estate 一词本身就有'房产用地'的意思,因此,"拍卖而得的天价房产用地"就可译为 the estate auctioned at an imperial price，但此种表达方式过于拖沓，所以不妨根据英语的构词习惯，将其简略为 imperial estate。Imperial 一词在英语中本来就有'帝王的'之意，在此以'帝王般的房产用地'喻'地王'，颇有相得益彰之处。"

其实，上面的译文让人感到莫名其妙，因为在一般人看来，所谓 imperial 就是指"帝王的"、"帝国的"、"皇家的"，该词与 estate 连用，给读者的最直接感觉是"皇室的地产"、"帝国的地产"、"皇帝的地产"，而非我们所说的"地王"。另外，"at an imperial price"作为一个短语的确有"高价"的意思，但单独一个 imperial 在与 estate 连用时却并不是这个意思。事实上，imperial estate 在英文中的确是指"皇室/帝王的产业"，下面几段引文均可证实：

During that time, the Nazi Germans robbed and vandalized **the imperial estate**; a special unit looted the palace and moved its valuable art collection to the Nazi Germany. Then the palace was destroyed by the Nazis using explosive devices.

German Encyclopedia

The Church of the Ascension was built in 1532 on the **imperial estate** of Kolomenskoye, near Moscow, to celebrate the birth of the prince who was to become Tsar Ivan IV ('the Terrible'). One of the earliest examples of a traditional wooden tent-roofed church on a stone and brick substructure, it had a great influence on the development of Russian ecclesiastical architecture.

UNESCO World Heritage Center

The Asian man's grave was found in a cemetery at Vagnari, which experts have determined became the site of an **imperial estate** at some point after the rise of Caesar Augustus in 27 B. C. and before the death of Nero in 68 A. D.

Winnipeg Free Press, 2010 - 02 - 28

有鉴于此，我们认为，"地王"还是应该遵照 *The China Daily* 等主流媒体的做法，直译为 land king，而不必费尽心思去寻找一个"地道"的英文说法，原因很简单，"地王"是一个具有中国特色的词汇，国外既然没

有这种现象,也就不会有其"地道"的说法。下面几句话是几个国内主流媒体报道的标题:

Land king loses MYM29.30m deposit in Beijing

The China Daily, 2010 – 02 – 02

New "**land king**" auctioned for 7 bln yuan in Shanghai

The People's Daily Online, 2009 – 11 – 11

New **land king** expected in Beijing's CBD

CCTV 9,2010 – 02 – 13

第 三 者

　　《现代汉语词典》(第五版)对"第三者"的定义为:(1)当事双方以外的人或团体;(2)特指插足他人家庭,跟夫妇中的一方有不正当的男女关系的人。我们这里所说的"第三者"就是指该词的第二个义项。现代社会充满着诱惑,"第三者",有时又戏称"小三"(尤指女性"第三者"),处处"插足",对正常婚姻构成了不小的威胁。尽管有人辩称"第三者"也有追求幸福的权利,但"第三者"总体而言还是过街老鼠,人人喊打。

　　很多出版物均想当然地将该词译为 the third party,或对其含义加以解释。如《现代汉语词典》(汉英双语 2002 增补本)的译文为:third party;person who has illicit sexual relations with either one of a married couple。再如《新时代汉英大词典》的译文为:person having an affair with either the husband or the wife; third party。然而,我们清楚地知道,英文中的 third party,是指(formal or law) a person who is involved in a situation in addition to the two main people involved。这明显是"第三者"的第一个义项。所以,third party 经常用来翻译合同的第三方、第三方物流(third party logistics)、法律中的"第三人"等。事实上,英语中很少用third party 来表示插足别人婚姻的"第三者",譬如,Wikipedia 列举了third party 的在不同语域中的各种用法,但却没有一项表示此义。

　　那么,涉足别人婚姻的"第三者"应该如何来译呢?英文中常见的说法为:the other man/woman,既简洁又传神。例如:*The New York*

Times 就曾专文讨论 the other man/woman 这个问题,下面的引文是这篇文章的前两句:

In general, society looks at **the other man/other woman** as being the responsible party in an affair. It's understandable that **the other man/other woman** become the target for the rage and anger the deceived spouse feels.

最新版的《牛津高阶英汉双解词典》显然也注意到了这一现象,特意收录了 other woman 一条,释义为:a woman with whom a man is having a sexual relationship, although he already has a wife or partner,与"第三者"的意思不谋而合。由此,我们也可以推出"other man"表示男性第三者,the other person 则可以泛指二者,例如下文:

Talking to **the other person** can cut both ways – sometimes it drives a wedge between a cheating spouse and his or her lover. And, sometimes it backfires; it can draw a cheating spouse and **the other person** closer together.

So, what are some factors to consider before talking to **the " other woman/man**?"

此外,还有人认为"第三者"应该译为 lover、mistress 或 concubine。但如果对照汉英两种文化对这三个词进行详细考察,我们很快就会发现,这些词均非理想的译文。首先,lover 通常翻译为"情人",但这样的翻译却往往会误导读者,因为"情人"在汉语语境中往往是一个贬义词,而 lover 在英文中则是褒义词。再看 mistress,这个词的意思倒是和"第三者"相仿,但却过于直白,没有后者来得委婉。同样的,concubine 的意思是:a woman who lives with and has sex with a man who already has a wife or wives, but who is socially less important,汉语中通常译为"妾"、"姨太太",与"第三者"大相径庭。当然,如果用了 mistress 或 concubine 还会把男性"第三者"排除在外,这也是一个问题。

事实上,除了前面谈到的 the other man/woman/person 之外,"第三者"还可采用委婉表达,译为 marital intruder。这无疑也是一个地道妥切的表达法,例如下面两例:

The lawsuit portrays the other man as a **marital intruder** who had sex with Altamont's wife and destroyed the happy family.

The injured spouse could consider filing a civil suit against the **marital intruder**, but that also is an "iffy" situation.

从上面的分析可以看出,"第三者"并非中国独有,西方国家也是层出不穷,而英语中除了上述对这种人的称呼外,还有不少其他有趣的表达(见下文中的黑体词),这从下面一段话中可见一斑:

A quote from my little book: "Whilst most women would rather stick hot needles in their eyes than be labeled a **home wrecker**, sadly there are some that have no such qualms. They have various tags, **the other woman**, **mate-poacher**, **marital intruder**, **trespasser** or **interloper**. But no matter what she's called you'll know exactly by her actions and intentions that she is a **home wrecker** by any other name. "

吊　诡

　　"吊诡"这个词近年来常见于报端,但很多大陆读者并不熟悉。而诸如《现代汉语词典》、《新华词典》、《现代汉语规范词典》等也未有收录。其实,"吊诡"一词在台湾甚为流行,含有反常、怪异、矛盾等多种意义,相近于大陆批评界所谓的"佯谬"、"悖论"、"反语"。该词的实际用法如下例所示:

　　1. **吊诡**的是,选择现代高科技及艺术美学和中外文化等有价值的专题演讲,并没有吸引大众,而换成几部古籍著作后,却引起了大众的亢奋与狂热。

　　2. 房价已经够**吊诡**的了,"房价预测"不能比房价还**吊诡**。

　　3. 不了解中国互联网的**吊诡**就开始做网络营销,并照搬一些美国的方式,显然会败多胜少。

　　4. **吊诡**的是,尽管外国人也对中国许多不规范的做法频有抱怨,但为了把事情办成,现在也越来越懂得"入乡随俗"。

　　5. 十分**吊诡**的是,面对死亡的勇气会释放出生存的能量。

　　其实,"吊诡"一词并非汉语新词,充其量只能算是旧词的重新启用。如果追根溯源的话,我们会发现,该词出自《庄子·齐物论》。庄子说:"梦饮酒者,旦而哭泣;梦哭泣者,旦而田猎。方其梦也,不知其梦也。梦之中又占其梦焉,觉而后知其梦也。且有大觉而后知此其大梦也,而愚者自以为觉,窃窃然知之。君乎!牧乎!固哉!丘也与女皆梦也,予谓女梦,亦梦也。是其言也,其名为弔诡。"这里的"弔诡"即为"吊诡"。

赵诚(1997)先生根据古人的注疏,联系"吊诡"所处的语境解释说,庄子所谓"弔诡"当指奇异而有一定道理的言论。然而一般人只感到其言论的奇异,而不识其有一定道理的深远之意。后世沿用,多用来表示怪诞、怪异、奇特、奇异之类的意思。

这样,"吊诡"就有了两类语用义。一个当用英语 bizarre 来对译,有稀奇古怪、不同寻常、离奇、奇特、不可思议、荒诞不经之类的意思;另一个当用英语 paradox 来对译,有似非而是的议论、反论、悖论之类的意思。

钓鱼执法

2009 年 9 月 8 日,上海白领张军(化名)因好心帮载自称胃痛要去医院的路人,结果却被城市交通执法大队的"钩子"诱人入瓮,认定为载客黑车,遭扣车与罚款 1 万元的处罚。这就是后来引起千夫所指的"钓鱼执法"的起源。这一黑幕曝光之后,随之各行各业中又冒出了不少"被钓者",大吐"被钓"的辛酸经历,从而引起了社会各界的强烈反响。鉴于社会舆论的巨大压力和对上海城市形象的影响,上海即将出台《上海市人民政府关于进一步规范和加强行政执法工作的意见》和《上海市行政执法人员执法行为规范》,明文禁止"钓鱼执法",并将切断"钓鱼执法"的源头。

"中文维基"对"钓鱼执法"的释义为:钓鱼执法,又称钓鱼式执法或倒钩(执法),一般指的是中国的行政、执法部门故意采取某种方式,隐蔽身份,引诱当事人从事违法行为,从而将其抓捕的执法方式,其形式类似其他一些国家的"诱惑侦查",但其性质却是利用公权为欺骗手段,谋取部门利益,属于"权力敲诈"。

当然,"钓鱼执法"也并非一无是处,譬如,不少国家的执法机关偶尔也会使用类似手段,比如香港的"放蛇"现象,就是指行政、执法部门故意隐蔽身份(例如假扮嫖客、妓女、赌客或其他顾客),于当事人从事违法行为时表露身份,从而将其抓捕的执法方式。"放蛇行动"包括警察假扮妓女,然后将嫖客逮捕,以及假扮嫖客,在答应性交易后将妓女逮捕的行为。

　　"钓鱼执法"的英译常见的有以下两种。第一种为 fishing law enforcement。但该译文明显并不高明,因为 fishing law 的意思是"渔业法",所以 fishing law enforcement 会让人误解为 enforcement of fishing law,即"渔业法的执行",这与该词的原义大相径庭。第二种译文出现在2010 年出版的吴光华先生主编的《汉英大词典》中,为 enforcing the law by angling/fishing。下面主要谈谈这种译法。

　　吴教授在接受《半岛晨报》的专访时特意提到该词的英译,他说:"中国的新词一般都有时代背景,如果单纯直译虽然简短好记,但很难让外国人明白,于是我们在本义之外还增加了引申义,虽然长一点,但表达更准确,阐述深层次问题。所以,每个新词都有至少两三种译法。"他举例说,"新词典收录的最后一个新词就是'钓鱼执法',如果直译就是 enforce the law by angling(fishing),意为通过钓鱼来执法,外国人肯定看不懂。于是有了引申义 enforce the law by preinstalling a trap,意为通过提前预设一个陷阱来执法,这就与曾经发生的上海'钓鱼执法'事件的真相基本符合了。"此外,除了 enforce the law by preinstalling a trap 之外,吴先生还给该词提供了另外一个译文:enforce the law by framing a case against the captured。

　　吴教授的解释有没有道理呢?从双语词典翻译中条目各译文语义互补的角度来说是有一定道理的,譬如,"桌子"的两个译文 desk 和 table 就相互补充,构成汉语"桌子"的完整意义。但首先,从译者的角度来看,enforce the law by angling(fishing)这个译文根本没有可用性。第二,enforce the law by framing a case against the captured 的意思是"给被捕者捏造罪名"的意思,与"钓鱼执法"在意义上并不对等。第三,enforce the law by preinstalling a trap 虽然基本译出了"钓鱼执法"的含义,但严格而言,这只是一种解释,而非地道的译文。

　　那么,地道的译文是什么呢?答案是 entrapment。Entrapment 是英美刑法中的一个概念,请看 Wikipedia 对该词的定义:

In criminal law, **entrapment** is constituted by a law enforcement agent inducing a person to commit an offense that the person would otherwise have been unlikely to commit.

再看 *Lectric Law Library's Lexicon*[1] 对该词的定义:

A person is "**entrapped**" when he is induced or persuaded by law enforcement officers or their agents to commit a crime that he had no previous intent to commit; and the law as a matter of policy forbids conviction in such a case.

这与我们所说的"钓鱼执法"百分之百契合!

事实上,国内诸如 *The China Daily* 之类的英文报纸也是用该词来报道"钓鱼执法",如:

Xu has asked for 100 yuan a month without a slice of any possible compensation, and intends to give his entire salary to the victim of a famous **entrapment** case in Shanghai. His other computer salary is 6,000 yuan a month.

The China Daily, 2009 - 12 - 21

A series of official investigations were then set off into the validity of the practice of entrapment. Sun cleared his name later that month when the district government apologized to him and admitted the illegal **entrapment.**

The China Daily, 2009 - 12 - 18

对该词英译的讨论还可以引起我们对归化和异化这两种翻译策略的再思考。近年来,不少学者认为在汉译英实践中,应注重异化的译法,因为翻译的目的不仅是为了交流,译者还应该注意目的语文化的传递。这种认识当然是正确的,但在翻译实践中,归化和异化的度应该如何把握是译者和译论研究者应该深入思考的问题。拿"钓鱼执法"这个词来说,汉语运用了"钓鱼"这一形象的表达,但如直译为 fishing,英美读者肯定不知所云,一头雾水,这样,交际的功能都丧失了,何谈汉语文化的传递? 这时,采用英文中对应的地道译文,尽管原词的形象在译文中已丧失殆尽,看来也是极为必要的。

---

[1] 见 http://www.lectlaw.com/def/e024.htm。

钓鱼短信

近些年来，国内各种"钓鱼"事件频发，让人防不胜防。这不，我们刚刚谈了"钓鱼执法"，就又出现了"网络钓鱼"、"钓鱼网站"、"电话钓鱼"、"语音钓鱼"以及最新的"桌面网络钓鱼"等诈骗手段。下面，我们主要谈谈与我们每个人的利益都息息相关的"钓鱼短信"，因为这种诈骗手段是通过手机短信的方式进行的，而手机又是现代人必备的"武器"之一，这就难怪有很多人上当受骗了。另外，我们还会顺便提提上面几种"钓鱼"手段的译法。

相信我们很多人都收到过诸如："尊敬的客户，你的银联卡在某商城消费1280元，已确认成功，如有疑问，请拨银行联合管理局电话＊＊＊找某先生"之类的短信，这就是"钓鱼短信"！据报道，这些骗子们发的手机短信大多很"无厘头"，没有称呼，字数也较少，内容多为"请把钱存入银行账户6227××××，户名张成，尽快!"据称，这些人中只要有一两个上当受骗的，骗子们就有盈利空间。

事实上，钓鱼短信属于广义的垃圾短信，是指行为人假定被害人正在进行资金汇转，向不特定多数人发送的关于收款银行账户的提示或变更信息。例如：不明来历短信注明：我银行卡磁条坏了，请速将钱汇到农行9558 8112 5258 963＊＊＊，户名刘荣。

那么，"钓鱼短信"的相应英文表达是什么呢？

要搞清楚这个问题，我们先得看看"网络钓鱼"的译法。所谓"网络钓鱼"，又名钓鱼法或钓鱼式攻击，是通过大量发送声称来自于银行或其他知名机构的欺骗性垃圾邮件,意图引诱收信人给出敏感信息(如用户名、口令、账号 ID、ATM PIN 码或信用卡详细信息)的一种攻击方式。这在英文中称作 Phishing,与钓鱼的英语 fishing 发音非常相近。请看下面 Wikipedia 对该词的定义和描述:

In the field of computer security, **phishing** is the criminally fraudulent process of attempting to acquire sensitive information such as usernames, passwords and credit card details by masquerading as a trustworthy entity in an electronic communication. Phishing is typically carried out by e-mail or instant messaging, and it often directs users to enter details at a fake website whose look and feel are almost identical to the legitimate one.

此外,我们知道,所谓"手机短信",通常译为 SMS(Short Message Service)。这样,我们就可以归纳总结出"短信钓鱼"的译法——Smishing,而"钓鱼短信"则为 smishing message。很明显,smishing 这个词是通过"拼缀法"(SMS + Phishing)而构成。现在,唯一的问题是:英文中是否有这样一个词呢? 如果有,是否就是"短信钓鱼"的意思。答案是肯定的。请看 Wikipedia 的相关表述:

Similar to phishing, smishing uses cell phone text messages to deliver the "bait" to get you to divulge your personal information. **The "hook"** (**the method used to actually "capture" your information**) **in the text message may be a web site URL, however it has become more common to see a phone number that connects to automated voice response system.**

The smishing message usually contains something that wants your "immediate attention", some examples include "We're confirming you've signed up for our dating service. You will be charged MYM2/day unless you cancel your order on this URL: www.?????.com."; visit www.?????.com if you did not make this online purchase"; and "(Name of a financial institution): Your account has been suspended. Call ###.###.#### immediately to reactivate".

Following is an example of a (complete) **smishing message** in current circulation: "Notice: this is an automated message from (a local credit union), your ATM card has been suspended. To reactivate call urgent at 866 -###-####."

上文中的第一处黑体部分告诉我们, smishing 原来是指通过发短信,让用户登录某个网址,从而泄漏自己的敏感信息,但现在却是直接通过电话,这与汉语的"短信钓鱼"完全契合。第二处黑体部分则为"钓鱼短信"的译法。

另外,上面提到的"网络桌面钓鱼"是一种更为隐蔽的欺骗方式,英文为"desktop phishing","钓鱼网络"则为 phishing site,而"电话钓鱼"则译为"phone phishing","语音钓鱼"译为"vishing"(voice phishing)。关于后两个词,请看 Wikipedia 的表述:

Phone phishing:

Not all phishing attacks require a fake website. Messages that claimed to be from a bank told users to dial a phone number regarding problems with their bank accounts. Once the phone number (owned by the phisher, and provided by a Voice over IP service) was dialed, prompts told users to enter their account numbers and PIN. **Vishing** (**voice phishing**) sometimes uses fake caller-ID data to give the appearance that calls come from a trusted organization.

最后,随着"钓鱼网站"日益猖獗,"钓鱼邮件"(phishing e-mail)日益泛滥,反网络钓鱼(anti-phishing)的软件也应运而生,比如微软就在 IE7.0 中加入了网络钓鱼过滤器(phishing filter)。但要想防止被骗,还需要我们平时多加小心。

钉　子　户

　　《现代汉语词典》(第五版)收录了"钉子户"的原意：指长期违规办事，难以处理的单位或个人。但该词现在更多地用来指代在城市建设征用土地时，讨价还价，不肯迁走的住户。"互动百科"认为，"钉子户"是指政府或房地产开发商在征用公民个人使用的土地、房产等过程中，无视公民个人的愿望要求，公民暂时像钉子一样不答应征用要求。根据以上表述，任何个人要求高于政府或开发商征用条件的**公民**，即被称作"钉子户"。

　　近几年来，关于全国各地"钉子户"的报道以及"钉子户"与"拆迁队(demolition squad/team)"之间的大战可谓不绝于耳，"涌现"出了一大批诸如"史上最牛的钉子户"、"钉子户自焚"、"老年钉子户被活埋"等社会群体事件，对社会的和谐构成了不小的威胁。

　　"钉子户"之所以成为钉子户，一般是认为拆迁补偿不多，要从开发商那里取得更符合自己利益的补偿。钉子户现象目前在中国尤为突出，其成因牵涉很多复杂的问题，非一句话可以说得清楚。但同样的情况在国外，如美国、日本等国，则完全不同，这些国家也有"钉子户"，但政府拆迁的成本如此之高，以至于政府根本就不考虑付费拆迁这个办法。所以，这些国家的"钉子户"往往"坦然"、"幸福"，让人羡慕。

　　要弄清"钉子户"的英译，首先要搞清楚其所指。从上面第一段的定义中，我们发现，"钉子户"既可以是"屋"，也可以是"人"。请看下列引述：

（1）成都一"钉子户"自焚死亡

《联合早报》,2009 年 12 月 3 日

（2）北京"最牛钉子户"奔波恳请拆迁

《工人日报》,2010 年 7 月 14 日

（3）昨日是法院通知杨武夫妇自行拆房期限之后的第一天,那幢被网友称为"最牛钉子户"的二层孤房依然孑立于工地中。

《新京报》,2007 年 3 月 24 日

很明显,上面三例中前两个是指人,而后一个则是指"屋"。因此,英译"钉子户",首先要分清楚其所指到底是"人"还是"屋",而后才能有的放矢。

关于该词的英译,争论较大,较有代表性的译文有《汉英词典》（第三版）的译文 nailed-down households、ChinadailyBBS"翻译点津"中的音译 *dingzi hu* 和 die-hard house-owner。下面做一简要分析:

首先,nailed-down households 这个译文是译者想当然的译文,完全错误。估计译者认为 nail down 的意思是"钉在某地不走",所以用了 nail 一词,然后为了强调,又用了 down 这个副词。然而,这里有两个问题,第一,nailed-down 是过去分词,所以 nailed-down households 应该解释为 households that are nailed down,意即被"钉下来"的 households,但我们知道,现实中的"钉子户"并非被"钉",而是自愿"钉下来"不愿搬迁。所以 nailed-down 一词所表述的内容与原词不符。第二,译者可能没有注意到,nail down 是英语中的一个习语,一般有两层意思:1. to force someone to say clearly what they want or what they intend to do（强迫某人表明意图）,例如:Before they repair the car, nail them down to a price.（修车前,先让他们把价钱讲明。）;2. to reach a final and definite decision about something（最终确定）,例如:Two days isn't enough time to nail down the details of an agreement.（要把协议的所有细节都确定下来,两天的时间是不够的）。也就是说,nail down 并没有"钉下来"的意思。

其次,"钉子户"是否可以音译为 *dingzi hu*? 答案是肯定的。但同时我们又要意识到,纯粹依靠音译有两个弊端,第一,对英美读者而言,纯粹的音译其实是没有意义的;第二,音译后汉语原词的形象丢失

殆尽,而且在翻译实践中需要大量的解释。譬如,笔者在为商务印书馆在国外出版发行的刊物《汉语世界》进行相关翻译时,就碰上了"钉子户"这个词,原句为"各地矿难此起彼伏,这是民生之痛;'最牛钉子户'引发热议,这是民生之重"。笔者只能勉强译为"Mine disasters occurred deeply saddening the people; the most stubbon 'dingzi hu' was a topic of heated discussion, drawing the attention of the enrite society."译完之后,对 dingzi hu 还得充分进行解释:Dingzi hu, literally "nail household", refers to residents who defy the local government's order to move out of their homes for resettlement elsewhere. These households are usually dislocated by some commercial projects and are compensated by the developers (or government) but, in many cases, the compensation is hardly enough to purchase a new home or apartment. Therefore, they refuse to move, even when construction is proceeding around their homes. 翻译的复杂程度,可见一斑!如此看来,尽管音译可以采用,但在翻译实践中却并非首选。

再次,die-hard house-owner 也不妥帖,因为 die-hard 是指那些拒不接受变化和新观点的死硬派,不仅在意义上与原词有出入,即使在文体上也与原词不符,die-hard 是一个彻头彻尾的贬义词,而"钉子户"最起码在大多数中国老百姓眼中没有贬义,否则,大家也不会为某些"钉子户"喝彩了。如果把 die-hard 和 house-owner 拼接到一起,给人的感觉就是那种拒不接受新观点的房主,这与当下国内"钉子户"的概念还是有一定距离的。

那么,"钉子户"应该如何翻译呢? 笔者经过调查,发现有以下译法:

1. 如果"钉子户"是指"屋",那就可以直译为 nail house。该译法首先见诸于 The China Daily,后来为 The New York Times 等西方媒体采用,现在已为 Wikipedia 所收录。请看下面的阐述:

A partially-demolished "nail house", the last house in the area, is seen at a construction site in Hefei, Anhui province February 2, 2010. The owner of the house is attempting to seek more compensation before agreeing to the demolition of their home, local media reported.

"'Nail house' seeks more compensation",

The China Daily, 2010 − 02 − 03

Still, the "**nail house**," as many here have called it because of the homeowner's tenacity, like a nail that cannot be pulled out, remains the most popular current topic among bloggers in China.

"Homeowner Stares Down Wreckers, at Least for a While"

The New York Times, 2007 − 03 − 27

A **nail house** is a Chinese neologism for homes belonging to people (sometimes called "stubborn nails") who refuse to make room for development.

Wikipedia

2. 如果"钉子户"是指"人",那就可以采用上例中 Wekipedia 所提到的 stubborn nails,或用 nail household。这里的 household 就是指 all the people who live together in one house。譬如下面关于京城第一外国人"钉子户"Tim Hilbert 的报道:

Tim Hilbert may have been the first foreigner holed up in one of China's famous "nail houses" — buildings occupied by stubborn tenants who refuse to leave despite the demolition of structures around them.

But he told *The China Daily* that he does not want to be tagged a "troublemaker".

"I am not proud to be a '**nail household**'. I just want to get justice and be normal," Hilbert said.

"1st foreigner 'nail household' in China",

The China Daily, 2009 − 09 − 03

Some residents, known as *dingzihu*, or "**stubborn nails**", refuse to give up their homes, resulting in violent show-downs with demolition squads. Two people burnt themselves alive last year and others have been killed fighting the demolition squads with homemade explosives.

"Chinese pharmacist stands up to eviction bulldozers",

The Observers, 2010 − 05 − 28

3. 此外,英文中的 holdout 一词在特定语境中也可以用来翻译指"人"的"钉子户"。"Holdout" refers to a person who refuses to budge (退让) unless his demands are met. 例如:

What drove interest in the Chongqing case was the uncanny ability of the homeowner to hold out for so long. Stories are legion in Chinese cities of the arrest or even beating of people who protest too vigorously against their eviction and relocation. In one often-heard twist, **holdouts** are summoned to the local police station and return home only to find their house already demolished. How did this owner, a woman no less, manage? Millions wondered.

"Homeowner Stares Down Wreckers, at Least for a While",

The New York Times, 2007 − 03 − 27

多 军

　　如果您是一位股票爱好者,您大概对"多军"、"空军"、"多头"、"空头"这些词并不陌生。例如,在股评节目中,我们常常听到诸如"空头不死,涨势不止、多头不死,跌势不止"以及"多空对弈"之类的说法。而且,这些股票用语现在似乎还被用到了房地产市场,例如:

　　地产"**空军**领袖"被曝购上海滨江豪宅

　　　　　　　　　　　　　　　　《每日经济新闻》,2010 年 9 月 15 日

　　在论坛中,支持房价下跌的网民被称为"**空军**",而支持房价上涨的被称为"**多军**"。在多数网站的论坛中,"**空军**"全面压倒了"**多军**"。

　　　　　　　　　　"新国十条"出台影响郑州楼市,市场成交量大幅萎缩",

　　　　　　　　　　　　　　　　　　河南新闻网,2010 年 7 月 15 日

　　"百度百科"认为:"多军"即看多或者看涨,多用于股市或房市中。多军即多头,与空军相对,空军即空头。在股市中,多军看涨买进,空军看跌卖出。在房市中,多军看涨,炒房或持有;空军看跌,观望或抛售。

　　这样看来,"多军"、"空军"、"多头"、"空头"既可以指一种看多或看空的"观点或看法",也可以指那些持有这些观点的"人"。因此,在探讨这些词的英译之前,我们首先应该区分其使用的语境:股票市场及房地产市场。其次,我们必须搞清楚它们所指代的到底是"人"还是"观点"

　　目前出版的汉英词典中均没有收录表示房地产市场上的"多军"和"空军",只是收录了股票市场上的"多头"和"空头",由于"多军"和"空

军"只是"多头"和"空头"的形象性说法,其译文应该和"多头"及"空头"一致,所以下面的讨论采用较为专业的表述"多头"和"空头"。《汉英词典》(第三版)和《汉英大词典》(第三版)对这两组词的处理分别如下:

多头:(on the stock exchange)bull; long

空头:(on the stock exchange)bear; short position; shortseller

多头:(买空的证券投机商)bull; long

空头:(预料证券或货价将跌,先售出期货,于跌价后再买进以获利的方式或人)bear; short-seller; oversold position

以上对这对词语的处理,无论从词典学角度还是从翻译学角度来看,均不恰当。从词典学角度而言,"多头"和"空头"属于封闭型的配套词(见赵刚,2005),其释义方式应该基本一致。譬如,既然"空头"的译文中出现了 short position,"多头"就相应地应该用 long position。从翻译学的角度而言,译者混淆了作为"人"的"多头"和"空头"以及作为"观点或方式"的"多头"和"空头",把多个译文简单地累积在一起,使读者无所适从。

有鉴于此,我们认为,股票市场上的"多头"和"空头"的英译应该分两种情况进行讨论:

1. 作为"人"的"多头"和"空头

当"多头"和"空头"指"人"的时候,"多头"应该翻译为 bull 或 long,而"空头"则应该译为 bear、short-seller 或 short。请看下列引文:

(1) A **short seller**, also referred to as a **short**, is a speculator who has sold a futures contract and has a short position in the market. These traders make money when the market goes down and they lose money when the market goes up.

(2) As the S&P 500 nears a long term trending resistance, weekly MA(50), and short term resistance, it may be time for **bulls** to take profits and **shorts** to pile in.

(3) Investors are '**long**' when they have bought assets in the hope that prices will rise and that they can sell them when prices have peaked.

2. 作为"方式或观点"的"多头"和"空头"

当"多头"和"空头""指"方式或观点"的时候,"多头"应该译为 long position 或 going long 或 bull position 或 overbought position,而"空头"则应该译为"short position"、"bear position"、"short-selling"或者"going short"或"oversold position"。例如:

(4) In finance, **short selling** (also known as **shorting** or **going short**) is the practice of selling.assets, usually securities, that have been borrowed from a third party (usually a broker) with the intention of buying identical assets back at a later date to return to the lender.

(5) In finance, a **long position** in a security, such as a stock or a bond, or equivalently to be long in a security, means **the holder of the position** owns the security and will profit if the price of the security goes up. **Going long** is the more conventional practice of investing and is contrasted with **going short**.

(6) A dealer on a financial market who expects prices to rise. A bull market is one in which prices are rising or expected to rise, i. e. one in which a dealer is more likely to be a buyer than a seller, even to the extent of buying without having made a corresponding sale, thus establishing a **bull position** or a **long position.**

此外,从上面(5)的引文中,我们还可以发现,作为"人"的"多头"和"空头"似乎也可以简单地译为 long/bull position holder,而"空头"也可以译为 short/bear position holder。

最后,再谈谈房地产市场上的"多头"和"空头"的英译。值得一提的是,*The China Daily* 的"新词语英译"一栏中将"空军"译为 no-house class 和 no-housers 其实是不确切的,因为实践告诉我们,"空军"并非只指那些没有房子的人,有房子但看跌房市的人也叫"空军",所以 no-house class 和 no-housers 只能说是"空军"中的一个重要部分而已。

笔者认为,既然房地产市场上的"多军"和"空军"是借用股票市场上的术语,我们不妨也借用股票市场上这两个词的英译 long position 和 short position 来译作为一种观点或看法的房地产"多军"和"空军",而作为"人"的"多军"和"空军"则可以译为 long position holder 和 short position holder, 至于这些人到底决定是否出手购买还是兜售房屋其实并不重要。另外, 从上面对 long position 和 short position 的定义(见上面第(4)和(5)个引文)中, 我们也可以看出, 这两个英文术语并非只指股票市场, 房地产市场上同样的行为应该也可以用它们来指代。

恶　搞

明星遭网友**恶搞**,黄晓明出书教英语,潘长江教增高。

《扬子晚报》,2010 年 7 月 28 日

"曹操这厮,智商绝对在 120 以上,丫还学孙武、吴起,就这样还在南阳、乌巢、祁山、黎阳吃过大苦头,然后才夺得现有的地盘。叔就这么点本事,不冒险是不行的,娃娃你到底懂不懂啊? 懂不懂啊? ……"看到这一股子江湖气息的句子,谁能想到这竟是千古名篇《后出师表》的白话文注解。近日,这类雷人的古文翻译正逐渐走红网络。**恶搞**古文、古诗的风气也似乎愈演愈烈。

文化中国网,2010 年 7 月 27 日

复杂的放假日程,本让人一头雾水,但在上班族带点**恶搞**与调侃的 PS 中,却变得一目了然。"个性假期表"最开始的版本只是简单的 QQ 表情,9 月 13 日到 10 月 10 日中的假日用笑脸代替,上班日则是沮丧的黑脸,哪几天哭、哪几天笑,看得倍儿清楚。比如今天本是周日,但定为工作日,就用黑脸表情表达自己的不满、沮丧。

"零碎假期遭**恶搞**:假期折腾我,我就折腾日历",
《北京晨报》,2010 年 9 月 21 日

读了上面几段引文,读者大概可以了解何为"恶搞"了吧? 所谓"恶搞",就是把一个完美或者严肃的事物,改造为庸俗的东西,通过两者之间的强烈反差达到意想不到的喜剧效果的一种做法。

"恶搞"的官方解释是"滑稽模仿及其引申发挥",而国内最出名的

一次"恶搞"要数大导演陈凯歌打造的《无极》被胡戈恶搞成《一个馒头引发的血案》。自此以后,恶搞之风就一发而不可收,愈演愈烈。开始,人们还是比较宽容这些虽然无厘头但不乏想象力与幽默感的恶搞,但直到像《闪闪的红星》这样的红色经典也遭到无情恶搞和嘲弄之后,善良的公众才开始愤怒起来!

"恶搞"肯定要有底线的,这个底线就是道德和法律。比如不能进行人身攻击,不能扰乱社会秩序。一旦"恶搞"成了真正意义上的"恶",那也会失去其本来的意义。如果对于公众人物连起码的尊重都做不到,那实在是挑战善良公众的忍耐底线。"网络暴民"破坏和谐的网络环境,就必须受到公众的谴责、舆论的鞭挞,甚至法律的惩罚。

一般认为,"恶搞"一词来自日语的 Kuso,由日本的游戏界传入台湾地区,成为了台湾地区 BBS 上一种特殊的文化。这种新文化然后再经由网络传到香港地区、继而全中国。但是,恶搞这种行为方式,早在"Kuso"出现之前在各国就已存在,它只是对古已有之的某种滑稽幽默的行为的另一种说法,很难证明与日本的"Kuso"有什么关系。

在 2010 年出版的《汉英词典》(第三版)中,"恶搞"被译为了 raise the mischief 和 play planks。很遗憾的是,这两种译文都是错误的。首先,play planks 属于低级的拼写错误,应为 play pranks。其次,raise the mischief 并非"恶搞"或"恶作剧",而是"惹事生非"、"大吵大闹"、"闹事"的意思。譬如下面两例:

Some of the big boys who were there "just to **raise the mischief**," would perhaps dare the master to go outside and fight.

This is one of the reasons which **raise the mischief** of an act of robbery so far above the mischief of a simple theft.

我们从这两种译文可以看出,译者认为"恶搞"就是"恶作剧(mischief)"或"开玩笑(pranks)"。首先,这种认识虽然并不为错,但并没有触及"恶搞"一词的本质,"恶搞"并不是简单的"开个玩笑"那么简单。譬如,曾几何时对英雄刘胡兰、董存瑞,甚至毛主席的恶搞,玩笑就开大了,引起了大部分国人的愤怒。其次,prank 和 mischief 这两个词选择不当,pranks,又称 practical jokes,往往是指那些令当事人感到很难堪的"恶作剧",它们通常是"做"出来的恶作剧(a practice),而非口头的或书面的(verbal or written jokes),譬如愚人节那天的"玩笑"或"恶作剧"。而"恶搞"的东西既可以是书面的,也可以是口头的,如上面引文中对《出师表》的恶搞便属于书面上的恶搞。Mischief 的意思则是"儿童的捣蛋和胡闹",英文释义为:bad behavior, especially by children, that causes trouble or damage, but no serious harm,这与我们常见的"恶搞"也大相径庭。

那么,"恶搞"应该如何翻译呢?答案是 parody、spoof、send-up 或 lampoon。请看下面 Wikipedia 对 parody 的阐述:

A **parody**, also called **send-up**, **spoof** or **lampoon**), in contemporary usage, is a work created to mock, comment on, or make fun at an original work, its subject, author, style, or some other target, by means of humorous, satiric or ironic imitation. As the literary theorist Linda Hutcheon puts it, "parody . . . is imitation, not always at the expense of the parodied text."

Parody may be found in music, art or culture, including literature, music (although "parody" in music has an earlier, somewhat different meaning than for other art forms), animation, gaming and cinema. Parodies are sometimes colloquially referred to as spoofs or lampoons.

从第一段对 parody 的定义我们可以看出,parody 与汉语"恶搞"在形式和性质上何其相似和契合! 从第二段中我们可以看出 parody 与"恶搞"的范围也几乎一致。

事实上,*The China Daily* 等媒体也用以上各词来表达"恶搞"。例如:

Video **spoofs** have become so popular that netizens have even coined a slang term, "egao," to describe the act of using real film clips to create mocking **send-ups.**

那么,"恶搞"为什么译为 parody 呢? 在《牛津高阶英汉双解词典》(第六版)中,该词的解释为"诙谐模仿的言语、文字或音乐"。这个词源自古希腊文学,前缀"par-"有反对的意思,"-ody"则表示歌曲,合在一起含有嘲讽原作的意思。近年来最受推崇的 parody 经典电影,就是那部连海报都损死人的《惊声尖笑》(Scary Movie)。而在互联网上,老外更爱使用"spoof"一词来表达相同的意思。

在 You Tube 上搜索"spoof",就可以领略美国网民们在"恶搞"方面的卓越才华。现在,最受欢迎的"受害者"包括苹果公司的 Mac 广告、孤独女生15,当然,还有经久不衰的星球大战以及总是说错话的美国前总统小布什先生。

最后,parody、spoof 这两个词既可以用作名词也可以用作及物动词,用作名词时常为 make a parody/spoof of sth./sb。例如,"The show spoofs/makes a spoof of commercials.(这场表演恶搞了商业广告。)"当然,它们也可以用作定语,如 spoof videos、spoof pictures、spoof articles 等等。

法 治

"法治"和"人治"应该说是热词,而非新词。"法治"建立在民主的基础上,崇尚的是宪法和法律,认为宪法和法律的权威高于个人意志,它坚持任何组织和个人不能凌驾于宪法和法律之上。而"人治"则建立在个人专断与独裁的基础上,主张的是个人的权威大于宪法和法律的权威,搞人大于法,权大于法。然而,这样一对重要的法律术语,却常常被错译。例如,*The People's Daily Online* 在翻译外交学院院长吴建民的演讲《中国是一个负责任的大国》时,把"法治"译成了 governance by law;一些权威的汉英词典(如《新时代汉英大词典》及《汉英词典》(第三版)等)把"法治"译为 rule by law、government by rule,把"人治"译为 rule of man、rule by individuals 以及 government by men,这些译文看似差别不大,但却都有问题。

先谈 rule by law 和 rule of law,这两个短语英文中都有,但意思上却区别很大。Rule by law,一般翻译为"依法而治",是指当权者按照法律治理国家,但这些法律不一定是由普通公民所组成的立法部门制订的。而 rule of law 才是真正的"法治",是指在某一社会中,法律具有凌驾一切的地位。所谓"凌驾一切",是指任何人,包括管治机构、法律制定者和执行者本身都必需遵守。法律本身被赋与一个非常崇高的地位,不能受到轻慢。政府(特别是行政机关)的行为必须是法律许可的,而这些法律本身是经过某一特定程序产生的。即,法律是社会最高的规则,没有任何人或机构可以凌驾法律。

对于社会上常见的违法或失序现象,尤其是以激烈的、游走于法律边缘的手段向政府争取权利的行为,政治官员常常会呼吁和要求人民"守法"以尊重"法治"。这其实是将"法治"的意义误解和窄化为"依法而治"。西方媒体在批评中国的法律制度时,常用 rule by law 的说法,例如,《纽约时报》2005 年 11 月 1 日就刊登了一系列文章,说中国是 rule by law 的国家,而非 rule of law 的国家。

再谈 governance by law 和 government by rule。按照上面的说法,governance by law 应该改为 governance of law,才和"法治"的意思相符。Government by rule 的说法本身就有问题,因为"法治"的"法"不是"rule",而是"law"。英文中正确的说法是 government by law 或 government by rule of law。当然,如果一定要用这个短语翻译"法治"也未尝不可,但最好改为 government of law。

最后,"人治"最好译为 rule by man,与 rule by law 相对应。而 rule by individuals 虽然可以用来翻译"人治",但却并不常用,现在常为 rule by man 所替代。例如,*Online Dictionary of the Social Sciences* 在定义 rule of law 的时候,就用到了其反义词 rule by individuals[1]。

RULE OF LAW

One of the cornerstones of democratic society, meaning that everyone is subject to the law. It is not just the rule that everyone is covered by the Criminal Code and must be charged and convicted if appropriate. It also means that no one in the society, the Prime Minister, cabinet, senior civil servants, judges or police has power except as it is derived from law. Authority can only come from law, namely the Constitution, a statute, legal regulations, Common Law, municipal by-law. There is a rule of law rather than rule by individuals.

综上所述,汉语热词"法治"的译文应该是"rule of law",间或可用"governance/government of law";而"人治"则应该译为"rule by man",

---

〔1〕见 http://bitbucket.icaap.org/dict.pl? alpha = R

间或可用"rule by individuals"。

另外,令人遗憾的是,国内一些汉英词典把类似"法治"和"人治"这样的其他一些成对词也译错了,这里仅举一例:

逃税:evade/dodge a tax

避税:evade tax；tax evasion

注:"逃税"和"避税"是两个不同的法律概念,但上面《汉英词典》(第三版)中所提供的译文却给人感觉二者完全相同。另外,《汉英大词典》(第三版)将"避税"译为:tax avoidance；evade tax,而把"逃税"译为:evade/dodge tax；tax evasion；tax avoidance；evasion of taxation,看来也是彻底混淆了这两个概念。事实上,"逃税"应为 tax evasion 或 tax fraud,而"避税"则应是 tax avoidance。如下面 Wikipedia 对这两个词的定义:

Tax avoidance is the *legal* utilization of the tax regime to one's own advantage, to reduce the amount of tax that is payable by means that are within the law. By contrast, **tax evasion** is the general term for efforts not to pay taxes by *illegal* means.

原载《辞书研究》2008 年第 6 期,有改动

房　奴

　　"房奴"这个词尽管出现较晚,但对大多数都市人来说并不是一个新词,因为环顾四周,因购房而大量贷款的人实在不在少数。"房奴"顾名思义为"房子的奴隶",是指城镇居民抵押贷款购房,在生命黄金时期中的 20 到 30 年,每年用占可支配收入的 40% 至 50% 甚至更高的比例偿还贷款本息,从而造成居民家庭生活的长期压力,影响正常消费。购房影响到人们的教育支出、医疗支出和老人抚养等,使得家庭生活质量下降,甚至让人感到奴役般的压抑。具有讽刺意味的是,目前在北(京)上(海)广(州)这样的国内一线城市(first-tier city)中,一套房子动辄几百万,很多人想当房奴却连资格也没有,因为他们连首付都付不起。

　　《汉语世界》2006 年第 1 期中将"房奴"译成了"house slave"。而 *Shanghai Daily* 用的则是"housing slave"这个译文。此外,还有人将这个词译为 room slave 或 apartment slave。最新出版的《汉英词典》(第三版)中则用了 house slave,并加上了注解:someone under the pressure of paying back housing mortgage loan。

　　从翻译的角度来看,这些译文都值得商榷。先来看看构词方式大致相同的 house slave、room slave 及 apartment slave。这三个译文的主要区别在于"房奴"的"房"如何译,那么,首先让我们看看"房奴"的"房"与 house、room、apartment 是否一样。我们知道,中国的"房"是公寓房 (apartment),而英文中的 house 则"通常至少有两层"(见英文词典对 house 的定义),room 则指 a division of building,是"房间"的意思。这样,我们便可以排除 house slave 和 room slave 这两个译文了。那么,剩下来的"apartment slave"是否就是正确的译文呢? 也不尽然。因为,"房奴"的深层意思并不是"房子的奴隶",而是说贷款者成了所贷之款的奴隶,为还清贷款而背负巨大压力,所以这种译法还是有望文生义之嫌。最后,house slave 本身就是一个固定的英文表达,表示在家里工作的奴隶,与在田地中工作的奴隶(field slave)相对。请看下列一段有关"house slave"的地道的英文表述:

Join me while I show you what house slaves were like in colonial America. House slaves were trained to do their work from childhood. They would be away from the other slaves. They would sleep on a pallet besides the masters' bedroom. The house slave was taught to believe that being a house slave was the best thing that could become of him or her. All older housemaids wore a key ring. On it, were all the keys to the pantry, the smokehouse, the cooling cellar, and other food storage's. Every house slave would walk in a way so that the keys would jingle to show how proud, important and trusted the slave was. Close to the kitchen was a large wooden building called the kitchen quarter in which the house servants ate. They also did the washing in the family and the unpleasant work such as scaling fish, cleaning and putting up pork, etc. Being a house slave was easier than being a field slave, but they had to work longer hours.

其次,再来看看"housing slave"。联系到"房价"为"housing price","房改"为"housing reform","房奴"译为"housing slave"似乎也未尝不可,但考虑到"housing"一词主要指"供给住房"的概念,与 slave 搭配似乎有点不伦不类。此外,上面提到的"房奴"实为"买房贷款"的奴隶,与"房子"本身其实关系不大。

那么,用什么来译"房奴"呢? 或许"mortgage slave"是个不错的选择。它抛弃了原文的表层含义,抓住了"房奴"之为"奴"的本质原因,而且表达地道、简洁,让人过目不忘。下面是一些主流报纸对中国/美国的"房奴"现象的报道:

Red-hot real estate markets have given birth to a new class of people, known as mortgage slaves, because the financial burden of buying into the middle-class dream of home ownership has suddenly become so great.

The New York Times, 2006 − 12 − 18

A Chinese term translated as "mortgage slave" has been adopted to describe those whose mortgage payment is more than half of their monthly salary. Most experts say the mortgage should be one-third of the household income.

The People's Daily Online, 2006 − 06 − 14

... This will inevitably create deeper societal divisions and, very likely, a permanent underclass of mortgage-slaves.... (Article titled "Hard Times Ahead For 'Mortgage Slaves'?")

The Atlantic Free Press, 2007 − 02 − 22

最后,再谈谈近几年出现的与"奴"相关的其他一些新词的翻译。我们常说的"卡奴"为 credit card slave,"孩奴"为 child's slave,"车奴"为 car's slave,"婚奴"为"marriage slave",而"墓奴"则为"tomb slave"。

非 礼

　　"非礼"一词本不算新词,意思是"所有不合礼法的行为",孔子所谓的"非礼勿视,非礼勿听,非礼勿言,非礼勿动"即为此意。《现代汉语词典》(增补版)中给该词的释义"不合礼节;不礼貌"基本上概括了这层意思。然而,在现实生活中,我们发现,该词又衍生出了新意:调戏;猥亵(妇女)。"维基百科"对此的定义为:非礼是指未经对方同意,同性或异性之间的身体接触,含性意识。所接触的部位可能但不限于是敏感部位,接触手、脚或其他部位同样有可能被视为非礼行为。在法律上,"非礼"的正式名称为猥亵侵犯,属刑事罪行。在香港地区,非礼罪成立可囚十年。下面是该词该义的一些用例:

　　(1) 今日网络疯传北京顺义五中几名男同学教室内公然**非礼**一女同学,其大胆程度令人咋舌。

　　(2) 香港警方公布的数据显示,今年第一季度的铁路**非礼**案较去年同期劲升7成。

　　(3) 据香港《文汇报》报道,现职香港中文大学生物化学系的一名副教授,涉嫌在过去3个月内,在同一条行经中环区路线的巴士车厢内**非礼**一名女乘客,案件8月12日在东区法院提堂。

　　"非礼"一词的新义,《新华新词语词典》已有收录,并提供了其英文翻译:assault。《新世纪汉英大词典》对"非礼"一词的新义亦提供了几种译文:harass sexually;take liberties with(a woman);assault;violate。下面对这些译文逐一进行分析,力图找出"非礼"一词新义的最佳译文:

首先,如有具体语境,用 assault 来译"非礼"较为恰当,如:

The suspect had a box cutter and gave the victim a choice——get cut or get raped. He then dragged her into the courtyard, where he **sexually assaulted** her.

Some say it happens all the time——women **sexually harassed, even assaulted** while riding a subway train, many in the middle of the day.

但如脱离语境,就词译词,单独一个 assault 并不能表示"非礼",因为从该词的定义 "to attack sb violently, especially when this is a crime" 来看,它并不一定涉及"猥亵"的意思。例如,在下面这个句子中,assault 就不是"非礼"的意思:

Two police constables were **assaulted** by a dozen unidentified men and robbed of their rifles and motorcycles.

其实,从上面的例子我们已经可以清楚地看出,"非礼"在英文中的表达应该是"sexually assault"或"sexually harass"。保留限定词"sexually",才能译出"非礼"的确切含义。

其次,violate 和 take liberties with 这两个表达法是否可以用来翻译"非礼"呢?答案是否定的。先谈 violate,该词本身就有性侵犯的含义,不需要借助其他词来缩小其语义范围,但该词在程度上似乎比汉语的"非礼"更为严重一些("非礼"一般而言是做下流的动作,不一定涉及"强奸"或"奸污")。例如,《牛津高阶英汉双解词典》(第六版)对 violate 一词的定义是(literary or old-fashioned) to force sb to have sex,一般译为"强奸、奸污"。再看 take liberties with (a woman),该短语在《牛津高阶英汉双解词典》(第六版)中的定义为:(old-fashioned) to be too friendly with sb, especially in a sexual way,一般译为"过分亲昵,放肆,狎昵,调戏",与"非礼"的新义似乎不谋而合。然而,细心的读者可能从这两个词的英语释义中发现它们在用法上的特点了:violate 是文学用语或古体风格,take liberties with 则是古体风格。而《现代汉语词典》(第五版)则清楚地标明"非礼"的这层意义为新义且为"方言"用法,所以 violate 和 take liberties with 与"非礼"并不能对应互译。

最后,还有一个词 molest 值得讨论,该词在汉语中虽然也译为"调戏、猥亵、作性骚扰",但通常是指对儿童的的性侵犯。例如《朗文当代高级英语词典》对该词的释义为 to attack or harm someone, especially a child, by touching them in a sexual way or trying to have sex with them,并举了一个例子:men who molest young boys。

综上所述,"非礼"一词的最佳译文应该是 harass sexually,其次应该是 assault sexually。当然,在具体语境中我们也可以使用这两种表达法的名词形式 sexual harassment 和 sexual assault。如果被骚扰的对象为儿童,则可使用 molest 一词。

负 翁

当年香港地区楼市泡沫破灭后,一夜之间发现自己的房产变成负资产的人们,第一次被媒体冠以"负翁"的称号。今天的都市里也有不少自嘲为"负翁"的人。他们收入不菲,积蓄却不多;买了房子和车子,却欠着巨额的债务。目前,这一群体正变得越来越庞大,一方面,这可能体现了"超前消费"的潇洒,但另一方面,如果一个社会"负翁"过多,生活压力过大,也会危及社会的安定。

"负翁"一词是仿拟(parody)人们常说的"富翁"而造的,"负"与"富"语音相同,但在意义上则正好相反,表示背负债务,听上去是富翁,其实是负债。该词现在常用来指代负债消费者这一新生的特殊人群,尤其是与"房奴"紧密相关。

The China Daily"英语点津"栏目中将"负翁"翻译为了 spend-more-than-earn;《辞书研究》2006 年第 2 期"新词新义荟萃"栏目中则将该词翻译为 young people with a big loan from a bank;另外,也有地方直接译为 a poor man 或 a person in debt。这些译法都是不确切的,首先,spend-more-than-earn 与其说是"负翁",不如说是"月光",因为日常生活中的"负翁"并非是指那些花钱比赚钱多的人,而是指那些背负(往往是巨额)债务(往往是房贷)的人,这些人中可能有一部分花钱比赚钱多,但大部分应该是赚的钱多于花费的钱,否则他们连当"负翁"的资格也没有。此外,该译文也无法在翻译实践中使用,譬如,你不可能把"我是一个负翁"就简单翻译为"I'm a spend-more-than-earn"。其次,young people with a big loan from a bank 不但是解释,而且语义不确,因为现实生活中的"负翁"可不一定只指 young people,还有不少是中年人。最后,a poor man 或 a person in debt 明显是过于泛化的翻译,而且与现实不符。要知道,目前都市中的"负翁"大多可不是真正意义上的"穷人",在房价迅猛飙升的今天,要做"负翁"也是要有资格的,没有几十万或近百万的资产,想做"负翁"也不够格!而谁又敢说这样的"负翁"是"穷人"呢?

那么,"负翁"应该怎么翻译呢?这里需要分情况对待。第一种情况是负债,但由于房价上升,净资产为正的那些"负翁";国内由于买房而沦落成"负翁"的人大部分属于此类。第二种情况是房产已纯粹沦为了负资产(negative equity),因而成为了名副其实的、悲惨的"负翁"。

第一种情况下可以译为(debt-ridden)mortgage borrowers,这里的 debt-ridden 为可选项,可根据负债的程度选用。之所以用 debt-ridden,是因为贷款买房者,少则几十万,多则上百万,绝对算得上"负债累累(debt-ridden)"了。当然,在这种情况下,汉语中"负"的修辞效果是译不出来了,但这就是翻译,永远存在缺憾。

第二种"负翁"在美国较为常见。事实上,作为"超前消费"源起国的美国,"负翁"的历史极为悠久,而这次经济危机爆发之后,更多的美国人为房产所累,沦为"负翁"。发现自己的房产已经变成了"负资产"之后,这些"负翁"们拒绝再向银行支付房贷,从而引发了所谓的"次贷危机(subprime crisis)"。而这些"负翁"在美国通常被称为 negative equity homeowners 或用更为形象的说法 underwater borrowers/homeowners(with their mortgages)和 upside-down homeowners。下面就这三个译文做一简单分析:

1. Negative equity homeowners 明显是"负翁"一词最为直白的说法,所谓"负翁"就是拥有"负资产",即 negative equity,而我们通常所说的"负翁"几乎无一例外是指那些贷款购房者,所以 negative equity homeowner 可谓译出了"负翁"之确切含义。当然,该译的缺点在于不够形象生动,也无法令读者产生与"负翁"一样的心理共鸣。

2. Underwater borrowers/homeowners(with the mortgages)以及

upside-down homeowners 与汉语的"负翁"可谓契合！一个 underwater 就极为形象地指出了这些"负翁"们所处的水深火热的境地：他们在水下拼命挣扎,希望不要溺水而亡,这与我们的"负翁"们何其相似？他们不敢辞职、不敢冒犯上级、不敢度假、不敢创新,而所有这一切的原因,只是因为他们还有房贷要还！而 upside-down 也很是形象,与 underwater 有异曲同工之美。

下面来自原版英文的引文,证明了这三种译法的合理性,也启发我们,"负翁"一词可用不同方式灵活表达：

1. This week, a new federal loan modification option went into effect that is aimed at helping people who **are underwater with** their mortgages – but who are still current on their payments.

——"FHA Short Refinance Option for **Underwater Borrowers**"

2. The homeowner must **be in a negative equity position**, and be current on the existing mortgage they are seeking to refinance

3. The large and growing number of **homeowners with negative equity** will increase the rate of defaults and foreclosures and therefore drive the downward spiral of prices.

4. Our concept of a homeownership gap reflects the dramatic growth in the number of **negative equity homeowners** —those who owe more on their mortgages than their houses are worth — in the current housing market.

5. Loan Modifications are only working for about 2% of the "**upside-down**" or "**negative equity**" **homeowners**.

6. The Federal Housing Administration (FHA) recently launched yet another foreclosure prevention program to address the plight of **underwater homeowners**, called a 'FHA Short-Refi Program,' the 'short' standing for a process also known as a *cramdown* or *strip-away* of excessive loan balances. The new conditions allow **upside-down homeowners** who are current on their payments to refinance into a new mortgage which the FHA will then insure.

最后,谨希望国内那些 debt-ridden 的"负翁"们不要沦为 underwater borrowers 或 be turned upside-down,也希望中国的房地产市场能够健康、繁荣地发展,让居者有其屋,人民安居乐业,社会和谐安定。

搞　定

　　"搞定"这个词大家一定都很熟悉。现实生活中,该词的使用范围很广,几乎什么都可以被"搞定"。"百度百科"将其定义为"新型口语,一种年轻的语言",常用于自我激励,表现自信或工作效率。《现代汉语词典》(第五版)中已收录该词,释义为:(方言)把事情办妥;把问题解决好。

　　目前,关于该词的英译,在网络上争议较大,出现了各种译文。另外,《汉英词典》(第三版)中收录了该词,其处理如下:

　　搞定:(方)arrange;settle;fix up 把计划搞定 work the plan out/把事情搞定 settle the matter

　　上面这个译文让人有点莫名其妙。首先,根据译者提供的三个译文,我们基本上可以断定译者认为"搞定"的意思就是"安排(好)",因为arrange 就是"安排",而 settle 和 fix up 都有"安排"的意思。但问题在于,"安排(好)"是"搞定",但"搞定"并不一定就只指"安排(好)"。例如在下面这些句子中,"搞定"并不能解释为"安排(好)"。

　　17 天**搞定** GRE 新单词。

　　金钱是怎么**搞定**我们的?

　　蔡振华能**搞定**中国足球吗?

　　几个销售小技巧,轻松**搞定** 98% 的客户。

　　其次,在第一个例证的翻译中,work the plan out 虽然语法上也讲的通,但更为地道的则是 work out the plan。

　　其实,"搞定"这个词并不难译,最常用的一个词为 fix,其后可直接跟 something 或 somebody。譬如,美国爱情喜剧片 *MR. Fix It* 就被译为《**搞定先生**》。再例如,下面句子中的 fix 均可以译为"搞定":

At the design stage, when you discover problems, you can **fix them easily**(轻松**搞定**)by editing a few lines of text.

If you have been a victim of identity theft, you may want to hire legal help versus trying to **fix the matter on your own**(自己搞定这件事情).

另外,还可以用 get something done/settled 或 something gets/is done/settled 这两种说法,譬如美国有一本书名为 *Getting Things Done: the Art of Stress-free Productivity*,国内则译为《搞定:无压工作的艺术》。再如,"这件事我可以搞定"可以译为 I can get it done. ;"票子搞定了"可以译为 The ticket is done;而"全部都搞定了"则可以译为"get everything settled/done"。

其次,在某些语境中,我们甚至可以将该词简单译为 It's done. 或 It's all set. 或 It's all settled. 在一些美国的片子中,我们甚至听到主人公只说"Done!"或"settled!"或"fixed"就可以表示"搞定"。

当然,像"搞定"这些词,在不同的语境下会有很多灵活的译法,译者只要平时多注意观察,就会发现不少英美人都在说"搞定"。譬如,下面这些英文句子中的黑体词均可译为"搞定":

As you will find out, all is now **settled**. 你将会看到这样的情况,一切都已搞定了。

Winder not **settled** yet. Someone kindly recommend a cheap one for it? 线轮还没搞定。哪位好心推荐一个不贵的来搭配?

Phoebe:(stirring pot)Ok, **all done**.(忙完了)好了,全部搞定。

Yes, **all finish**. Disconnect hose now. 是,全搞定,拆管子吧

Hiya, Rog. Frank, you **all set**? 嗨,你好,罗格。佛兰克,你都搞定了吗?

After completing the installation process, you simply need to type one more command and you are **all set**. 安装完成之后你只需要再输入一行命令就全部搞定了。

No prob. It's cool. I can **handle** it. 没问题,挺好,我能把它搞定。

Come on May, let's **sort this out**. 来吧,梅,我们把它搞定。

关键先生

篮球等体育比赛中双方势均力敌、相持不下时,能在关键时刻挺身而出,突破僵局,赢得关键比分,使球队获胜的球员通常被称做"关键先生"。譬如大家熟知的火箭队的特雷西-麦克格雷迪(Tracy McGrady)、湖人队的(Kobe Bryant)科比·布莱恩特等都堪称"关键先生"。《京华时报》2004年4月27日报道:"虽然弗朗西斯2罚1中双方战成88平,但科比再次成为了"关键先生",他的上篮又迫使泰勒犯规,再次打3分成功,奠定了胜局。"

《辞书研究》2006年第2期"新词新义荟萃"一栏中把"关键先生"译成了"key player"。这个译文看似正确,其实值得商榷。首先,"key player"可以回译为"关键球员",而一个球队中首发上场的球员均应算该队的"关键球员",但"关键球员"却并非"关键先生"。此外,"关键先生"在命名上生动形象,译为"key player"则显得索然无味、形象尽失。

其实,所谓"关键先生",像硬件(hardware)、软件(software)一样,乃语意借词(semantic loan),英文中本已有其表达,只要查看原版的体育报道,就能找到地道的表达。著名的美国体育电视台"娱乐体育电视网"(ESPN)就曾撰文"Who's Mr. Clutch?"[1],对NBA现役球员中的"关键先生"进行分析。文章指出,现役NBA球员中的十大关键先生为:Kobe Bryant、Mike Bibby、Tracy McGrady、Steve Nash、Allen

---

〔1〕 见 http://espn.go.com/page2/s/rosen/030501.html

Iverson、Jason Kidd、Paul Pierce、Stephon Marbury、Tim Duncan、Shaq O'Neal。这篇文章标题中的"Mr. Clutch"就是"关键先生"的地道英文表达。

此外,如果不考虑形象的传译,该文中提到的"clutch shooter"、"last-shot hero"、"finisher"也不失为"关键先生"的精当译文。请看下面相关的表达:

1. The best **clutch shooters** in the history of the game are（in alphabetical order）Larry Bird, Michael Jordan and Jerry West. While none of today's mega-stars match that Big Three, here is my ranking of the best modern-day money men.

2. **Tracy McGrady**：Young and oh-so-talented, T-Mac has everything in his favor except a proven track record in the postseason. Perhaps this is the year he establishes himself as a bona fide **last-shot hero.**

3. **Jason Kidd**：An erratic shooter except when a game is up for grabs. Kidd also goes left as well as anybody in the league and is a reliable **finisher.** And who is more adept at creating dunk shots for his teammates?

最后,有些读者可能会问:既然"先生"应该译为"Mr.","关键"为"key",那么"关键先生"是否可以用最简单的译文"Mr. Key"? 我们查证的结果是:尽管网络上有很多华人用"Mr. Key"来表示"关键先生",但该表达很少见于原版英文,最为常见的应该是 Mr. Clutch。这从《篮球先锋报》2005 年 1 月 3 日对 NBA 球员霍里的报道中也可见端倪。霍里很满意中国球迷给他的"关键先生"封号,但他有些不好意思,说到:"NBA 有 MR. CLUTH 的评选,只有杰里·韦斯特这样的人才有资格叫做'关键先生'。"但是他很高兴地透露:"我在老家是不折不扣的关键先生,在那里大家都喜欢叫我 Mr. Key,因为大家都记得我在火箭和湖人时候的投篮。"

韩　流

　　韩流，谐音"寒流"，是人们对于韩国音乐、电视剧等大举登陆中国以及整个亚洲地区后的一种形象说法。曾几何时，韩流势不可挡、不容小觑，看看电视上热播的韩剧，尾随明星身后的汹涌人潮，听着震耳欲聋的尖叫声，你会深深感叹其兴盛之势！韩流滚滚，其内容在不断丰富，形式也日趋多样化，从喜欢看韩国电视剧，听韩国劲歌，"追星"，进而发展到追求韩国的商品，如韩国的化妆品、结婚礼服、传统美食以及韩剧服装等等。

　　"韩流"一词目前在各主要汉英词典中均有一个译文：South Korean trend。但如果仔细考察，我们会发现这一译文其实并不到位，而翻译这一新词的关键在于"流"如何来译。通常情况下，这里的"流"可以理解为"潮流"。而"潮流"在英文中的对应词通常有 fashion、trend 和 fad。下面结合"韩流"的意义，具体分析这三个近义词，并厘定"韩流"的英译。

　　首先，fashion 一词确指"潮流"，但它指的一般是衣服、头发等的流行样式、行为等的时尚、时髦，即 the popular style of clothes, hair, behaviour, etc. at a particular time, that is likely to change。例如，Hats are in fashion again this year. 由于 fashion 的这个基本含义，该词有时甚至可以用来指代"时装"或"时装业"，如 men's fashions 为"男士时装"，the fashion industry 则为"时装业"。因此，fashion 不能用来译"韩流"的"流"。

其次, trend 一词往往指一件事的发展趋势、动态、倾向等等, 即 a general direction in which a situation is changing or developing。和该词构成的搭配一般有 economic/political trends、development trend、underlying trend 等。Trend 一般所表示的是一种规律和趋势, 人们往往需要作出很大的努力才能 reverse a trend, 这就说明 trend 一般持续的时间比较长, 力度也较大。用 trend 来译"韩流"的"流"也不是好的选择, 因为, 韩流的"流"不是这样的一种趋势或动态, 而主要是指一种时尚热潮的一时风靡和普及。当然, "韩流"这股"寒流"可不像表层化的 fashion, 它甚至包括韩国文化在中国的认同和仿效。

最后, fad 一词用来翻译"韩流"的"流"则较为确切,《牛津高阶英汉双解词典》(第六版)对该词的释义为: something that people are interested in for only a short time, 意即"一时的风尚或爱好"、"短暂的狂热", 它往往是指 an interest followed with exaggerated zeal。例如, Will Tom continue to collect stamps or is it only a passing fad? 再如, 下面关于 handbag 的选择的一段话更是说明了 fad 的易逝性及其与 trend 的区别:

In my never ending search for the perfect handbag, I have decided to emerse myself head first into the **trend** of today and strongly consider an animal print handbag. But, before I shell out hundreds of dollars for such a lavish purchase, I have to ask: are animal print bags just **a fleeting fad**, or will I be able to wear it for many seasons to come? How do I select the right handbag?

这样, 我们便可以很清晰地看到 trend 和 fad 之间的区别与联系。诚然, fad 是一种 trend, 但它和 trend 本质上的不同在于 fad 有"life span"(生命长度), 而且一般较为短暂 (short-lived), 在英文中常与 passing、fleeting、fading、temporary、short-lived、momentary 等词连用, 而 trend 所表示的时间感则相对薄弱。另外, 在审美层面上, trend 可以说是审美时尚的萌芽状态, fad 则是人的审美情感的进一步唤起, 它表明一种具有审美特性的生活方式、行为模式、文化精神等为少数领潮者所拥有和操纵, 并成为众多赶潮者纷纷追随和效仿的对象。这与"韩流"的"流"则不谋而合。我们知道, 韩流是近些年出现并风靡起来的, 其先锋部队便是时尚因素。这点特质 fad 能够体现出来,trend 则不具备。再者,"时尚决非是现存恒定的,而是总是在生成变化。"(齐奥尔格,2000)虽然当今韩流风行,但人们,包括韩国文化界和经济界的一些人士,都对"韩流"能够持续多久表示怀疑。因为"韩流"主要是在青少年中出现的一种现象,而青少年正处于心智、思想与兴趣爱好剧烈变化的阶段,他们大多数也没有收入来源,经济能力有限。此外,随着韩流影响的加深,别国政府会不会采取限制措施也不得而知。另外,如果韩国文化界自身拿不出更多有吸引力的精品,也会使"韩流"失去后劲,最终昙花一现。

　　事实上,近年来已经有不少媒体注意到了韩流在中国的没落,譬如,香港《紫荆》杂志 9 月号刊文"'韩流'缘何悄然退热?"说,"韩流"在中国内地和港澳台悄然退热,成为昨日黄花,原因是韩星都到中国了。其实,"韩流"退热也有其内因。一些有识之士甚至在 2008 年的时候就断言:韩流在中国还会存在一段时间。这个周期大概是五年左右。五年后我相信中国的大众会对来自韩国的文化产品产生真正的审美疲劳。韩国人编写的东西文化深度毕竟不够,格局太小,加上其所反映出的偏执的民族主义,更加速了其被中国人抛弃的进程。这一切都决定了它难成大器。

　　由此可以看出,韩流是有 life span 的,trend 在表述这方面意义上则有所欠缺,不够准确。因此,通过分析词语字面意义以及其后所承载的文化含义,我们认为"韩流"一词应该译为"South Korean fad"。

黑　车

　　《现代汉语词典》(第五版)对"黑车"的定义为:指没有牌照的或非法运营的车辆。这个定义告诉我们,黑车有两类,一类是没有牌照的车辆,另一类则是非法运营的车辆。这两类黑车在现实生活中确实存在,但尤以第二类为多。譬如,国内外大城市中,如北京、上海、伦敦、纽约等,几乎都有"黑车"的踪迹。尽管"黑车"屡遭政府部门打击,但不可否认的是,"黑车"现象也反映了政府在改善城市交通方面还有待提高。

　　关于"黑车"的英译,主要有以下几种:

　　《汉英词典》(第三版)将该词译为:unlicensed vehicle;unlicensed taxi

　　《汉英大词典》(第三版)将该词译为:black taxi (a taxi that carries passengers illegally and without a business license)

　　《新世纪汉英大词典》则将该词译为:vehicle without registration;unlicensed vehicle

　　这几种译文中,vehicle without registration 明显与"黑车"的定义不符,而且有解释之嫌,可以不用讨论。Unlicensed vehicle 应该是第一类"黑车":"没有牌照的车辆",译文也没有问题。而关于第二类"黑车",即非法运营的车辆,上面出现了两种译文:unlicensed taxi 和 black taxi。很明显,前者是译意,而后者是译形。《汉英大词典》(第三版)之所以采用译形的方法应该是有据可循的,因为 *The China Daily* 上就曾如是翻译,请看:

A crackdown on Beijing's **black taxis**—private vehicles illegally carrying passengers for money—kicked off on Monday in a bid to stop the disarray in public transportation and improve the capital's traffic system.

下面首先讨论一下 unlicensed taxi 和 black taxi 这两个译文,然后再提出关于"黑车"的其他译法:

首先,unlicensed taxi 的确是"黑车",请看 Wikipedia 对该词的阐述以及对伦敦一个相关案例的报道:

(1) **Unlicensed cabs** may be found cruising the residential streets of a city, typically in the working class neighborhoods. Sometimes, drivers will also wait at a location where taxi service is in demand, such as airport or train station arrival areas or shopping centers, asking arriving passengers if they need a ride. **Unlicensed taxis** often do not have meters, so the fare is usually agreed to at the beginning of the ride. The car itself is usually large, similar in feel to a licensed taxi.

(2) A judge at the Old Bailey in London has sentenced **unlicensed taxi** driver Astor Murray, 49, to eight years in prison for the rape and indecent assault of a passenger of his illegal taxi business in 2003. He forced the 22-year-old student, who cannot be named, to perform oral sex on him before raping her in the back of his car and was linked to the crime when he was arrested for unrelated offences last year.

其次,"黑车"是否就是 black taxi 呢? 英文中有 black taxi 这个说法吗? 答案是 black taxi 在英文中也有,但却不是指"黑车",而是指合法运营的出租车! 请看下面 Wikipedia 的说法:

In London illegal cabs are called **gray cabs**, as the licensed legal cabs are called **black cabs**. Usually black is associated with black market, but in this case the black cabs are the legal ones, officially called Licensed Hackney Carriages.

这段引文不但说明了 black cab/taxi 不是"黑车",而且还提供了一个和"黑车"比较形似的表达 gray cab。如此看来,"黑车"应该用 gray cab/taxi 来译,而非 black cab/taxi。当然,"黑车"是否可以译为 black taxi,这是一个有争论的问题。例如,*The China Daily* "英语点津"栏目就认为:black taxi 中的 black 应该是"非法"的意思,所以 black taxi 就是"黑车"。笔者认为,这个说法虽然有一定的道理,但并不全面,如英文中的 black market、black mail、black economy 等中的 black 的确都有"非法"的意思,但同时,更多由 black 构成的短语则没有此意,如 black humor、black goods、black box、black belt、black top 等等,这种过分总结归纳(overgeneralization)的方法其实在翻译实践中并不可取,很容易造成汉语式的译文或翻译中的"假朋友",尤其是当英文中本来就已有类似表达的时候。

当然,"黑车"除了 unlicensed taxi 和 gray taxi/cab 以外,还有其他的表达法,如 illegal taxi/cab、White card(香港的用法,原因是合法运营车辆的牌照颜色和"黑车"牌照的颜色不一样)等。下面是关于这两种译法的相关表述:

Illegal cabs tend to be more prevalent in cities with medallion systems, which restrict the number of legal cabs in operation. **Illegal taxi/cab operation** is generally seen as a victimless crime although it may affect the economic value of licensed taxis, and safety regulations may be bypassed. Both the drivers and passengers of **illegal cabs** are taking this risk. However, passengers sometimes find **illegal cabs** to be more available, convenient, or economical than licensed ones.

In Hong Kong, **illegal cabs** are usually referred to as **White card** due to different plate appearance between commercial and non-commercial vehicles.

黑　哨

　　"黑哨"是一个富有中国特色的、非常形象的表达,是指裁判员因收受某一方俱乐部的黑钱或好处,为了"知恩图报",在执法足球比赛时明显偏袒该方球队的行为。该词一般直译为 black whistle,但也有人认为(赫迎红,2007)认为,black whistle 是一种爱尔兰生产的黑色的金属笛子,与"黑哨"风马牛不相及。正确的译法应该是 a corrupt referee。

　　那么,"黑哨"是否应该是 a corrupt referee 呢?并不尽然。

　　首先,该译彻底归化,从而使原词中所包含的生动形象消失殆尽。

　　其次,corrupt 一词含义宽泛,译"黑哨"不一定正确,因为"腐败"一词包含各种意义,权钱交易叫"腐败",权色交易也叫"腐败",权权交易更是"腐败",所以"腐败的裁判"不一定是"黑哨",虽然"黑哨"肯定腐败。

　　最后,上面黑哨的定义显示,黑哨只指偏袒一方的"行为",尽管我们偶尔也可把某个实施这一行为的裁判称为"黑哨",如"我们还了解到有个杭州裁判,现在已经被停哨,此人是个黑哨。"等。赫译用 referee,没有照顾到"黑哨"作为"行为"的意思。

　　那么,用 black whistle 来译"黑哨"是否错误呢?也不尽然。

　　首先,翻译形象生动、富有民族特色的词汇,最好采用异化,因为翻译的目的不只是意义的传递,更重要的文化的传递。成功的译例如"纸老虎"(paper tiger)、"走狗"(running dog)、"丢脸"(lose face)、"crocodile tears"(鄂鱼的眼泪)、"hardware"(硬件)、"dark horse"(黑马）等。当然，对那些形象差异很大的词汇，如"白骨精（白领、骨干、精英）"等，如无法直译，那就只能用 office elite 等译文了。

此外，"黑哨"的"黑"和赫先生所说的"足球裁判实际使用的哨子大都是黑色"实在没有什么直接的联系，这里的"黑"应该是"非法的、不公开的"意思。而英文中，black 的确有这样的意思，如 black market 为"黑市"、black spot 为"交通黑点"、black economy 为"地下经济活动、黑市经营"等。所以，黑哨的"黑"译为 black，取其"非法、暗箱操作"的含义，可谓恰如其分。当然，这样处理的另外一个原因是英文中没有"黑哨"一词形神兼备的对应表达法。

第三，赫先生认为由于 black whistle 在英文中另有他义，所以不能用来译"黑哨"，这种说法也站不住脚。一者这是语言间的巧合，此 black whistle 与彼 black whistle 没有任何关联，我想在一定的语境下，没有哪个英美读者会把二者混淆。二者，类似情况在翻译实践中也不少见，《新华新词语词典》用加拿大和澳大利亚等国特有的术语 Affordable Housing Project 来译"安居工程"就是一例。

最后，国内的主流英文媒体都用 black whistle 来译"黑哨"，如 The China Daily、People's Daily 等。例如，

Debuted 10 years ago and hailed as the milestone in China's soccer history, the much-touted domestic league is still a mess, plagued by numerous problems, such as the "**black whistle**" and "money-bought goals."

——"AFC official apologizes for tirade of misunderstanding",

The China Daily, 2004 - 07 - 20

国外的刊物如 *Columbia Law Review* 在 2005 年 1 月第 105 卷中也用 black whistle 来说明中国的"黑哨"现象[1]。有趣的是，该刊对 black whistle 的解释为：referees who accept money to affect the outcome of matches。这样看来，black whistle 既可指这种"行为"，也可以指实施这一行为的人，与汉语原文何等之契合！

---

〔1〕 见 http://www.columbialawreview.org/pdf/Liebman-Web.pdf

　　值得一提的是,翻译中国特色词汇时,很多人喜欢采用归化的手法,惟恐外国人看不懂。事实情况是,在全球化迅猛发展的今天,译者不必太低估译语读者的理解能力,他们可能刚开始看不懂,但逐渐都会理解的。"福娃"的译文从最初的 Friendlies 改为最终的 Fuwa 便是明证。

回 头 率

所谓"回头率",简单而言,就是指人们回头的频率。具体地讲,就是人们在行进中,迎面而来的人虽然已经从身边走过,或观察者已经走出被观察者的视线,却仍然要回过头来再看看。在日常生活中,美女或外国人、外族人、残疾人等通常"回头率"较高,当然,也不乏一些商品,如拉风的汽车、精美的首饰等,由于其豪华、精致或美丽,也常常"回头率"较高。"回头率"是一个很有意思的概念,它反映了某种社会现象,不同人的内在文化、心理和生理上的差异。

"回头率"在现版的各种参考书中,均被译为 rate of second glance。这个译文没有问题,例如:

The rate of second glance when wearing the boots is definitely 100% , believe many people may ask you where you buy them!

An appropriate hair style can increase your rate of second glance.

然而,尽管如此,我们还会禁不住自问,既然"回头率"并非文化局限词(culture-specific word),那为什么不能直译为 head-turning rate 呢? 英文中有没有 head-turning rate 这个说法呢? 有的话是否就是"回头率"呢? 带着这些问题,我们进行了相关的调查,结果发现 head-turning rate 也是翻译"回头率"的一个绝妙选择! 甚至连 head-turning 也已经作为独立的条目,为英语词典所收录! 下面先看 head-turning 的英文释义,再看 head-turning rate 的用法实例。

1. head-turning 的词典释义:

head-turning: *adj.* extremely noticeable, attractive

Dictionary. com

head-turning: *adj.* extremely noticeable or attractive

The Concise Oxford Dictionary (Ninth Edition)

2. head-turning rate 的用法实例:

(1) Owing to the individual style of Ed Hardy, people who are wearing Ed Hardy **obtain a high head-turning rate.**

(2) Just think about it, if you wear one of these Jeans and walk along the streets, apparently you will **get the highest head-turning rate**, keeping warm do not need to say, you can also become a charming flower girl this winter.

(3) As she really feels proud and extremely satisfied if **retaining a good head-turning rate**, or male's peeping in the office or on the street. The probability of getting others' focus is the standard she adopts to judge the risk of decision, and a few really blood-pumping photos were posted by her on the Internet.

(4) A stay across from Madison Square Garden for MYM139 (pre-tax) per night, for a well-equipped (e.g., free WiFi) room? Indeed, it is possible. The New Yorker Hotel, at 34th Street and Eighth Avenue in Manhattan, is **offering that head-turning rate** in January and February, and it'll throw in a free Continental breakfast too.

上面这些例子不但说明了美女、靓服的"回头率"可用 head-turning rate 来译,甚至宾馆的"回头率"也可以用该词来译。看来"回头率"最形象的译法应该是 head-turning rate,而 rate of second glance 只能退居其后了。

家庭影院

    "家庭影院"这个概念我们都不陌生,但它究竟是指什么,并不是每个人都很清楚。事实上,所谓"家庭影院",是利用现代电子技术把 20 世纪 70 年代后期发展起来的专业多路环绕立体声影院设备,经简化后做成的家用产品。一套家庭影院一般由环绕声放大器(或环绕声解码器与多通道声频功率放大器组合)、多个(4 个以上)扬声器系统、大屏幕电视(或投影电视)及高质量 A/V 节目源构成。

    商务印书馆 2003 年出版的《新华新词语词典》把"家庭影院"译为了 family cinema,这个译文乍一看没有什么问题,但略加考证即会发现它是一个纯粹的"假朋友",是译者想当然的硬译,因为英文中根本就没有 family cinema 这样的说法。

    事实上,"家庭影院"的正确译文为 home theatre 或 home cinema。请看 Wikipedia 对这两个词的定义:

    A **home theater** or **home theatre** is a theater built in a home, designed to mimic(or exceed)commercial theater performance and feeling, more commonly known as a **home cinema.** Today, **home cinema** implies a real "cinema experience" at a private home.

    Home cinema, commonly referred to as **home theater** or **home theatre**, are home entertainment set-ups that seek to reproduce movie theater video and audio feeling in a private home.

    为了加深印象,我们可以再看一些关于如何使用 home theater 的例子：

He blew a lot of money on his new **home theater.**

他挥霍了很多钱在新置的**家庭影院**上。

We may spend our precious dollars on consumer goods—fancy cars, **home theater** systems, and other disposable items that depreciate and lose value over time.

我们可能把宝贵的美元花费在——汽车、**家庭影院**及其他容易折旧和贬值的东西上面。

Build Your **Home Theater** In A Weekend.

建立您的**家庭影院**，在一个周末。

Home cinema fans are in for treat today, as Sony have announced the launch of not one, but three new pieces of kit to turn your living room into a multiplex.

本文是"也评《新华新词语词典》的英译"一文中的一部分，载《双语词典新论》（四川人民出版社，2007）

经济适用房

  "经济适用住房"是指已经列入国家计划,由城市政府组织房地产开发企业或者集资建房单位建造,以微利价向城镇中低收入家庭出售的住房。它是具有社会保障性质的商品住宅,具有经济性和适用性的特点。经济性,是指住房的价格相对同期市场价格来说是适中的,适合中等及低收入家庭的负担能力;适用性,是指在房屋的建筑标准上不能削减和降低,要达到一定的使用效果。和其他许多国家一样,经济适用房是国家为低收入人群解决住房问题所做出的政策性安排,而另一种以出租为主的住宅政策则称为廉租房(low-rent housing)。

  "经济适用房"这个概念起源于上世纪 50 年代,正式成形于 1998年。通过 60 年的发展,经济适用房逐渐成为中低收入家庭住房的重要选择。当然,近年来由于种种原因,经济适用房遭到了广泛的质疑,不少专家在争论是否应该取消经济适用房,因为他们认为经济适用房已经成为滋生腐败的一个温床。

  关于经济适用房的英译,学界也争论不休。譬如,《新华新词语词典》的译文为 economically comfortable housing,金其斌(2003)先生对该译文进行考察后,认为该词应译为"affordable housing",而 *The China Daily* 以及 *Guangming Daily* 等主流媒体则采用"comfortable housing"的表述。

  首先看看流传甚广的 affordable housing。评判这个译文的关键在于 affordable 一词作何理解。众所周知,affordable 的意思是"可以承受得起的;可以负担得起的",这样就产生了一个问题,"可以承受得起的;可以负担得起的"是一个相对的概念,很难界定。譬如说我有 5 万元,因而承受不起 50 万元的房子,而总价 50 万元的房子在目前中国的一线城市,如北京、上海、深圳等,可能只能属于经济适用房了。但是如果我有 100 万的资产,500 万或上千万的房子对我来说仍然是 unaffordable,但有资产 100 万的中国人,估计也没有资格申请所谓的经济适用房了。所以,affordable housing 一词问题较大。另外,affordable housing 碰巧是英文中的一个习惯表达,如下面的一篇报道[1]:

The Affordable Housing Program provides loans or grants to non-profits, local governments, and public housing authorities to:

1. build new rental units for persons that have a low to moderate income,

2. adapt a building from another use such as an old school or hotel to housing,

3. rehabilitate an existing rental property owned by a non-profit or public housing authority to meet local building codes and Housing Quality Standards,

4. administer a downpayment assistance program,

5. develop new single family housing for homeownership, including infrastructure, and

6. purchase homes, rehabilitate to meet local building codes and Housing Quality Standards and provide downpayment assistance to a new homebuyer to purchase the homes,

7. administer a program to assist homeowners in rehabilitating their houses.

由此看来,英文中的"affordable housing"与汉语中的"经济适用房"并非一个概念,尽管有小部分重合。所以,把经济适用房翻译为"affordable housing project"确属不当。

然后再看看 economically comfortable housing 和 comfortable

---

〔1〕见 http://crd. neded. org/communty. html。

housing。前者逻辑上就有问题,什么叫 economically comfortable 呢? 到底是讲经济状况好还是不好的家庭呢? 从这个译文中无从看出。后者似乎问题更大,经济适用房是否 comfortable 这是一个仁者见仁、智者见智的问题,与豪宅相比,它肯定不是那么 comfortable,但与没有房子的人的相比,应该也算是 comfortable 了,至少心理上的感觉如此吧。

那么,经济适用房应该怎么翻译呢? 笔者认为译为 economical housing 或 housing for low-income urban residents" 倒是不错。后者是一个解释性译文,应该没有什么争议,主要看 economical housing 是否恰当。下面一段来自华盛顿 2006 年 6 月的一份 Growth Policy Staff Report 以及来自 *The China Daily* 的一段报道或许可以帮我们解开这个谜底:

Regulations that increase housing choice by providing the opportunity to **construct more diverse and economical housing to meet the needs of low and moderate income families.** Such regulations often require a minimum percentage of housing for low and moderate income households in new housing developments and in conversions of apartments to condominiums.

Growth Policy Staff Report

Housing sold at low prices to low-income earners to get them affordable shelters. Starting in 1998, the central government decided to offer favorable policies to housing developers so that they could build apartments of specified sizes and prices. Families with living floor space or income under given standards could apply for purchasing the apartments at prices much lower than the market prices. Eligibility standards for purchasing economical housing are set by provincial authorities according to local situations. **Economical housing** is subject to special clauses for trading in market, which discourage profiting from the property. It is an integrated part of the State efforts to shelter groups with limited financial resources.

The China Daily

本文是“因特网与汉英词典编纂”一文中的一部分,载
《西安外国语学院学报》2005 年第 1 期

绝　杀

　　所谓"绝杀",是指篮球或足球在比分胶着的最后时刻或接近最后时刻球员投进致胜的一球,而这样一个事关比赛胜败的投球则称为"绝杀球"。有时候,"绝杀"本身也可以表示所投进的"绝杀球",如"西蒙斯将球传给哈里斯,后者带球直奔前场,在还剩 1 秒时投中一记**绝杀** 3 分,最终篮网以 98—96 逆转对手。"

　　篮球方面的"绝杀"有:费舍尔零点四秒绝杀马刺,科比绝杀雄鹿,科比 7 秒绝杀凯尔特人,科比 4.3 秒绝杀灰熊,乔丹绝杀骑士,大卫-李 0.1 秒绝杀,麦迪 35 秒 13 分,米勒 8.9 秒 8 分,爵士菜鸟甘尼斯 3 分绝杀骑士,约什史密斯补篮绝杀魔术和火箭,科比压哨绝杀国王;足球方面一个经典的"绝杀"发生在 2010 年 3 月 31 日举行的欧冠四分之一决赛第一回合,当时拜仁慕尼黑坐镇主场迎战曼联,拜仁前锋奥利奇最后 1 秒绝杀曼联,拜仁最终 2:1 获胜。

　　关于"绝杀"一词,只有《汉英词典》(第三版)中有所收录,其译文为:(1)give a fatal blow; knock out;(2)deadly strike; fatal move(as in chess, etc.)。由于没有例证辅助说明,这种译文表意极为模糊,另外,从第二个译文中的第二项 fatal move(as in chess, etc.),我们似乎可以看出,译者想翻译的是象棋比赛中的绝杀,但第一个译文 deadly strike 却又让人感到莫名其妙,因为它与象棋比赛又没有什么关系了。

　　此外,还有些地方将该词译为 kill shot,这是一个误译,因为 kill shot 是"射杀"的意思。另外,该词在网球、羽毛球等比赛中也可以表示

"扣杀"。

最后,有些人还认为"绝杀"应该译为 make the last shoot 或 critical shoot,其实这种译法也有问题,last shoot 就是最后一投,这可不一定是"绝杀"性的一投。Critical shoot 就更不合适了,因为严格来说,球场上的任何一投都 critical,否则绝难赢球。

那么,体育比赛中的"绝杀"应该怎样翻译呢? 笔者认为,我们应该区分作为名词的"绝杀"和作为动词的"绝杀":

首先,作为名词,"绝杀"可以翻译为 buzzer beater、clutch shoot、game-winner 以及 last-gasp goal。下面一一说明:

1. buzzer beater:尽管 buzzer beater 同时还可以表示"压哨球",而"压哨球"与"绝杀球"又有所区别:比赛的每一节都可能有"压哨球",但只有最后一节决定胜负的"压哨球"才是"绝杀球"。这一点,Wikipedia 讲得很明白:

In basketball, a **buzzer beater** is a shot taken just before the game clock of a period expires, when the buzzer sounds. **The term is normally reserved for baskets that win or tie the game, but also refers to shots that beat an end of quarter or halftime buzzer.**

2. clutch shoot:这个译文容易理解,因为我们前面才探讨过"关键先生"及其译文"Mr. Clutch",a clutch shooter 就是投入"绝杀球"的球员,而 clutch shoot 就是"绝杀球"。例如:

There are a lot of players that become a big star because mastering the three points shoot technique. Let's say Larry Bird in the 80's, Reggie Miller in the 90's, Peja Stojakovich in early 2000, and Jason Kapono in the 2006 until now. They offer superb three points shoot and **clutch shoot** in the perimeter area.

3. game-winner:投中一球,即 win the game,这就是为什么 game-winner 可以译为"绝杀"的原因所在。另外,该词的一个常见搭配是 hit the game winner,例如:

Unlikely Gaines **hit the game-winner** at the buzzer, allowing the Jazz to overcome second-half injuries sustained by both starting point guard

Deron Williams and starting small forward Andrei Kirilenko, and beat the Cavaliers 97—96 in a late-starting, TNT-televised game at sold-out Energy Solutions Arena.

"Utah Jazz: Sundiata Gaines hits game-winner at buzzer to beat Cavs", *Desert News* 2010 - 1 - 15

4. last-gasp goal:这一说法十分形象,是指在比赛的最后时刻攻破对方球门,对方已没有反扑的机会。last-gasp 形象地形容出了"最后一搏"的紧张激烈状态,比如 The team were at their last gasp when the whistle went.(球队正做最后拼搏,这时哨声响了)。关于该译,请看 *The China Daily* 的报道:

England shook off a traumatic start to the World Cup on Wednesday to beat tiny Slovenia and squeeze into the second round while the United States booked their place with a **last-gasp goal** against Algeria.

其次,作为动词,"绝杀"可以译为 clutch shoot 及 buzzer-beat。Clutch shoot 既可以用作名词,也可以用作动词。而既然"绝杀球"为"buzzer beater",那么,作为动词的"绝杀"就应该是 buzzer-beat。请看下面两例:

Jordan could score, dunk, rebound, pass, defend and **clutch shoot** better than Kobe.

The Nets are now 0-12 and Lawrence Frank hasn't been fired yet. They were this close to beating the Heat, but Wade **buzzer-beat** them.

啃 老 族

曾有这样一个谜语:"一直无业,二老啃光,三餐饱食,四肢无力,五官端正,六亲不认,七分任性,八方逍遥,九(久)坐不动,十分无用",打一类人。这个谜语的谜底就是本文所要谈及的"啃老族"。

"啃老族"是近几年国内出现的一个使用频率极高的新词,指那些23到30岁,往往大学毕业,有谋生能力,却仍未"断奶",还得靠父母供养的"成年孩子"(adult children)。"百度百科"认为:啃老族也叫"吃老族"或"傍老族"。他们并非找不到工作,而是主动放弃了就业的机会,赋闲在家,不仅衣食住行全靠父母,而且花销往往不菲。社会学家称其为"新失业群体"。当然,在现实生活中,"啃老族"中不乏那些无奈而"啃老"的成年人,这些人由于种种原因,虽已成年,但仍然找不到工作,只能呆在家中,依靠父母生活。

统计显示,在城市里,有30%的年轻人靠"啃老"过活,65%的家庭存在"啃老"问题。"啃老族"很可能成为影响未来家庭生活的"第一杀手"。

据中国媒体调查,目前"啃老族"主要有以下六类人:

一是大学毕业生,因就业挑剔而找不到满意的工作,约占20%;

二是以工作太累太紧张、不适应为由,自动离岗离职的,他们觉得在家里很舒服。占10%左右;

三是"创业幻想型"青年,他们有强烈的创业愿望,却没有目标,缺乏真才实学,总是不成功,而又不愿"寄人篱下"当个打工者。占20%;

四是频繁跳槽,最后找不到工作,靠父母养活着。占 10% ;

五是下岗的年轻人,他们习惯于用过去轻松的工作与如今紧张繁忙的工作相比,越比越不如意,干脆就离职,约占 10% ;

六是文化低、技能差,只能在中低端劳动力市场上找苦脏累工作,因怕苦怕累索性呆在家中,占 30% 。

"啃老族"这个词的英译,目前只有《辞书研究》2006 年第 2 期中有其英译,译文为 young people relying on their parents,但这纯粹是解释,还算不上翻译。而在其他正规出版物中,笔者还未见及"啃老族"的英译,如 2010 年出版的《汉英词典》(第三版)和《汉英大词典》中均未收录该词。然而,在一些非正式的文献中,该词的英译却不时可见,例如,有些地方将其译为了 adult dependent children。但这个译文其实也是不恰当的,因为该英文表达的意思是"有心理缺陷或生理缺陷,需要抚养的成年子女",比"啃老族"含义要宽泛。例如:An adult dependent child is one who is incapable of self-care because of a mental or physical disability. 那么,"啃老族"这个词如何翻译呢? 我们认为有以下几种选择:

第一,如果仅从译意的角度而言,该词完全可以译为 adult children living off their parents 或者 adult children living at home。譬如,Dr. Phil Foundation 所出版的 Message Board Newsletters 中就提出了这样一个问题,让读者回答:Do you or someone you know still have an adult child living at home either out of necessity, or just plain laziness? 从读者的回答中,我们可以明显看出,adult child living at home 与我们所谓的"啃老族"完全契合。另外,《纽约时报》在报道美国的"啃老族"时也是如是说:

In the United States alone, nearly 16 million families had at least one child over the age of 18 living at home in 2003, marking a 7 percent jump since 1995, according to the Census Bureau's American Housing Survey.

第二,进一步调查则发现,其实"啃老族"在西方及日本这些国家中早已有之,并非新鲜事。而在英文中也已有固定的表达 NEET group。NEET 是一个首字母拼音词(acronym),全称为"Not in Education, Employment or Training",指那些不上学、不就业、也不参加就业培训的,整天呆在家中,依靠父母生活的年轻人。该词源于英国,通常是指 16—24 岁的年轻人,但目前已传至日本及中国等一些国家。在日本,"啃老族"的年龄基本是在 15—34 岁之间,而在中国,一般是指 23 岁到 30 岁之间的年轻人。

根据 2010 年 8 月 18 日 BBC News 一篇题为 "Fall in number of 'Neet'" youths, official figures show"的报道,目前,作为"啃老族"一词发源地的英国,"啃老族"的比例正在下降: The proportion of 18-24-year-olds in England who are not in school, college or work has fallen, figures from the Department for Education indicate。而另一方面,日本和中国等国家正在沦为"啃老族"的重灾区。据报道,NEET 人群在日本近年来扩大的速度相当惊人。根据日本 2004 年经济白皮书公布的数字,2002 年 NEET 人口为 48 万人,2003 年增至 52 万人,而日本全国失业总人口不过 148 万而已。另据日本劳动政策研究所的调查,2004 年,日本 15—34 岁 NEET 人数达到 75 万,这一数字是 10 年前的 10 倍。而在中国,虽然"啃老族"还没有具体的统计数字,但"啃老族"数量在不断快速上升却是一个不争的事实。

第三,"啃老族"在美国也存在,但美国人却用了一个完全不同的形象来表示: boomerang child/kid。请看 Wikipedia 对该词的定义:

Boomerang child: A young adult, especially a college graduate, who has returned to the parental home, especially from college due to unemployment.

Boomerang 是一个来自澳大利亚的词,意思是:抛出后可飞回的飞镖,用它来指代那些父母期望读完大学可以自主独立的,但事实上却"飞回来"的成年儿女,确实十分形象。然而,这些"归巢族"却给父母带来了沉重的精神和经济负担。下面摘自 2005 年 6 月 25 日 *The New York Times* 上题为 "Boomerang children: when the nest isn't empty anymore" 中的一段话,就说明了这些"啃老族"父母们的尴尬:

The financial implications of **boomerang children** can be enormous as parents struggle to keep their own finances on track and help their children become more responsible - while at the same time not allowing them to grow too comfortable under the family roof.

　　老人把孩子拉扯成人，已属不易，孩子成人后却还啃老，确实不该，这不，2011年1月20日，《江苏省老年人权益保障条例（草案更改稿）》颁布，更改稿新增了对"啃老"现象的规定："有独立生活能力的成年子女要求老年人经济资助的，老年人有权拒绝。子女或者其他亲属不得以物业或者其他理由，骗取、克扣或者强行索取老年人的财物"。希望通过这样的立法，能真正制止"啃老"现象的发生。

雷　人

　　"雷人"一词对大多数年轻人来说并不陌生,而且很多人在日常谈话中也经常用到该词。笔者甚至在中央四套的新闻节目中听到节目主持人也使用该词。下面是一些媒体(包括官方主流媒体)中使用该词的实例:

　　(1)昨日(3 日),全国政协十一届三次会议开幕,而网上关于部分政协委员"雷人提案"的议论却仍在继续。

　　　　另眼相看"雷人提案",《长沙晚报》2010 年 3 月 4 日

　　(2)公职人员"雷人"话语频出,暴露了其任职素质的欠缺,背后是对公开政府信息、维护人民知情权、参与权、表达权、监督权的抵触。面对公众关切,公职人员只有讲真话,才能有效引导舆论,化解矛盾,才能真正维护政府形象和公信力。

　　　　公职人员说话别太"雷人",《解放日报》2010 年 1 月 13 日

　　(3)最近,动辄大话"雷人"的干部时不时地见诸媒体。视监督如无物的干部,看来并不鲜见。他们的言行,"雷"坏了党风,"雷"伤了群众的信任。

　　　　有些干部为何专"雷"群众,《人民日报》2009 年 7 月 21 日

　　上面的"雷人"(有时候就用一个简单的"雷"),到底是什么意思呢?根据"百度百科"的释义,雷人的本义是云层放电时击倒某人,但目前网络上流行的"雷人"则为该词的新义:出人意料且令人格外震惊,甚至无语。这个词语类似晴天霹雳的意思,但又与晴天霹雳不同。晴天霹雳多

用于惊闻噩耗的时刻,而雷人则用于表达喜剧性的或无奈的、尴尬性的场合,将个人感受描述为于无声处听惊雷的状态,极度夸张地表达了个人对喜剧、无奈、尴尬场合中行为和语言的感受。现实生活中"雷人"的例子实在是太多了,下面略举几例:

"一人超生,全村结扎。"

"该扎不扎,见了就抓。"

"宁添十座坟,不添一个人。"

"人民罪犯人民爱,人民罪犯爱人民。"(山东聊城监狱的标语)

"严禁触摸电线,5万伏高压,一触即死,不死法办。"(某变压器上的标语)

"宜春,一座叫春的城市。"(宜春市曾经的宣传标语)

"雷人"一词目前未见于任何汉英类辞书,关于它的英译也极为少见。我们认为,"雷人"一词的最佳译文应该是 thunderstruck,其次还可以根据具体语境翻译为诸如 shocking、shocked、get stunned、astonished、astonishing 等。下面简要说明:

首先,之所以说 thunderstruck 为最佳译文,原因有二:一是因为该译与汉语中的"雷人"一词可谓形似:thunder 为"雷",struck 为"打击",二者合一则为"雷人"。二是因为二者完全神似:英文中的 thunderstruck 也有令人感到极为惊讶的含义,而且往往是因为 amazement。这从 thunderstruck 的英文释义可见端详:affected with sudden astonishment or amazement;completely taken aback;amazed or shocked。再看下面这个例子,与汉语中的"雷人"何其相似!

I watched the *Who Killed the Electric Car* documentary last night and was **thunderstruck** by the "ad" that GM made when California made them make electric cars against their will.

其次,诸如 shocking、shocked、get stunned、astonished、astonishing 这样的词在不同语境中也可以用来翻译"雷人",形虽不存,"神"却仍在。例如:"你雷死我了"似乎可以翻译为:I'm shocked to death! /I'm stunned! 而"雷人的提案"则可以译为:astonishing/amazing proposals。

另　类

　　"另类"这个词其实流行时间已经不短了。2005年出版的《现代汉语词典》（第五版）也已经收录了这个词语,并给出了如下两个不同词性的义项:

　　另类:(1)名词:另外的一类,指与众不同的、非常特殊的人或事物:这样的女孩可以归入~｜这部片子是当代电影中的~。(2)形容词:与众不同;特殊:~服装｜她打扮得很另类。

　　在大多数人的印象中,"另类"是年轻人的专利,是率意直为,是想穿什么就穿什么,想说什么就说什么,想做什么就做什么。是酷毙了,帅呆了,是靓,是爽,是怪,是现代的新潮和荒诞,是对传统的否定和背叛。该词刚出现的时候,由于大众还不太适应,可能还带有些许的贬义,但现在却已为人们所普遍接受和理解,认为"另类"也是一种生活方式,只要个人喜欢,"另类"也没有什么不好。

　　"另类"这个词如何英译呢? 先看看《汉英词典》（第三版）和《汉英大词典》（第三版）的译文吧。

　　另类:1. 名词:the other kind: ~女孩 nonconformist girl　2. 形容词:alien;unconventional;offbeat:打扮得很~ dress in an offbeat way

《汉英词典》（第三版）

　　另类:a different, special, completely new of fashionable type or trend

《汉英大词典》（第三版）

　　先看《汉英词典》（第三版）的译文。从词典学的角度来看,这个词条的译文处理得很不科学,首先,第一个义项为名词,但配例中的"另类"却是形容词,丝毫也看不出名词的用法。其次,把"另类"翻译为 the other kind 也让人莫名其妙,难道我们可以把"这样的女孩可以归入另类"这个《现代汉语词典》中的例子译为:This girl belongs to the other kind. 吗?最后,第二个义项中的译文 alien;unconventional;offbeat 倒是可以用来翻译"另类",但例证的译文 dress in an offbeat way 一点也不地道,在英文中根本就不存在。再看《汉英大词典》(第三版)的译文。可以说这个译文简直就是令人匪夷所思,不仅意义不明,而且语法错误。作为一本享有盛名的大型汉英词典,这个错误错得让人难以置信。

那么,"另类"该如何英译呢?我们先来探讨其作为名词的译文。笔者认为,作为名词的"另类"首先可以用 peculiarity 来表示,该词的意思是:something that is a feature of only one particular place, person, or situation,即所谓"与众不同"的意思。上面《现代汉语词典》中的两个例子似乎就可以译为"This girl is peculiar."和"This film is a peculiarity of modern films"或"This film is peculiar of modern films"。译文中用 peculiar 只是反映了翻译中的灵活变通。此外,还可以用作为名词的 offbeat 来译,譬如:He liked the offbeat in fashion. (他喜欢另类时尚。);So, unless you like the offbeat simply because it's offbeat, 8 1/2 Women (注:划线部分为电影名) may not be the best choice for an evening's entertainment.

而"另类"作为形容词,则可以用 offbeat、unconventional、peculiar 甚至 bizarre 和 way-out 等词来译。其中 offbeat 的意思为:unusual and not what people normally expect(不同寻常的、异常的、不落俗套的);unconventional 的意思是"非传统的";peculiar 的意思则是:strange, unfamiliar, and a little surprising, especially in a way that is unpleasant or worrying;bizarre 的意思为:strikingly unconventional and far-fetched in style or appearance;way-out 的意思则为:extremely unconventional or experimental;avant-garde(前卫)。这些词意都与"另类"相符,而且这几个词在语义上相互补充,共同揭示出"另类"一词可能包含的褒贬含义。这里需要注意的是最好不要用 alien 这个词来译"另类",因为该词已经

有了汉语对应的表达"异类",而且该词给读者所产生的心理联想也不恰当:异域的、外星人的。下面看看以上这些词的具体用法:

　　peculiar residence plan for the urban poor 城市贫民的另类居住方案

　　peculiar historical documents 另类的历史文件

　　peculiar literary phenomenon　"另类"文学现象

　　unconventional wedding gowns 另类时尚婚礼服

　　unconventional career 另类职业

　　unconventional remedy 另类疗法

　　offbeat music 另类音乐

　　offbeat news 另类新闻

　　offbeat rock 另类摇滚

　　offbeat wit and charm 另类的智慧和魅力

　　bizarre pet 另类宠物

　　bizarre clothing 另类服饰

　　way-out music 另类音乐

　　最后,英文中还有另外一个词也常用来翻译"另类",那就是 alternative。该词的英文释义为: not based on or believing in the established social or moral standards。譬如,我们常说的"另类投资"为 alternative investment,"另类视角"为 alternative perspective,"另类的生活方式"为 alternative lifestyle 等等。下面再看一些用 alternative 来翻译"另类"的例子:

　　另类摇滚/音乐 alternative rock/music

　　另类投资市场 alternative investment market

　　另类金属 alternative metal

　　另类医学 alternative medicine

　　另类疗法 alternative therapy

　　另类思维 alternative way of thinking

　　另类科学 alternative science

留守儿童

留守儿童,全称为"农村留守儿童",是指父母双方或一方外出到城市打工,而自己留在农村生活的孩子们。他们一般与自己的父亲或母亲,或者与上辈亲人,甚至父母亲的其他亲戚、朋友一起生活。

留守儿童问题是近年来国内一个突出的社会问题。随着中国社会政治经济的快速发展,越来越多的青壮年农民走入城市,在广大农村也随之产生了一个特殊的未成年人群体——农村留守儿童。留守的少年儿童正处于成长发育的关键时期,他们无法享受到父母在思想认识及价值观念上的引导和帮助,成长中缺少了父母情感上的关注和呵护,极易产生认识、价值上的偏离和个性、心理发展的异常,一些人甚至会因此而走上犯罪道路。

近几年来,关于农村留守儿童的悲剧时有发生,应该引起整个社会的关注。例如,2008年2月25日,安徽太湖一12岁少年在祠堂边自缢身亡,留下遗书称想念外出打工的父母,自缢前深情吻别陪伴自己的爷爷。2009年11月,新华社报道广西某农村的鞭炮作坊发生爆炸,2死12伤,除一名老人外,其余都是留守儿童,最小的只有7岁。2010年7月5日《华商报》报道,陕西扶风县杏林镇5名小学六年级的学生,相约到一古庙里喝农药自杀,幸被过路村民发现后及时送往医院。2名学生经抢救后脱离危险。其他3人检查无恙后回家。记者了解到,5个孩子中4个是农村留守儿童。

根据权威调查,中国农村目前"留守儿童"数量超过了5800万人。

57.2％的留守儿童是父母一方外出,42.8％的留守儿童是父母同时外出。留守儿童中的79.7％由爷爷、奶奶或外公、外婆抚养,13％的孩子被托付给亲戚、朋友,7.3％为不确定或无人监护。

"留守儿童"用英文应该如何表达呢? 笔者可以看到的译文可谓五花八门,有些地方(如吴光华先生主编2010年版《汉英大词典》)用leftover children,有些地方用home-alone children,有些地方用abandoned children,还有一些地方用的是unattended rural children、stay-at-home children、left-behind children等等。

这些译文怎么样呢? 我们下面一一简单进行分析:

首先,leftover children这个译文不足为取,因为leftover的意思是: remaining after all the rest has been used, eaten, etc.(未用完的、未吃完的),常构成的搭配为leftover vegetables/food(剩菜/饭)。Leftover和children搭配一起,不仅不能表达"留守儿童"的含义,而且显得不伦不类,因为children既不能吃,也不能用。

其次,abandoned children也不恰当,因为该译的意思为"被抛弃的孩子"。"留守"儿童并未被抛弃,只是不能常伴父母身边,接受父母的影响和教育而已。

第三,home-alone children是英文中一个固有的表达,其极端形式有时也称作latch key children,因为这些孩子的父母只是每天都出门工作,但晚上一般会回家。请看下列表述:

Every day thousands of children arrive home from school to an empty house. Every week thousands of parents make decisions to leave children home alone while they go to work, run errands, or for social engagements. It is estimated over 40％ of children are left home at some time, though rarely overnight. In more extreme situations, some children spend so much time without their parent(s) that these children are labeled "latch key children", referring to the house or apartment key strung visibly around their neck.

"Home Alone Children" from American
Academy of Child & Adolescent Psychiatry

　　从上面的引文可以看出,home-alone children 及 latch key children 用来指代那些城市里白天见不到父母的"留守儿童"才是最为合适的。汉语中现在也出现了一个新词"挂钥匙儿童",估计就是从 latch key children 翻译过来的。例如"人民网——市场报"2003 年 3 月 4 日的一篇题为"从容潇洒地回家谋生——解读'粉领丽人'"的报道中就出现了"挂钥匙儿童":有人认为,居家工作的出现,标志着**挂钥匙儿童**时代的结束。在家工作,既能在生活上独立自主,又能尽心抚养孩子,这正好可以实现他们的期望。

　　第四,unattended rural children 这个译文乍一看没有问题,有些国内的英文媒体在报道时也用该译文,例如,

　　CHANGSHA, Dec. 3（Xinhua）—A senior government official has called for showing care and love towards **unattended rural children** whose parents have left their hometown to work in other parts of the country to support the family.

www. chinaview. cn,2007－12－04

　　但如果仔细思考,该译文明显也与"留守儿童"不符,因为这些儿童的父母虽然不在身边,但他们通常是其父母委托上辈亲人,甚至父母亲的其他亲戚、朋友来照顾的,并非 unattended。

　　第五,stay-at-home children 事实上也未能表达出"留守儿童"的概念,因为该译文只说明了这些孩子是呆在家中的,不是在外面的,譬如在外面玩耍等。而留守儿童则不一定是 stay at home,他们完全有出门的自由,该词表达的核心不是孩子是否呆在家中,而是其远离父母。此外,我们从另一个角度也可以佐证该译文的不合理性,例如,在英文中有 housewife 的说法,我们通常翻译为"家庭主妇",但现在汉语中又有了"家庭妇男"的说法,是指那种妻子赚钱养家,丈夫在家照顾孩子,操持家务的现象,而这种说法在英文中的相应表达则为 stay-at-home dad/ father,所以,stay-at-home 似乎与"留守"并没有太大的关系。

　　最后,再看 left-behind children 这个译文。该译文的使用频率较高,如 2005 年 10 月由社会科学文献出版社出版的《关注留守儿童》一书的英文版就用了 *Left-behind Children in Rural China*。另外,诸如 *The*

People's Daily Online 等英文媒体也用该译。然而,如果仔细研究英文 left-behind children,我们就会发现,该表达在英文中早已名花先有主了,用来指学习上落后的儿童。正如何俊(2008)指出"美国布什政府施政以来,最为人称道的改革称为"No Child Left Behind",即"不让任何一个孩子掉队"的改革,该政策于 2002 年已成为法案。当美国读者看到 "left-behind children in rural China"时,很容易会产生中国农村小孩在学习等方面赶不上城镇小孩的联想;同时在特殊语境下还可能误解成中国农村掉队的小孩,因此该译法值得商榷。

那么,"留守儿童"应该如何翻译呢? 笔者认为,该词为文化局限词,不可能在英文中找到一个现成的说法,而应该根据其含义,进行创造性翻译。有鉴于此,笔者建议将该词译为 left-in-hometown children in China's rural areas,并适当加以解释。该译文中的 hometown 一词点名了 "留守"的地点:家乡,相对而言信息量最为充分,也能较容易地激起译入语读者的思考:为什么这些孩子被留在了家乡? 为什么这个现象会出现在中国的农村? 这些思考会促使他们进一步阅读,直至弄清楚该词的确切含义。事实上,中华人民共和国外交部网站和中华人民共和国驻立陶宛共和国大使馆的网站都在相关的报道中采用了该译法,例如,在一篇题为"The Left-in-Hometown Children Celebrates Their Festival on June 1 and the Little Children Loves Diplomacy"的报道中就有下面的表述:

On the afternoon of June 1, 2007, over 120 children including **the left-in-hometown children（the children who are left behind in their rural villages when their parents migrate to cities in search of work）** from 10 provinces and the young pioneers from the capital walked into the compound of the Ministry of Foreign Affairs, where they spent a special International Children's Day.

面子工程

　　看到"面子工程"这个词,我们很容易就联想到了"形象工程"。在现实生活中,我们往往也会误解这两个概念,认为它们指的是一回事。但仔细想想,二者又有很大的区别。众所周知,"形象工程"是某些领导干部为了个人或小团体的目的和利益,不顾群众需要和当地实际,不惜利用手中权力而搞出的劳民伤财、浮华无效却有可能为自己和小团体标榜政绩的工程。而"面子工程"虽然也有形象方面的考虑,却无论如何也算不上"形象工程",譬如下面第一个报道中的"华山刷漆"事件就是"面子工程",而非"形象工程";而第二个报道中的"丰城新区建设"则一般称为"形象工程"。

　　在陕西省华县秦岭北麓,一家采石场为了让被毁坏的山体好看些,竟然刷上绿漆"遮羞"。这一"面子工程"最近引发人们质疑。

燕赵都市网,2010 年 9 月 6 日

　　对于一个县级市来说,丰城新区建设确实是"大手笔":规划总用地3.3 万亩,目前已征用 1.1 万亩,"预征"7000 亩。新区的新城大道宽100 米,紫云大道宽 80 米,人民广场面积达 176 亩,百年老樟树进城"安家",当地群众形容丰城新区是"道路超过北京三环,广场超过天安门广场"。

《新闻晨报》,2004 年 7 月 21 日

　　关于这两个词的关系,秦海先生(2008)在杂文"形象工程和面子工程"一文中不无幽默地说道,"'形象工程'和'面子工程'是相辅相成和

各得其妙的。'形象工程'给自己树立光辉，'面子工程'则为自己掩盖丑陋。光'形象'不'面子'，不行；光'面子'不'形象'，也不行；只有'形象'加'面子'，才能只见光辉而不见丑陋。"这真是一语中的！

然而，在《汉英词典》(第三版)中，笔者却不无遗憾地发现，译者对"面子工程"和"形象工程"的理解恰好相反了。前者被译为 image project，而后者则被译为 vanity project。而《汉英大词典》中则未收录"面子工程"，"形象工程"同样被译为了 vanity project。

有鉴于此，笔者建议把这二者的译文对调才比较合适："面子工程"为 vanity project，而"形象工程"则为 image project。或者至少不要把"面子工程"译为"image project"。

当然，如果有读者认为 vanity 一词为"虚荣"之意，而"形象工程"也是"虚荣"的一种表现的话，那么不妨采用另一种方式来译"面子工程"，那就是 face job。请看下面关于 face job 的引文：

Known as hiring "**a face job**," or a "white guy window dressing," some Chinese companies have started hiring foreigners with a light complexion to portray employees or business partners to get an edge in the business world. The actors are hired to appear in some second-tier Chinese cities where their presence is needed to fulfill a claim of being an international company, or impressing local officials. Many of the individuals hired to fill the roles are English teachers, out-of-work models, or actors.

CNN, 2010 - 07 - 06

上面这篇报道就是最近广为流传的不少中国企业"租借"白种人老外撑门面的事情，报道中把这种现象称为"面子工程"。

裸　婚

　　最近,随着电视剧《蜗居》的热播,"裸婚"一词也热了起来,何为裸婚? 就是既没车又没房,依然要结婚,就像《蜗居》里的海萍和苏淳。"互动百科"认为,"裸婚是近年来(2008年)诞生的新名词,是指结婚'无房无车无钻戒,不办婚礼不蜜月'"。

　　"裸婚"一词的出现有其社会条件和语言学条件。从社会条件来看,首先,这是新一代年轻人(主要是80后)对日益高涨的社会压力,如高企的房价、排场的婚礼、有房有车的要求等的一种无奈抗争。据最新调查显示,即将年满30岁的职场人中将近五成人无房无车,而在1981—1984年出生的人群中,无房无车的人的比例达到了七成。其次,"裸婚"也可看作是80后追求返璞归真的爱情的一种体现,因为他们认为,婚姻幸不幸福,跟结婚的仪式隆重不隆重没关系,跟结婚的日子也没关系,关键还是看人。如果人合适,不摆酒席,不度蜜月,不拍结婚照,都可以。最重要是两个人心在一起,两个人开心就行了。从语言学条件来看,该词的出现并非偶然,因为诸如"裸官"、"裸捐"、"裸奔"、"裸身"等"裸"文化已经渗透到了我们生活的方方面面,而"裸婚"只不过是通过"仿拟(parody)"而构造的另一个新词而已。

　　像"裸婚"这样的概念属于文化局限词,在英文中大概不可能找到对应的成分,因为在英美国家中不存在这样的现象。所以,建议将该词直译为 naked wedding,再配以解释性译文 get married without a house, car, diamond ring or grand wedding ceremony。当然,如果该词出现在特定的语境中,释文则可省略。下面 CCTV International 2009 年 12 月 25 日的一个报道,即可佐证该译文的普遍适用性。该报道的题目为: "Naked" wedding: a blessing or a disaster?

BEIJING, Dec. 24 — "**Naked wedding**," a popular catch phrase in China coined amid the background of skyrocketing property prices, reflects the reality of many young people in China today. It refers to a marriage without a house, a car, diamond ring, and fancy wedding ceremony—just a nine-yuan marriage certificate.

值得一提的是,有些地方把"裸婚"翻译成了 nude wedding,这就大错特错了! 请看 Wikipedia 对 nude wedding 的释义:

Nude weddings are weddings that may include the couple, bridal party, and / or guests involved with the wedding being in the nude. Participants may choose this style of wedding because they are committed to their nudist lifestyle, or just an average couple that want a different and unusual kind of wedding. Though nude weddings have occurred throughout history, the first documented nude wedding was celebrated in Elysian Fields, California in 1942. Since this event, the number of nude weddings being performed has risen across the globe.

和"裸婚"一样,"裸官"(指那些把妻子和儿女都迁居到国外,钱也带到国外,而自己一个人留在国内的官员)、"裸替"(指电影或电视剧中的裸体替身演员)、"裸奔"、"裸泳"、"裸聊"这些词均可以采用上面的方法,分别翻译为:naked official (officials whose family members have all emigrated abroad)、nude stand-in、dash naked、swim naked / in the nude、nude web-cam session。值得一提的是,"裸替"在英文中还可译为 body double,下面是 Wikipedia 对该词的定义:

A body double is a general term for someone who substitutes for the credited actor of a character in any recorded visual medium, whether videotape or film. **The term is most commonly used in the context of head-to-toe (or nearly) shots involving nudity.**

当然,naked / nude 等词也不可能全部通吃,有些"裸"则要根据情况具体翻译,譬如,"裸退"(指干部退休后不担任任何职务)就应该译为 complete retirement(thoroughly retire and refuse to accept any post or title)、"裸泳"还可以译为 swim in the raw 或口语体(skinny-dipping)、"裸捐"(把特定范围的个人资产全部捐出)则应该译为 all-out donation、而上面所说的"裸奔"还可以用 streak 来翻译、"裸检"(指机场为安全检查配备全身扫描设备,对乘客进行严格检查)则应该译为 full-body scanning。

　　本来对"裸"字所引发的一系列新词的讨论就到此为止了,但一大早打开电脑就看到了"上海热线"上的一则报道,题为"潘洁早逝事件余波未了,沪部分白领毅然弃高薪**裸辞**",讲的是前两天上海交大毕业的美女研究生刚入职场半年即过劳而死(death from overwork),受此影响,好几位供职于"四大"和 500 强企业的白领在论坛里发帖,表示受到此事触动,已放弃原本数十万年薪的"超高压"岗位,打算休息一阵子或再去寻找一份低薪、环境轻松的新工作。看来我们还得再讨论一下"裸"家族中的另外一个新成员:裸辞。

　　所谓"裸辞",指的是还没找好下家就辞职,不考虑后路,意味着毅然决然地离开。关于"裸辞",人们有不同的看法,有些人,尤其是人力资源专家们,认为"裸辞"是冲动之举,对第二次就业影响很大,不宜提倡,在这些人看来,"裸辞"应译为 irrational resignation 或 resign irrationally 才算达意。但另外一些人则认为,"裸辞"也没啥大不了,辞职后一样混得好。在这种情况下,不妨把"裸辞"直译为 naked resignation,然后再加上解释:resign without finding work / a new job 或 quit a job without finding another one,或干脆抛弃"裸"的形象,将其意译为后者。如此看来,"裸"字家族中的这个成员由于人们看法的不同,英译还较为复杂,应根据具体情况具体对待。

驴 友

　　"驴友"一词源自网络,最初由新浪"旅游论坛"传出,其中的"驴"是旅游的"旅"的谐音,泛指参加旅游、自助游的朋友。这类朋友互称为"驴友"。但现在更多地是指背包客(backpackers),就是那种背着背包,带着帐篷、睡袋穿越、宿营的户外爱好者。简单地说,"驴友"就是户外运动的爱好者。在我国开展的主要户外运动包括远足、穿越、登山、攀岩、漂流、越野山地车等。这种属于"驴友"的运动中多数带有探险性,属于极限和亚极限运动,有很大的挑战性和刺激性。因为可以拥抱自然、挑战自我、锻炼意志及团队合作精神,提高野外生存能力,所以这些活动深受青年人的喜爱。随着人们生活水平的提高,户外运动和"驴友"越来越受欢迎,日益成为关注的焦点。

　　一般旅游与"驴友"的户外运动的差别在于,一般旅游是指出门以旅游的方式享乐的活动,交了钱别人可以为你安排一切,不用担心吃喝拉撒睡,放心享受旅游的乐趣就可以了。而"驴友"则通常自己计划安排衣食住行,以体验大自然为目的,自备各种必需的旅游用品,所以"驴友"的活动方式是一种更为自由、更为独立的旅行方式。之所以用"驴"一词,大概除了谐音的因素外,还因为汉语中的"驴子"总是吃苦耐劳,不畏艰辛,这与这些热衷于探险的"驴友"大有共通之处。

　　"驴友"有些地方采用直译的方式,译为 donkey friend,这种译法对国内略懂英文者而言,理解无甚难处,但相信西方读者肯定是丈二和尚摸不着头脑,因为 donkey 在西方文化中是"固执"和"无知"的代名词(in western culture the donkey is a symbol of stubbornness and stupidity）。此外,还有一些地方直接用 backpackers 来译"驴友",但根据上面对该词意义的探索,我们知道 backpackers 只是"驴友"的一种而已,这种译文显然犯了以点盖面,以偏盖全的错误。此外,笔者偶尔还看到诸如 travel mate、travel partner、travel companion 之类的译法,但考虑到 mate、partner 以及 companion 的本义,用它们来译既诙谐又传神的"驴友"一词,似乎也有点牵强,因为这些词所表示的人际关系都十分亲近,而"驴友"之间的关系则比较生疏,至少最初如此,例如下面摘自《汉语世界》中的一个例子就能说明问题:

上个周末,小王第一次参加"驴友"活动,现在回忆起整个旅行经历,他还显得很兴奋。"大多数人互不认识,我们在网上约好时间和地点,见面时只说网名。"在中国,很多"驴友"活动都需要自带食品和生活必需品,虽然一起行动但基本不互报姓名、职业、年龄等个人信息。大部分"驴友"们选择的路线都有一定的危险性,所以在出发前,他们还可能会写一份"后果自负"的声明。

上面这个例子告诉我们,"驴友"之间大多数之前并不认识,他们的活动甚至可能只是在网上的一个约定,彼此并不的熟悉,也不太关心相互的个人信息,他们关心的只是一起上路探险旅游而已。此外,"驴友"所表示的诙谐、非正式含义 mate、partner 及 companion 这三个词也难以表达。

那么,"驴友"一词如何翻译呢? 或许我们可以从"笔友"的英译 pen pal 中得到启发,从而想到 travel pal 和 tour pal 这两个词。然而,当我们把 travel pal 输入到 *Google* 中进行验证时我们发现该词在英文中通常并不指人,而是指旅游时使用的手册和一些保障安全的工具,有时甚至指旅游公司。例如:

Travel Pal is the ultimate travel companion for the professional and the casual Palm traveler.

Travel Pal lets you keep track of local and home times across different cities and time zones while synchronizing your Palm device time to your trip itinerary.

Travel Pal will manage your trips allowing transportation management (flight, sail, train, car & bus details) to specific destinations, lodging details management and auto rental details management. Travel Pal lets you define the cities you travel to, the currencies you use, your trip itinerary and allows full control of time management.

With **Travel Pal** you won't forget your flights, hotel arrangements and auto rental reservations and by letting it manage your Palm time your Palm will be always synchronized to your local time and so will your schedule.

——Travel Pal Description[1]

Travel-Pal fits between two child car seats and it's big enough to hold everything for both children. Travel-Pal is the best way to keep your backseat tidy, toys within reach and everyone happy.

这样看来,"驴友"一词的最佳译文就应该是 tour pal 了。首先,pal 一词指代"朋友"为非正式用法,与"驴友"的语体风格相似,另外,tour pal 的译法也得到了外国专家的肯定。笔者应邀翻译商务印书馆双语刊物《汉语世界》的一个栏目"流行新词语"时,就将"驴友"译为了 tour pal,而负责审稿的外国专家后来则解释说:Tour pal refers to the increasing number of backpackers who team up for budget tours after making the arrangements over the Internet rather than through a travel agency.

---

[1] http://pda. wareseeker. com/Travel/travel-pal-1. 5. zip/321419。

买壳上市

　　2003 年出版的《新华新词语词典》把"买壳上市"定义为"在股票市场上非上市公司通过购买已上市公司的股份,从而获得对已上市公司的控制权,实现间接上市。"这个定义并没有太大的问题,但该词典为"买壳上市"提供的英文翻译"go public through buying a shell"却让人啼笑皆非。这里的 buying a shell 缺乏语境,不知指的是买果壳还是买贝壳,竟然可以让一个公司上市。很显然,这种译文不但生硬,而且不符合法律英语的规范性要求。"买壳上市"中的"壳"不能直译成"shell",不然很容易引起误解。

　　那么"买壳上市"中的"壳"究竟源自何处呢?只有追根溯源,搞清楚"买壳上市"这一术语的的历史和内涵,译文才可能地道确切。

　　在美国,上市可分为直接上市(IPO 首次公开上市)和间接上市(买壳上市)两种方式。从 1934 年起,"买壳上市"在美国就成了一种简捷的合法上市方法,属于公司收购合并的一种正常形式。买壳上市,又称为反向收购(reverse merger),指非上市公司通过收购一家壳公司 shell company(已上市公司)的股份控制该公司,再由该公司反向收购非上市公司的资产和业务,使之成为上市公司的子公司,从而使原非上市公司达到间接上市的目的。

　　在西方资本市场,通过"买壳上市"这一方式进行资产重组和上市融资的商业案例不胜枚举,所以我们很容易就能在英语刊物中找到这一术语地道的表达。请看下面两例:

1. "The **reverse mergers** in biotechnology are meant to help private companies **go public** at a time when market conditions have made it virtually impossible for them to pursue conventional initial public offerings. "

The New York Times, 2009 – 03 – 09

2. "Big-ticket IPOs in New York and Hong Kong for Chinese banks and insurance companies make headlines. But in recent years another class of Chinese company has been quietly tapping the international capital markets. Enterprises that don't have the heft or profits for a splashy initial public offering are finding they can **get a coveted overseas listing through a reverse merger.** "

Businessweek, 2007 – 03 – 05

由此可见,"买壳上市"正确的译法为,"go public through a reverse merger"和"get a listing through a reverse merger"。其名词形式则为"a reverse merger"。

此外,和"买壳上市"紧密相关而又有所区别的另外一个术语是"借壳上市",是指上市公司的母公司(集团公司)通过将主要资产注入到上市的子公司中,来实现母公司的上市。借壳上市和买壳上市的共同之处在于,它们都是一种对上市公司壳资源进行重新配置的活动,都是为了实现间接上市,它们的不同之处在于,买壳上市的企业首先需要获得对一家上市公司的控制权,而借壳上市的企业已经拥有了对上市公司的控制权。"借壳上市"也不是什么 borrowing a shell,而是 back-door listing,意即"后门上市"。

脑 残

我们这里所说的"脑残"可不是指某个人真的脑袋受了伤害,而是指某人大脑残废,突发奇想,一般用于讽刺别人。该词出现于 2006 年,那时日本 NDS 上的《脑锻炼》类游戏正在大流行,由于这类游戏最初推出时打着"开发脑力、锻炼智力"的旗号,因而有人戏称玩这类游戏的人都是因为智力低下或脑力有缺陷,故而被称为"脑残者的游戏"。曾几何时,该词流行于网络,用来归总、评价两会代表委员们的提案,成为一些网友所热衷的新锐、时尚的言说方式。

据《成都晚报》5 月 3 日报道,"80 后"领军人物韩寒已正式启动了杂志的征稿工作,其千字 1000—2000 元的稿酬标准让国内同类杂志望尘莫及。有意思的是,韩寒还在杂志中开辟了"脑残稿"栏目,即写得最臭的文章,韩寒也予以发表,并给出了千字 250 元的"戏谑"标准,声称"杂志完全不认同作者的观点,认为作者脑残,杂志也会发表此类文章示众。"

网络上对"脑残"有一个非常有趣的语义双关的释义:Your brain has two parts: the left and the right. Your left brain has nothing right, and your right brain has nothing left.

"脑残"一词目前还没有词典收录,笔者在其他地方见到的也是该词作为医学术语的译文,如 brain damage、brain disfunction 以及 brain deformity 等。有鉴于此,就该词该义的英译,笔者提出以下建议:

1. 直译为 brain-damaged 或 brain-impaired。这样的直译在语义上

不难理解,也反映出了这一汉语新词独特的表达方式,译文放在特定的语境中,应该能为英语读者所理解。当然,作为名词,"脑残"似乎也可以译为 damaged / impaired brain。

2. 意译为 brain-dead。Brain-dead 在英文中的字面意思是"脑死亡",比喻意为 stupid and uninteresting,即"愚蠢的"、"不会动脑子的"。该译文的优点在于它与"脑残"一词在形象和意义上均基本吻合,所以不失为一个较为理想的译文。

最后,随着"脑残"的流行,还出现了一系列与其相关的新词,如那种通过把汉字拆开和改变其部首来展示作者个性的文体被称作"脑残体",通常可意译为 leet 和 leetspeak 或直译为 brain-impaired writing style。下面是 Wikipedia 对 leet 一词的英文释义,笔者另外附之以 leet 和汉语"脑残文"各一个例子:

1. **Leet**, also known as **eleet** or **leetspeak**, is an alternative alphabet for the English language that is used primarily on the Internet. It uses various combinations of ASCII characters to replace Latinate letters.

2. TEh INTeRn3T i5 THr3@ + EN1N9 t0 Ch@ n93 thE W4Y wE $ p34k. (The Internet is threatening to change the way we speak.)

3. 莓天想埝祢巳宬儑1 种溍惯(每天想念你已成为一种习惯)。

另外,*The China Daily* 也报道了"脑残体",其报道如下:

This term "nao can ti", meaning literally "**brain-impaired writing style**," is the Chinese answer to "**leetspeak**" in English. It's a language used by some netizens who mix traditional and simplified Chinese characters with symbols, numbers and alphabets. It is so hard to read that it looks like the writing of a mentally impaired person.

而那些"非主流(non-mainstream)"们所写的爱情"诗"之类的,则被称为"脑残文",就是指他们的"诗"无病呻吟,作者脑子有问题,英文可以译为 brain-impaired essays / poems;"脑残儿"则是指这些"非主流"的作者,可以用 the brain-dead / impaired / damaged 来翻译。

农 家 乐

　　"农家乐"这个词相信对大多数都市人而言并不陌生。大城市（譬如上海）的周围现在几乎遍布各式各样的"农家乐"，为那些难得偷得一日闲的都市一族提供各式各样富有乡村风情的娱乐服务。譬如，上海周边的一些农家乐便以体现绿色、自然、健康为内容，突出田园特色。游客可以参与农事活动，如摘菜、摘果、农耕等，也可以享受农家灶头饭菜，还可以参与农家传统娱乐项目，如钓鱼、钓龙虾、划木船、参观中国第一颗试验火箭发射基地、参观东海大桥、滴水湖和南汇嘴，内容丰富，可供随意选择。

　　"互动百科"认为：农家乐是一种新兴的旅游休闲形式，是农民向城市现代人提供的一种回归自然从而获得身心放松、愉悦精神的休闲旅游方式。一般来说，农家乐的业主利用当地的农产品进行加工，满足客人的需要，成本较低，因此消费就不高。而且农家乐周围一般都是美丽的自然或田园风光，可以满足舒缓现代人的精神，因此受到很多城市年轻人的欢迎。

　　"农家乐"旅游的雏形来自于国内外的乡村旅游，并将国内特有的乡村景观、民风民俗等融为一体，因而具有鲜明的乡土烙印。同时，它也是人们旅游需求多样化、闲暇时间不断增多、生活水平逐渐提高和"文明病"、"城市病"加剧的必然产物。中国农家乐最初发源于四川成都，后来发展到整个成都平原、四川盆地，直至全国。

　　然而，"农家乐"一词的英译却并非易事，争论不小。譬如，邓巨

（2009）在指出了诸如 a wonderful visiting in the farm、a trip to the countryside、country life、the style of country life、happy farm life、enjoyment of country life、farmers' joy、happy farmhouse、nongjiale、rural grand time、happy farmer's house 等译文的问题后,认为在不同的语境中该词可以译为 farm hotel 和 rural tourism。另外,《中国日报》"英语点津"一栏中则把该词译为 farmer's home inn,并给出了如下解释:During the weeklong golden holidays, people often cannot find hotels in popular sites, so some farmers will lend their houses to tourists, which are cheaper than normal hotels. Tourists can also eat with the farmer's family and do farming chores for fun. 事实上,笔者自己在给上海市农委翻译材料时也常常碰到这个词,鉴于时间关系,也通常将其简单译为 Happy Farmer's House。

那么,"农家乐"究竟应该如何翻译呢？笔者赞同邓巨先生的观点,即译者应该根据该词出现的语境综合考虑译文。那么,农家乐通常出现在什么语境中？表现为什么形式呢？"互动百科"为我们提供了答案。它认为,中国的农家乐有以下分类:

1. 农家园林型:这些农家乐往往本身就是全国的花卉、盆景、苗木、桩头等的生产基地。

2. 花果观赏型:主要是农家果园游乐。游客可以采摘果品,购买鲜花等。

3. 景区旅舍型:提供低档次农家旅舍,价格低廉,游客感觉仿佛把自己的家搬到了风景区,花费居家度日的钱,享受景区的自然环境。

4. 花园客栈型:这些农家乐把农业生产组织转变成为旅游企业,把农业用地通过绿化美化,改造成园林式建筑,配以功能齐全的配套设施和客栈式的管理,使之成为在档次上高于"农家乐"低于度假村的一种休闲娱乐场所。

如此看来,所谓"农家乐"至少应该有 4 种译文,分别体现这四种不同的表现形式。另外,笔者注意到,"农家乐"旅游的雏形来自国内外的乡村旅游,所以很有可能这个旅游的形式国外早已有之,只不过国内给它起了一个形象生动的名称而已。事实上,国外的"农家乐"发展更为

成熟,也大致包括了国内这四种"农家乐"的形式。譬如,美国加州大学
(University of California)就有一个 Small Farm Program。该 program 中
就有针对不同形式的"农家乐"的命名,或许可以给我们提供一些借鉴。
请看该文(有删节):

Helpful Agricultural Tourism（Agritourism）Definitions

by Ramiro Lobo, *Farm Advisor*

Agricultural Tourism：Refers to the act of visiting a working farm or
any agricultural, horticultural or agribusiness operation for the purpose of
enjoyment, education, or active involvement in the activities of the farm or
operation.

Farm Stays：The activity of visiting a farm for overnight stays and for
the purpose of participating in or enjoying farm activities and / or other
attraction offered.

Farm Visits：The activity of visiting a farm for short periods of time
for the purpose of participating in or enjoying farm activities and / or other
attraction offered.

U-Pick or Pick-Your-Own Operations：These are fruits and farms or
orchards where the customers themselves harvest the fruits or products. The
prices they pay for the volume harvested will be usually higher than what
the grower would get from a broker.

Rural Tourism：Recreational experience involving visits to rural
settings or rural environments for the purpose of participating in or
experiencing activities, events or attractions not readily available in
urbanized areas. These are not necessarily agricultural in nature.

这样看来,农家园林型的"农家乐"似乎可以用 agricultural tourism
或 agritourism 来译,游客在这种"农家乐"中既可以娱乐,又可以了解农
业知识,还可以参与到农业活动之中。而花果观赏型的"农家乐"则可
以用 U-Pick 或 Pick-Your-Own Operations 来表达,游客可以自己付费,

采摘果品,购买鲜花等。而景区旅舍型的"农家乐"可以根据游客居留时间的长短分别译为 farm stays 或 home visits。而最后一种花园客栈型的"农家乐"根据定义似乎比较高级,而且已不局限于"农业"的特性,似乎可以用 rural tourism 来表达。

当然,笔者认为,把形象生动的"农家乐"按照字面翻译为 Happy Farmer's House 有时也不失为一种恰当的选择,因为汉语中的一个"乐"字所表达的意境远比那些冷冰冰的 visit、stay、tourism、inn、hotel 要深远得多。事实上,*The China Daily* 等英文媒体也常用该译,例如:

Down the river, you may find thousands-of-years-old camphor, Santan loquats, Jiusha old village, folk houses in New Yangcun, old workshops, Longmen waterfall, Dachuan Island and Phoenix Island. There are also many interesting activities to try out at the **Happy Farmer's House**: catch a Hui Opera in Miantan, try your hand at picking loquats, oranges and tea leaves, or check out how silkworms are being bred, or try making some soybean milk. All of these activities will ensure that you will have a delightful time when visiting **Happy Farmer's House**.

陪　聊

　　陪聊,顾名思义就是陪人聊天,它也可以指陪人聊天的人。陪聊在国内一直被认为与三陪服务一样,是一种色情服务,因为不少以前的"三陪女"现在改头换面,成为了"陪聊女"。有鉴于此,国家也从来没有批准过所谓的"陪聊公司",尽管陪聊服务在社会上屡禁不止。然而,世易时移,从 2010 年 2 月 20 日起,陪聊职业在上海正式获批,美其名曰:心理陪护师。当然,我们希望,有关部门能对该行业加强监管,避免心理陪护师们沦为"陪聊先生"或"陪聊小姐",更不应该让他/她们涉及陪旅游、陪购物之类的超范围服务。

　　"陪聊"这个词目前还未见有其英语翻译,但我们可以根据与其相关的其他一些词语的英译尝试翻译该词。譬如,在《新世纪汉英大词典》中,"陪酒"被翻译为:accompany（a guest）in drinking;"陪练"作为动词被译为:accompany sb in training; be a training partner,作为名词则被译为:training partner; sparring partner（in boxing）;"陪舞"则被译为:be a dancing partner。

　　首先,我们不能将"陪聊"译为 accompany sb in chatting,因为这样的译文太过生硬;其次,sparring partner（in boxing）只能适用于特定的语域,所以也不适用。剔除这两种译文之后,我们似乎可以借鉴上面三种译文中的 partner 一词,从而把"陪聊"的名词形式翻译为 chat partner,而将其动词形式用 be a chat partner 来表示。

　　Chat partner 这个译文并不一定带贬义色彩,所以合法化之后的"陪聊"似乎可用该词表达。另外,英语中常将网络上的"聊伴"用 chat partner 来表示,所以就有了 msn／QQ chat partner 等表述。例如:

These friends, confidants, and sometimes lovers are all part of the same e-society and become a "**chat partner**" or someone with whom you regularly communicate. This site is just up so those who are looking to meet others can become more informed on just what it is to make friends and develop **chat partners** across the world.

如果我们想表示含有贬义色彩的"陪聊",那么或许可以根据英文中 call girl(应召女郎:a woman prostitute hired by telephone)、street girl(妓女:a prostitute who attracts customers by walking the streets)和 working girl(妓女:a woman prostitute)的表达形式,译为 chat girl(陪聊女)或 chat boy(陪聊男)。事实上,英文中的确有这两个词,而且均含有色情服务的意思。例如:

This particular scam evolved over the course of an entire hour. The webcam **chat girl** posed as a real WooMe user trying to meet new people and eventually tried to lure her victim to an external video chat site where he was required to divulge his full name, address and banking information.

这样看来,"陪聊"一词既可用 chat partner 这个中性词来表达,也可以用 chat girl／boy 这样明显带有贬义色彩的词来翻译,而读者在具体使用时则需分清语境,根据自己所要表达的内容谨慎选用。

劈　腿

　　"劈腿"本来是一个体操术语,指两腿最大限度地分开,一腿与另一腿成一直线触及支撑面。然而,当我们把该词输入 *Google* 进行搜索,就会发现,与该词本义相关的内容几乎踪迹全无;相反,可以搜索出大量如下的例证:

　　爆马雅舒**劈腿**,不断抢洋老公

环球网,2010 年 7 月 3 日

　　情感剖析:智慧女 VS **劈腿**男

千龙网,2009 年 7 月 6 日

　　范植伟曝王心凌疑曾**劈腿**

星岛环球网,2010 年 4 月 25 日

　　刘嘉玲**劈腿**地产富豪?!

福建电视台,2010 年 7 月 27 日

　　在这些语境中,"劈腿"一词的新义呼之欲出:形容对爱情不专一、脚踏两条船的人或者这种行为。一般而言,"劈腿"在狭义上是指与一人以上有明确的交往关系及行为,而广义来说则是泛指对感情不忠的人,包括心灵与肉体的不忠。现实生活中,造成"劈腿"的主要原因有环境、人性两个因素。工作环境不同,接触到的对象也就不同,若再加上不专一、不忠实等个性的弱点,就会造成"劈腿"行为的产生。

　　关于"劈腿"一词,有翻译为 cheating 的,也有翻译为 have the third person 的,还有翻译为 player 的,更有直译为 get on with two girl / boy friends 的。这些译文中,除了 have the third person 为中式英语外,cheating 和 player 均语义过于宽泛,而 get on with two girl／boy friends 则一方面过于直白,另一方面并未充分表达出"劈腿"一词的含义。譬如,有些"劈腿达人"精于此道,乐此不疲,可能与几个异性保持"劈腿"关系。

"劈腿"一词因其语意一望即知、见则会意,而被八卦媒体广泛应用。由于该词过于鲜活生动,在英文中可能难以找到一个完全对应的形象,只能用英文动词 two-time 来译,而那些"劈腿者"则可译为 two-timer,"劈腿"这个行为则是 two-timing。下面是朗文英语词典中 two-time 的定义和配例,可以帮助我们更好地了解该词:

two-time：*vt. informal* to have a secret relationship with someone who is not your regular partner：If you're **two-timing** me, I'll kill you I swear.

再看 *The Free Online Dictionary* 对 two-time、two-timer 以及 two-timing 的定义:

two-time：*tr. v.* two-timed, two-timing, two-times *Slang*：To be unfaithful to（a spouse or lover）.

two-timer：*n.* someone who deceives a lover or spouse by carrying on a sexual relationship with somebody else.

two-timing：*adj.* not faithful to a spouse or lover；"adulterous husbands and wives"；"a two-timing boyfriend".

下面,再看看这几个词在具体语境中如何使用:

1. When a married person **is two-timing his or her partner**, the two-timing spouse is considered to be deceptive and sexually unfaithful.

2. Nick Jonas, the **two-timer**, now has two older women wanting him all to themselves.

3. The TV Matchmaker **two-timed me** and left my life in ruins.

"劈腿"这个词听来俚俗,却是大众文化的精妙创意。想象一下,那些肢体僵硬的男人／女人,弯下腰手指也许还碰不到脚趾,却乐此不疲地在感情上追求高难度的动作。他／她们以为自己在感情中可以左右逢源,游刃有余,劈开两腿踩上两条船,而最后得到的下场很可能只是"咕咚"一声落水,落得个浑身湿透,狼狈不堪。

票 贩 子

　　"票贩子"是指那些倒卖车票、船票或入场券等并从中非法牟利的人。其方言形式为"黄牛",《现代汉语词典》(第五版)对后者的解释是:指恃力气或利用不正当手法抢购物资以及车票、门票后以高价出售而从中取利的人。"票贩子"(或黄牛)历史悠久,他们在解放前倒黄金,在"文革"时倒诸如缝纫机、自行车、电视机等各类票证。目前,"票贩子"行业似乎有了更大的发展,开始倒月饼票,倒大剧院戏票,倒热线火车票,直至倒世界第一的磁悬浮列车票。从某种意义上而言,他们直接导致了春运期间的"买票难"。

　　"票贩子"一词目前在各主要汉英词典中均有一个译文:ticket broker。同时,也有学者(金其斌,2003)撰文指出,"票贩子"应该遵循《英汉大词典(补编)》中的译文,译为"ticket broker"。那么,这里的"ticket broker"是否就是我们所谓的"票贩子"呢? 答案是否定的。"Ticket broker"和汉语中的"票贩子"其实是指完全不同的两个概念。譬如,在一篇题为"Why Buy from a Ticket Broker"的文章中[1]我们就可找到佐证。根据该文,"ticket broker"与"旅行社"或"股票经纪人"类似,它根据客人的具体需要,提供专业的服务(A ticket broker is similar to a travel agent or a stock broker in that they provide service along with a

---

〔1〕见 http://www.jivha.com/blog/archives/2004/05/11/is-bharti-turning-into-a-shell-company.html。

product. Ticket brokers are event experts. They are trained to provide recommendations tailored to a customer's specific needs.)。另外,"ticket broker"具有营业执照、固定的营业地点和营业时间。从"ticket broker"那里买票,比从"street scalper"那里买票要安全,服务也更为周到(Purchasing tickets from a reputable broker like Show-Me Tickets provides a safety net against any potential problems. We recommend purchasing tickets from a licensed broker and a business in good standing with the Better Business Bureau. Reputable ticket brokers maintain normal business hours and a permanent location, to ensure assistance with any consumer complaints. While purchasing tickets from a "street scalper" whom you will probably never see again puts you at serious risk for fraud, dealing with a reliable broker ensures the highest degree of customer service.)。

  另有一篇文章"Ticket Brokers and Scalpers—How to Get Hard-to-Find Tickets"[2]对"ticket broker"做了更为详细的说明:By using an authorized ticket broker you can avoid certain risks. Tickets are guaranteed, delivery is fast and brokers often have good seats available. Remember these are ticket resellers and you will pay more—sometimes much, much more—than the price printed on the ticket when buying from them. 这说明,人们在一票难求时,可以高价从"ticket broker"处购买,但同时,"ticket broker"是经过授权的(authorized)售票机构,因而是安全可靠的。这和我们心目中的票贩子完全是两个概念。

  既然"票贩子"不能译为"ticket broker",那么应该如何翻译呢?其实上面第一篇文章中已经给出了答案,那就是"street scalper"。顺着这个线索,我们还可以找到美国英语中该词的表达"tout"。朗文词典对tout 的定义为:*derog* a person who offers tickets that are in short supply for sale at a price higher than usual,并提供了例证:A **ticket tout** offered me a £5 Cup Final ticket for £60. (一个票贩子向我索价 60 英镑,兜售原价为 5 英镑的杯赛决赛门票。)

---

〔2〕见 http://phoenix. about. com/od/attractionsandevents/a/scalper. htm。

此外,《新世纪汉英大词典》中还提供了两个译文,一个是 ticket speculator,另一个是 ticket shark。二者均可用来翻译"票贩子"。例如,一本英文词典就是用"Ticket speculator"来解释"ticket scalper"的:an unauthorized ticket speculator who buys tickets to a performance or sports event and resells them at inflated prices。"Ticket shark"非常形象,但用得较少,它的英文意思为:someone who makes money buying tickets under price and selling them overprice。

综上所述,"票贩子"可以翻译为:(street / ticket) scalper、(ticket) tout、ticket speculator、ticket shark。

本文是"因特网与汉英词典编纂"一文中的一部分,载《西安外国语学院学报》2005 年第 1 期

拼　车

　　把"拼车"一词输入 *Google*，信息之多，让人眼花缭乱。什么"上海拼车"、"北京拼车"、"深圳拼车"，甚至"拼车网"比比皆是。那么，什么是"拼车"呢？我们这里讨论的"拼车"可不是什么"黑车"载客的违法事件，而是指小区邻居、单位同事等熟人之间的"合乘"行为。他们由于乘车路线相同，为了节约费用和时间，同乘一辆出租车上下班或出游，而车费则由他们平均分摊。当然，"拼车"也不一定非要"拼"出租车，"拼"私家车也未尝不可。譬如，近几年春节前夕，由于火车票一票难求，而且火车上拥挤不堪，不少在沪工作的外地人就相互联络，同乘一辆私家车回老家过年，这些"拼客"只需分担私家车车主沿途的油费和高昂的过路费即可。

　　"拼车"是一个新兴事物。据报道，韩国、希腊及欧美国家的出租车已尝试"合乘制"。在美国，多人乘坐同一辆出租车是被鼓励和支持的，因为这既有利于环保，有利于缓解拥挤的城市交通，又有利于乘客。我国很多大城市中已经开拓了拼车服务，而且相应的注册服务机构也已应运而生。

　　既然美国等英语为母语的国家也有"拼车"的现象，那么就应该有该词的相应表达。"拼车"怎么说呢？地道的英文叫 carpool 或 carpooling，前者是动词，后者则是其名词形式。下面是 Wikipedia 中的相关表述：

　　Carpooling is the shared use of a car by the driver and one or more passengers, usually for commuting. **Carpoolers** use pool members' private cars, or a jointly hired vehicle, for private shared journeys.

Carpooling reduces the costs involved in repetitive or long distance driving by sharing cars, sharing rental charges, or paying the main car owner.

Inflexibility in **carpooling** can arise in accommodating en-route stops or changes to working times / patterns. Some larger **carpools** offer "sweeper services" with later running options. A further backup can also be a "guaranteed ride home" arrangement with a local taxi company.

这段话中不但说明了 carpooling 在英文中的意义,而且告诉我们,所谓的"拼车族"英文即为 carpooler,而所谓的"拼车公司/组织"则为 carpool。而关于 carpool 的动词用法,从下面的句子中可见端详:

(1) I **carpool** to save money on gas.

(2) You can share the ride with co-workers or people you live with and **carpool to work** from home, day care or school.

(3) Why should I **carpool**? The real question is "why not **carpool**?" You'll save money on gas and parking by splitting driving costs among two or more commuters. Sharing the ride makes those long commutes feel much shorter.

为什么用 pool 这个词表示"拼"呢? 因为该词原意是指"水池",例如 swimming pool(游泳池),通常引申为"集中起来共享的资源库",类似的用法还有 talent pool(人才库),data pool(数据库),oil pool(油库)等等。当然,如果一定要强调是乘坐出租车,我们也可用 taxipooling 这个词,例如:

Taxipooling is similar to carpooling which is based on the idea that sets of users having the same travel destination and sharing vehicles.

事实上,在英语中,"拼车"这个概念除了用 carpool 表达外,还有其他一些说法,如 car/taxi-sharing、ride-sharing、lift-sharing 等,例如:

(1) **Car sharing** is racing ahead full-throttle in the US market as Americans look for ways to cope with record fuel costs and be

environmentally friendly at the same time.

（2）**Ridesharing** brings a fun and social alternative to driving alone. Sharing the ride also means sharing the cost of gas and the driving.

（3）"**Lift sharing**", "**ride-sharing**", "**car-sharing**" or "**carpooling**" —it doesn't matter what you call it, it boils down to the same thing—two or more people sharing a car to get from A to B rather than driving alone. The benefits are numerous both for yourself, your family, your community and the environment. You save money on running costs, you save time looking for parking spaces and you help to save the planet by reducing your carbon footprint.

最后,值得指出的是,"拼车"在西方是政府鼓励的一种交通形式,而在国内,由于种种原因,"拼车"有时被看作是"黑车"运营,甚至遭到打压。譬如《深圳特区报》2009 年 4 月 24 日就曾报道了和几位邻居、朋友"拼车"的市民王先生遇到了相关部门的执法检查,执法人员以"非法营运"的名义向他开具了高达 3 万元的罚单的事情。事实上,市民"拼车"出行,无非就是通过成本分摊的方式降低出行的成本,这相当于一种人际互助形式,不能算作经营行为,所以"拼车"中发生的费用分摊问题不能按"非法营运"来处理。

拼 客

前面我们谈到了"拼车"的英译,事实上,"拼"这个概念在我们日常生活中使用极广,有的人"拼车",有的人"拼房"(即合租),有的人"拼购"(即团购[group purchasing])、有的人"拼游"(即拼团或自助游),也有的人"拼饭"(即拼餐),有的人甚至还"拼婚"(集体拍婚纱照、购买结婚用品等)。大家"拼"在一起只有一个目的,就是节约费用、分摊成本。这些人我们统称为"拼客"。例如:

"两人合买一张通票,每人就能省5毛钱,多划算啊!"张小姐刚刚大学毕业,是一名公司职员,也是一名忠实的"**拼客**"。平时张小姐很喜欢研究各种"拼"的方案,其中包括"拼票"坐地铁的方法。

> "白领"拼票"坐地铁 一张通票两人用",
> 《国际在线》2007年3月21日

"拼客"这种理念最初来源于 AA 制,即"拼客"们实行 go Dutch 或 split the cost 的做法。然而,如果我们把 AA 制看作一种消费观念的话,"拼客"则代表着一种流行的、积极的,甚至是低碳环保的生活方式。

由于上面的原因,"拼客"似乎等同于 AA 制,因为二者采用相同的费用分摊方式。然而,首先,很明显的是,"拼客"是指人,而 AA 制是指一种方式,二者在语言使用实践中无法相互替代。譬如,在"我是一个小拼客哦,希望和大家成为拼友"这个句子中,"拼客"就难以用 go Dutch 之类用来翻译 AA 制的表达形式来替换。其次,"拼客"们并不一定在任何情况下都实行 AA 制,拿"拼车"作个例子吧。今年春节很多人"拼"

私家车回老家,私家车主可能只要求这些"拼客"们共同支付诸如过路费、油费之类的开销,并非像 AA 制那样明晰地结算分摊每一项成本。

有鉴于此,我们不妨根据"拼客"的语音,生造一个英语译文:那就是 pinker。在这个译文中,pink 是音译,而 – er 则是地道的英文后缀,指"从事某项工作的人"。二者合二为一,恰当地凸显了"拼客"的含义,堪称妙译!

另外,该词之所以如此翻译,而不是套用英文中已有的某些表达,如 Algebraic Average(简称 AA),还有一个原因,即英美国家和中国对待"拼"的态度有所不同。英美国家一般认为"拼客"是一种节约的消费形式,例如"拼车"可以缓解交通拥挤状况,体现人文关怀等,所以这些国家的城市中往往设有 Carpool 站点,方便那些不想开车或没有私家车的人出行。而在中国,由于种种原因,有关部门对"拼"并不感冒,反而采取一些措施进行限制,而且由于缺乏相关的规章制度制约,有时也会"拼"出问题,导致"拼客"上当受骗。这样看来,采用一个生造的词来翻译这种具有中国特色的词实在是大有必要!它必将得到英语国家人士的认可而进入英语词汇,与 Fuwa、kowtow、Haibao 等词一样,最终丰富英语的表达。当然,这也是翻译行为的一个重要功能。

从另一个角度来看,"拼客"一词如此翻译,也体现了全球化的背景下,对民族文化中"异质"成分的尊重和认可。翻译和其他外事工作一样,译者既要"求同",考虑译文的可接受性,也要"存异",凸显"异质"文化的独特性。这是每一个从事文化交流工作者都应该谨记的原则。

无独有偶,笔者刚刚在"沪江英语"网站上还看到一篇短文,题为"读新闻学翻译:'拼一族'的英语表达"。文中说"层出不穷的'拼'在英语中正好有个单词 pool 对应",所以建议将"拼票"译为 ticket-pooling,将"拼团"译为 a group made up of individual tourist。首先,这种滥用 pool 来翻译"拼"的做法可要不得,拿 ticket pooling 来说吧,英文中确实有这个表述,但却经常与 lottery 一道构成 lottery ticket pooling,意思是"拼彩票",而这个"拼彩票"与我们一般意义上的"拼票"是完全不同的两个概念。前者是指通过挖补、拼接旧彩票的方法,制作当期的中奖彩票,是一种违法行为。例如:

通过挖补、拼接旧彩票的方法,制作当期的中奖彩票,骗得他人数万元。日前,西城警方破获了全市首例**拼接彩票**诈骗案,追缴赃款 1.4 万余元。

"**拼彩票**骗钱 嫌疑人被控制",《新京报》2010 年 11 月 11 日

其次,a group made up of individual tourist 这个译文很奇怪,group 肯定是由 individuals 构成的,否则如何能成为 group? 所以这个译文根本没有任何意义。

潜 规 则

"潜规则"一词最早见于吴思先生的《潜规则：中国历史中的真实游戏》(2001)。作者在书的自序中说："'潜规则'是我杜撰的词。我还想到过一些别的词，例如灰色规则、内部章程、非正式制度等等，但总觉得不如"潜规则"贴切。"而该词为大众所熟知则和女演员张钰2006年爆料娱乐圈内导演与演员的性交易密切相关。一时间，"潜规则"一词广为流行，甚至突破娱乐圈的范围，扩大到了社会各个领域。

吴思先生在其第二本书《血酬定律》(2009)中尝试着给"潜规则"下了如下的定义：

"潜规则"也称为"游戏的规则"，是指没有显现出来但已是心照不宣的某些规矩，不成文、不公开在各自的领域内得到大多数人的默许和遵守成为相关法律、法规之外的另一套行为准则和规范。各行各业游离于法规之外的"行规"和"惯例"，实质是非规则、反规则，"拿不上台面"、"见不得阳光"(比如招生潜规则、官场潜规则、足坛潜规则等)。

目前，"潜规则"的英译有多个版本，且不易判别。以下几种比较流行：

1. potential rule

2. underlying rule

3. casting couch 及 hidden rule

4. unwritten rule

5. built-in rule

6. insidious rule

7. tacit rule

8. latent rule

9. underlying code of conduct

10. off-the-record regulation

下面做简要分析：

1. potential rule：译文错误。Potential 虽译为"潜在的"，但与"潜规则"的"潜"却无关。其英文意思为：that may happen or become so, although not actually existing at present，意即"有……的可能性"，所以有可能成为客户的人称为"potential customer"，有可能发生的危险称为"potential danger"，但"潜规则"明显不是"可能发生的规则"。

2. underlying rule：译文错误。Underlying 虽可译为"潜在的"，但实际意思却是"根本的；最重要的"。《麦克米伦高阶英语词典》认为：underlying causes, facts, ideas, etc. are the real or basic ones, although they are not obvious or directly stated。其实，我们还可从 underlying 的动词形式 underlie 分析。"underlie"的词典定义为：to be the real or basic cause of or reason for something。看来，"underlying"与"潜规则"的"潜"根本无关。另外，笔者曾就"underlying rule"请教一位美国教师，她说：An underlying rule is a rule that is the basis of an action。这与"潜规则"相去甚远。

3. casting couch 及 hidden rule：用 casting couch 来译娱乐圈内的"潜规则"，形象生动、一针见血。《麦克米伦高阶英语词典》对该短语的定义为：a situation in which someone agrees to have sex in return for getting a job as an actor。而一些英文网站的解释则更为直白：The term casting couch means, in simple term, taking a girl or a woman aspiring to become a film star to bed in return for the favor of giving her an opportunity to act in a film or for recommending the aspirant to film producers for a role。而用"hidden rule"来译"潜规则"也不错，不但 *The China Daily* 上有相关报道，而且英国《镜报》(*Mirror*) 中的一篇文章也有谈及。该文在谈完一些"显性规则"（如 Keep quality high、Respond to

user needs、Work hard、Keep promises 等）后说:... but there are also hidden rules at work. These hidden rules work on us without our noticing. They are universal, or nearly so; though they are never stated, we all understand them. When a hidden rule is in conflict with one of our publicly stated rules, the hidden rule almost always wins out。这更佐证了"hidden rule"译成"潜规则"的合理性。

4. unwritten rule:译文错误。英文中确有此表达,但却并非"潜规则",因为它的意思是:a rule that is so obvious that it is not written or goes without saying(太明显而没有必要写下来的规则)。例如:You do not tell a girl she is fat, even if she is; you do not swear in the presence of a lady; you take your hat off during the national anthem. 这些例证都是英美人对"unwritten rule"的理解,显然与"潜规则"相左。

5. built-in rule:译文错误。Built-in 本身的意思是:"作为固定装置而建造的,固定的,内置的"。此外,美国人对 built-in rule 的理解为:a rule that is written in the constitution or by laws。与"潜规则"无任何关联。

6. insidious rule:译文错误。英美人认为"insidious rule"是:a rule that is more dangerous than appears on the surface。

7. tacit rule:勉强可用的译文。Tacit 的意思为:expressed or understood without being said directly,这与"潜规则"的定义基本契合。另外,中国政府网站(http://english. gov. cn/index. htm)在谈及商业贿赂时也用到该词:It was quite common for those bidding for business in China to offer potential customers or partners kickbacks ranging from cash and luxury goods to paid holiday travel. Many companies believed that the practice was a "tacit rule" of the Chinese market until a Los Angeles company was fined in the United States for paying bribes in China. 然而,该短语最好的译文似乎还是"默认的规则",因为在原版英文中,该短语似乎很难理解为"潜规则"。例如下面的说法:In *To Innovate——Break a Rule*, Thomas Ordahl recommends changing the "rules of the game" in an industry to make a difference. He cites the example of Barnes & Noble,

which challenged the tacit rule of the retail book industry that bookstores had to be quiet and stuffy, and reading was discouraged.

8. latent rule：译文错误。"latent"的释义为：present but not yet noticeable, active, or fully developed,而这些特征与"潜规则"得到行内普遍认可和实行的特征不符。

9. underlying code of conduct：译文错误。其对应的中文为"潜在的行为准则",这些行为准则主要来源于心理学、社会学和人类学,与"潜规则"无关。

10. off-the-record regulation：译文错误。Off-the-record 的意思为：不留记录的；非正式的；不准公开发表的,与"潜规则"毫不相干。

综上所述,"潜规则"一词在娱乐圈内的译文应该为：casting couch,而在其他领域的译文则以 hidden rule 为最佳。其次,间或也可使用 tacit rule。

原载《辞书研究》2007 年第 5 期

翘　课

"翘"在《现代汉语词典》(第五版)中的释义为:一头儿向上仰起。一般我们只说"翘辫子"、"翘尾巴",但现在该词却为学生,尤其是大学生所活用,创造出"翘课"一词。而那些在公司工作的白领们似乎也不甘寂寞,很快发明了"翘班",与"翘课"遥相呼应。

一般来说,"翘课"就是我们以前所熟知的"逃课",指学生在没有任何正当理由的情况下在应该上课的时候不去上课。甚至有人认为,"翘课"是大学生在大学期间必做的三件事或九件事之一。"翘"这个词之所以如此活用,可能是因为该词鲜活生动,充分迎合了大学生猎奇创新的心态吧。

"翘课"怎么译呢? 我们可能首先想到的是 skip a class / classes / school 以及 play truant 等大家都相对比较熟悉的表达。这些表达肯定都没有问题,但除此以外,我们还可以找到其他的说法,从而进一步丰富"翘课"的表述。

首先,可用采用 play hooky from class 这个说法,因为 play hooky 就是 play truant from work or school。例如:

He used to **play hooky from class**, now he plays hooky from life.

I decided to **play hooky from class** and work and spend the afternoon with my dog.

He recalled his days as a schoolboy when he used to **play hooky from class** — except carpentry.

其次, bunk off class / classes / school 也不失是一个好的译法。朗文英语词典对 bunk off 的解释为: 非正式的英国英语用法, 意思为: to stay away from somewhere such as school or to leave somewhere early without permission, 并给出了例证: I think I'll bunk off classes this afternoon. 下面再看几个例子:

If a new report is to be believed, then around 69,000 children in the UK **bunk off school** every day.

I have a Greek lesson this evening and am already thinking up excuses to **bunk off class**.

第三, 可以用 bump off classes 来译, 该词也是英国英语的用法, 通常有两层意思。第一层是 kill someone, 第二层则为 play truant。例如:

One of the negative comments about this system raised by pupils is that it will be very hard to **bump off classes** with this new technology.

第四, 还可以用 cut class / school 来译"翘课"。根据 The Free Online Dictionary, cut class 或 cut school 的意思为: to skip a school class or a day of school without an excuse, 该词典还提供了两个例证:

As a joke, one day all the students **cut their math class** and went to lunch.

Jane was grounded after she **cut school** last Friday.

第五, 澳大利亚英语中还有一个词也可以用来译"翘课"一词, 它就是 wag, 英文释义为: not go to school, either for a class or classes or the entire school day。该词既可以作动词, 也可以用在 play the wag、hop the wag 中作名词。例如: Have you played the wag before? (你以前逃过学吗?)

最后, "翘课"、"逃学"等词还可以用 bun off school、ditch school, 甚至 truant 作动词来译。请看下面的例子:

Who should I keep an eye on, the little old lady over there or this group of kids **bunning off school**?

Young people who **truant** regularly are less likely to do well at GCSE.

然而,关于以上这些译法,译者在具体使用时有如下两点需要考虑:

1. 美国人传统上用 skip school、ditch school 或 play hooky 来表达"翘课"、"逃学"这个概念,而 truant 则一般为警察或校方使用的官方用语。

2. play the wag 是个不错的短语。不过,这个俚语只适合给英国人听,美国人则更愿意说 play hooky。

值得一提的是,通过对"翘课"一词英译的讨论,我们基本上也知道了"翘班"(有意旷工。一般是在应该上班的时候,没有正当理由和解释而不去上班;在上班途中找借口或偷偷地离开工作岗位和工作地点)的译法,那就是 play hooky from work 或 bunk off work。

"翘课"虽一时感觉爽快,但是你认为可能没有用的课程在以后的工作学习中可能还会有用处,所以"翘课"并不是一个好的选择。古人云:"书到用时方恨少"还是很有道理的! 所以该上的课还是要去上的!

亲子鉴定

  当今社会,"亲子鉴定"这个概念对很多人而言并不陌生,尽管这一举措有时候是必要的,但不少家庭的悲剧也因此而起。据报道,中国第一起采用 DNA 方法进行的亲子鉴定案例发生在上世纪 90 年代初,但最近两年却突然"流行"了起来。而《沈阳日报》2009 年 12 月 23 日题为"亲子鉴定:三成以上为非亲生"的报道则更把这个话题推上了高潮。"亲子鉴定"是否挑战伦理道德我们暂且不谈,这里只谈谈该词的英译问题。

  "亲子鉴定",又称"亲权鉴定"或"父权鉴定",就是利用医学、生物学和遗传学的理论和技术,从子代和亲代的形态构造或生理机能方面的相似特点,分析遗传特征,判断父亲与子女之间是否是亲生关系。"亲子鉴定"在中国古代就已有之,如滴骨验亲,滴血验亲等。而现代医学则通常采用 DNA 鉴定(DNA identification)和组织分型(tissue-typing)的方法进行鉴定。

  《新华新词语词典》将"亲子鉴定"翻译为 identification in disputed paternity。这个译文意思上似乎没有问题,但却不是地道的英语表达。另外,从该译文的形式上来看,也更像解释,而不像规范的法律术语。

  事实上,像"亲子鉴定"这样的科技和医学术语,本就来自英文,其地道的表达叫做 paternity test/testing,下面是 paternity test 的两个定义:

  Paternity test is a test especially of DNA or genetic traits to determine whether a given man could be the biological father of a given child.

A **paternity test** establishes genetic proof whether a man is the biological father of an individual.

当然,既然有了"父权鉴定",那也应该有"母权鉴定"。英文中的 maternity test／tesing 即为此意,这个短语的英文释义为:a maternity test establishes whether a woman is the biological mother of an individual。

最后,英文中还有 parental testing／test 或 parentage testing／test 的说法,意即检验某个人是否与其父母有生物上的子/女——父/母关系,它其实涵盖了"父权鉴定"和"母权鉴定"这两个方面。例如:

Parental testing is the use of genetic fingerprinting to determine whether two individuals have a biological parent-child relationship.

Austudy Payment provides assistance to full time students aged 25 years and older who are undertaking an approved course of education. All students are automatically independent and there is no **parental test** of any sort. There is a partner and personal income and assets test.

The primary goal of **parentage testing** is to identify the biological parent of a given child. It is done to determine an individual's parent or parents in, for example, cases of adoption or alleged paternity.

Who may require a **parentage test**? Any person who wishes to prove or disprove that they are the biological parent of a child.

青 春 饭

　　"青春饭"这个词不算太新,大家也都不陌生。传统意义上的"青春饭",大多是服务、娱乐业,如演员、空姐等。所以很多人认为,"青春饭"虽然也是正当的职业,但由于这些职业总是与从业者的外貌体型紧密关联,便让人觉得既不太高尚,也不稳定,因为青春易逝,容颜易老。然而,如今的"青春饭"已远远超出了传统的范畴,IT 程序员、网络编程员、经纪人、基金经理、时尚类媒体记者、卡通画家、时尚分析师等正组成新的"青春饭"一族。他们受过良好的教育,具有广阔的知识面和较高的专业水平,善于沟通和交际,办事讲究策划和创意,拥有较高的薪水和社会地位。他们年轻、精力充沛、有活力;思想前卫,不盲从他人;他们甚至相貌亮丽,风姿绰约,气度不凡。

　　吃"青春饭"的人所从事的职业一般都发展变化较快,若想取得成功,便需要投入比其他工作更多的精力、体力和时间。此外,行业之间和同事之间的竞争非常激烈,长时间进行高强度工作,往往使得这些从业者身心疲惫,焦虑不安,甚至失眠、抑郁。其次是强烈的危机感。"青春饭"更多拼的是脑力和体力,年龄稍大,便会感觉体力、精力、工作速度等都比不上新员工。这种力不从心时刻提醒他们,稍有放松就有可能要被淘汰出局,于是便产生了随时会失业的危机感。

　　"青春饭"并未进入汉语词典,但几乎所有大型的汉英词典均收录了该词,而网络上关于该词的翻译也有不少讨论。譬如,《新世纪汉英大词典》的译文为 jobs for young people only;《汉英词典》(第三版)的译文

为 job for young people。此外，*The China Daily* BBS 上还有网友译为
（make a living by）selling one's youthful body、live on one's youth、youth-hot-post、youth-hot-professional、a career where age matters、job（exclusively）for the youthful 等。最后，还有网友译为 beauty-for-food，并解释说："青春饭"指那些短期的，只适合年轻人（一般为 18—30 岁）做的工作。某些行业需要年轻力壮或者年轻貌美的人，这些人就是所谓"吃青春饭"的人。

以上译文中有不少明显是错误的，因为它们要么太片面，如（make a living by）selling one's youthful body 和 beauty-for-food，要么汉语味道太浓烈，如 youth-hot-post、youth-hot-professional，要么译文不地道，如 live on one's youth 这种搭配在英文中是没有的。这里简单谈谈剩下的几个译文，尤其是见于汉英词典的两个译文。

首先，a career where age matters 这个译文不确切，因为 age 在这里并不一定只是指"青春"，也可能指"中年"。举一个不太恰当的例子，要做到国家主席这个职位，age 肯定 matters，但国家主席是"青春饭"吗？

其次，剩下的三个译文 jobs for young people only、job for young people、job（exclusively）for the youthful 倒是不错，但也存在几个问题。首先，当我们谈到"青春饭"时，我们往往指的是某种职业，而非某个具体的"工作"。譬如，当我们说"模特是个青春饭"时，我们指的是模特这个职业，而非某个特定的工作。其次，job for young people 可不一定是"青春饭"，譬如，如果我找人干一些诸如搬运的体力活时，有一个老年人来应聘，我会告诉他，"This is a job for young people（only）."难道你可以理解为"这是'青春饭'"吗？最后，年轻人应该是 the young 或 young people，而非 the youthful。

那么，"青春饭"怎么翻译呢？基于以上的讨论，我们认为，该词应该译为 a profession／professions for the young／young people。其实，西方人在讨论这一主题的时候也常用此表达，例如：

1. When you make a living（such as it may be）in **a profession for the young**, which has a very short life expectancy, there are usually a lot of years left during which you have to make a living. Unless, of course,

you are at the top（like LA）, or started out independently wealthy（like another five time TdF winner）.

2. Is IT **a profession for the young**? "If you are over 40, be very afraid. Your experience is not wanted, and your talents are of no value."

3. Ballet is **a profession for the young**; by the time a dancer is in their mid-teens, industry standards demand a very high level of technical ability and physical control in order to compete for the limited amount of existing jobs.

4. Acting and gladiatorial combat were **professions for the young**; they were what we would call "career choices" today.

5. Ageism is an issue in IT, if only because it's seen as **a profession for young people** and is having to deal with an ageing working population.

　　最后,我们再看看"吃青春饭"应该如何来译,其实上面的引文中已经给出了答案:make a living in **a profession for the young**。当然,在具体翻译实践中,译者也可以灵活处理为诸如 engage in a profession that lasts as long as one's youth 等译文。

群　租

　　"群租"是房地产市场上出现的一个新词,目前似乎还没有准确的定义和权威的解释。它与"转租"、"合租"等概念相似,但却又更多地和"群居"、"杂居"等词意义相近。在房价高企的大城市,例如北京、上海、广州等地,由于居住成本高昂,"群租"目前已经愈演愈烈。"群租"的好处显而易见,租房者可以摊低成本;房东(有时是二房东)往往通过把大房子分割为小间,分别出租,以获取更大的利润。当然,"群租"所引发的问题也不容忽视,如邻居生活受扰、安全隐患倍增、小区环境恶化、设施损坏严重、楼盘品质下降等。

　　目前,"群租"现象在上海已经很普遍,成为都市"拼一族"继"拼车"、"拼饭"之后的又一时髦话语。群租客说,为了"降低成本",苦并忍受着;房东说,与其空关,不如出租;二房东说,雁过拔毛,天经地义;邻居说,活在陌生人的世界,夜半歌声投诉没人理;管理者说,穷尽对策,却无力解决……。

　　尽管上海2007年已出台了一些措施来制约"群租",如规定民房出租,一间房只能出租给一个家庭或一个自然人居住、人均承租面积必须符合标准,业主不得擅自改变房屋原设计功能和布局等,但专家们仍然认为:"群租"不违法,不能随意定性;对于"群租",宜疏不宜堵。安全隐患、相邻纠纷等问题不仅仅是"群租"独有的,因此不要"妖魔化"群租。

　　"群租"一词目前尚未见诸汉语或汉英词典,但有些国内的英文媒体和网站上已有所报道,如 CRIENGLISH. com、Virtual China 以及上海政府的官方网站等。它们都用了"group renting"这个译文。另外，*The China Daily* BBS 上还有网友建议使用 joint rent、cooperative rental 等译文。这些译文中，joint rent 和 cooperative rental 明显有误，因为"群族客"之间并不存在"联合（joint）"租房或"合作（cooperative）"租房的问题，他们之间往往并不认识。而 group renting 这个译文则最具诱惑性，一则因为其"形似"，二则因为其使用频率极高。然而，经过调查，我们发现 group renting 其实是一个"假朋友"。首先，英文中并没有这样的搭配；其次，该译文让人觉得租房者组成一个 group 去 rent，因为我们知道，group purchase 就是"团购"，即大家组团购物，以期价格更为优惠。所以，该译文难以表达汉语"群租"的含义，而且容易引起误解。

其实，我们所谈论的"群租"不仅中国有之，西方国家也很普遍，但可能一方面由于西方人居住的主要是 house，而非我们所居住的拥挤的 apartment，另一方面可能由于国外"群租客"的素质相对较高，而且"房东"也没有某些国人这样"聪明"，把大房间隔小，以谋取更高的利润，所以"群租"并没有引起社会的普遍关注。在西方，人们把这种租房形式称作 shared renting（of a house），而非 group renting，其目的也是摊低房费。当然，西方国家，如澳大利亚，也有二房东，可以把自己租的房子再出租，以降低房租，但与国内不一样的是，二房东在转租之前，必须获得房东的同意。请看下面的一段引文[1]：

Shared renting is living with other people in the same house and sharing the monthly costs for the household. This way, all the renters pay a lower rent. The major benefit of sub-renting for people newly settling down in a city is that you're not obligated to the usual 1 + year minimum lease term. Sharing as a sub-renter can give you more freedom. However, it is not always allowed by the landlord, so make sure you've got his / her approval before you start sub-renting your place yourself.

此外，*Shanghaiist* 上也发表了一篇由英语本族人所撰写的题为"Share an apartment and break the law!"的文章，提到了目前上海禁止

---

〔1〕见 http://www.immigration-2-australia.com/living/housing/living-in-a-shared-arrangement

"群租"的现象。文曰：

　　... but today we came across an article from *The Oriental Morning Post*（《东方早报》）that may be the reason behind our landlord's latest move. In the article entitled 上海治理群租再出新招 朋友也不能合租一间房（"Shanghai begins to control **shared renting of apartments**, now even friends are not allowed to co-rent"）：上海治理群租再出新招，上海市房地局昨天表示，该局近日下发通知，对 2005 年版的《业主公约》、《业主临时公约》示范文本进行增补，新增一些制约"群租"的新条款……。根据该规定，民房出租，一间房只能出租给一个家庭或一个自然人居住。（Shanghai has begun to control **the shared renting of apartments** and recently the Shanghai Municipal Housing, Land and Resource Administration Bureau（SMHLRA）announced that it has made amendments to the 2005 version of the "Landlord Regulations" and the "Provisional Landlord Regulations". New regulations for shared renting of apartments have been added... According to those new regulations, each private apartment can now only be rented out to a single individual or a family）.

　　搞清楚了"群租"的英译后，我们还可以顺便看看"转租"和"合租"的翻译。其实，"转租"的英译已经在第一篇引文中出现了，那就是 subrent（a house／apartment），而"转租者"，我们称为"二房东"则为 subrenter。

　　在翻译"合租"之前，我们有必要先弄清楚"合租"和"群租"之间的区别。《无锡商报》2007 年 8 月 29 日刊登了一篇题为"合租群租不是一回事，无锡暂不对共同租房说不"的文章，对这两个概念进行了区分，请看下文：

　　业内人士表示，"群租"与"合租"虽然只有一字之差，但两者之间有很多不同。一般来说，主要反映在以下三个特征：一是签约主体，群租是一套房子同时签有几份租赁合同。二是入住人数，群租对于入住的人数基本没有限制。三是出租的具体操作方式，合租不需要改变原房屋结构进行房间分隔，而群租为了让更多的人住进来，则需要对房屋作一定分隔。

搞清楚这二者的区别之后,笔者认为,"合租"一词可用 co-rent(a house／apartment)来翻译。譬如,CCTV. com 上就曾刊登题为"Ants, another name for post-80s university graduates"的报道,其中有云:

Huang is a native of Zengcheng, Guangdong Province. After graduation, he found a job developing software. Now he earns a monthly salary of more than 3,000 yuan, but he still chooses to **co-rent an apartment** with his university roommates in a village located in Tangxia. The three young men now live in a 70-square-meter apartment consisting of two bedrooms and two living rooms. The apartment is well equipped, including a kitchen, a washroom, a balcony and cabinets. Although the apartment is spacious, the rent is quite low at only 900 yuan a month.

再如下面一句:

They even encouraged me to **co-rent a house** with Daisy, so that I could befriend her and stay close by.

上面两段话中的 co-rent an apartment 应该都不是"群租",而是"合租"。

惹 火

　　"惹火"一词现在常用的一个意思是"指女人的身材火辣、性感",如"惹火的身材"、"惹火车模"、"惹火美女"、"惹火尤物"等等。该词的这个义项从何而来尚不清楚,但很有可能是从其本意"把某人惹得生气"发展而来:以前说某女把某男给惹火了,这个某女就麻烦大了。今天若说某女惹火,那就是夸她身材棒,惹得男人都"上火"。

　　《现代汉语词典》(第五版)中尚未收录"惹火"一词,只收录了"惹火上身",可能编者认为"惹火"为自由搭配,尚未成词的缘故吧。新出版的《汉英词典》(第三版)从汉英词典中翻译的角度出发,不但将该词单独立目,而且加收了上面谈到的新义项,并提供了译文 provocative 和 eye-catching。这两个译文中的 eye-catching 并不恰当,难以译出"惹火"的形象和内涵。provocative 倒是不错,该词本身就有 intended to make someone sexually excited(挑逗性的)的意思,如 provocative clothes(挑逗性的衣服)、provocative movement(挑逗性的动作)等,这与"惹火"一词在汉语中的用法很是一致,如"新型**惹火**人体彩绘衣服"、"精品小妹穿什么衣服都**惹火**"、"这个姑娘身材火爆,又喜欢穿吊带衫、露脐装之类**惹火**的衣服,回头率相当高"、"此刻,邓晓琳刚好又换了一身**惹火**的衣服"等等。所以如果用 provocative 来译衣服、动作、图片等的"惹火",可谓恰当之至。英文中也有这样的用法,如:

　　1. He said: Bottom line, I feel that if you feel comfortable with your body and look good in **provocative clothes**, go ahead and wear them.

2. Very often in the street I see young girls (clearly underage, I'd say around 13 - 15) who wear very revealing and **provocative outfits**. Bared shoulders, low cut tops, underwear visible, etc. I wonder if the clothing retailers are "sexing-up" the young generation with a commercial goal in mind, or is the society simply allowing the hormone-fuelled teenage behaviour to take over?

3. Federal Minister for Children Larry Anthony today called on parents to boycott padded bras, low-cut tops and other **provocative clothes** aimed at girls as young as eight.

4. Many motorists and beguiling passers-by thus became victims of fatal accidents due to billboards blaring slogans in captivating words and images and showing snippets of dramas in digital pictures in multidimensional movies as the victims looked away from onrushing traffics during crucial moments while gaping at an attractive lass in her **provocative posture** on digital billboards.

当然,"惹火的衣服"往往比较"节省布料"或"薄露透"。参透这个实质后,我们也可以用 skimpy clothes 或 revealing clothes 来译"惹火的衣服"。例如:

1. Beautiful girls in **skimpy clothes** and creepy guys taking pictures of them from behind. What more can you ask for on a summer day?

2. Why do girls wear **revealing clothes** to attract others? Can't they do so with clothes that do not reveal?

当"惹火"用来修饰"身材"、"女人"等时,skimpy 和 revealing 就不能用了。Provocative 尽管也可以用,但此时用 hot 可能更为形象,而且 hot 一词语体上也更为合适。Hot 是一个俚语,意思是 sexually excited or exciting。此外,该词从本意上而言有"热"、"辣"的意思,译"惹火"一词可谓形神兼备。例如下面的例证:

1. She has been recognized on multiple occasions for her **hot figure** and bootylicious curves. Her measurements are 33-26-42 and she is almost 5′7 inches tall.

2. **Hot pics** of TV queen Sangeeta Ghosh on the beach with Manav Gohil in **skimpy clothes** showing her **hot figure** from the forthcoming movie *Bhanvraa* directed by Dharmesh Darshan.

3. She became famous quickly on the Internet for her **hot figure** and charming face.

4. Do you want to be whistled at when you walk by? Then this is the article that you should read! Read here on how to become a **hot girl**.

5. There I met his sister, Hannah, a **provocative girl** with long black hair and bright eyes. I was hesitant to speak of my attraction to her, knowing how the Jews felt about interracial romances; but after several months of silence, after her face revealed that she was attracted to me as I was to her, I talked with Amos. He said that he had no authority in his family, but he encouraged me to go to her father.

最后,还有些网友建议使用 inviting 一词。该词的确是一个不错的建议,而且经常和"身材"、"身体"连用,如 He smiled at the thought and eyed her **inviting figure** and knew his attention would please and maybe appease her. For only she knew that he had an old score to settle, and that his desire to marry and tame her arose only from his devastating desire for her **inviting body**. 但考虑到"惹火"一词的语体特色以及 inviting 的本义,该词和"身材"、"身体"连用时译为"迷人的"似乎更为合适。

热　点

　　"热点"是指"某时期引人注目的地方或问题"。目前常见的搭配有"热点地区"、"旅游热点"、"投资热点"等。该词用于此义时，一般汉英词典中都提供了 hot spot 这个译文。《汉英词典》(第三版)中甚至用了一个例证：旅游热点：tourist hot spot。然而，张健教授(2003)则撰文指出 hot spot 不应滥用，他说，一见"投资热点"就不假思索地译作 investment hot spot 是会出问题的。须知，hot spot 也指"(可能)发生动乱的地方(至少这一意思是主要的)，而 heat spot 则是医学上的'热觉点'。正确的译文应是 popular investment spot"。

　　那么，"热点"是否就是 hot spot 呢？"旅游热点"和"投资热点"等是否可以用 hot spot 来译呢？

　　首先，我们发现，张教授上面所言确实是有道理的。Hot spot 一词确实是"可能发生动乱或战事的地区，多事地区"，其英文释义为 a place where there is likely to be trouble，fighting，etc. 。所以，上面的"热点地区"如指"多事地区"，用 hot spot 来译可谓恰如其分。例如，"中东是世界上的热点地区"一句就完全可以用 hot spot 来译。

　　其次，"旅游热点"和"投资热点"的确可以用 popular tourist spot 和 popular investment spot 来译，但后者更为常见的修饰语不是 popular(在 *Google* 中输入 popular investment spot，得到的无一例外都是国内网站的译文)，而是 top。例如：

　　A surprise choice for **top investment spot**：Forbes magazine is out

with its annual list of best places in the world to invest in real estate and its
top pick is a bit of a surprise—Washington D. C.

——*The New York Times*, 2009 - 01 - 29

第三,用 tourist hot spot 和 investment hot spot 来译"旅游热点"和
"投资热点"也并非不妥。首先,hot spot 除了"多事地区"这层意思外,
还有一个意思:受到人们欢迎的地区(a place of more than usual
interest, activity, or popularity)。例如,*Merriam-Webster Dictionary* 中
就提供了这样的例证:The new restaurant is the latest hot spot in town.
而原版英文资料中用 tourist hot spot 和 investment hot spot 的也不在少
数。例如:

1. A grim **tourist hot spot**: Chernobyl

The New York Times, 2005 - 06 - 15

2. The best **tourist hot spot** on the planet is probably New York City,
after all the Big Apple is dubbed the Capital of The World. So, naturally
millions of visitors flood the city each year and in turn, the city strives to
satisfy their sight seeing needs. The top ten most visited sites in New York
City are the Empire State Building, Statue Of Liberty, Grand Central
Terminal, Rockefeller Center, Ellis Island Immigration Museum, Staten
Island Ferry, American Museum of Natural History, Central Park,
Metropolitan Museum of Art, and the Museum of Modern Art.

The New York Times, 2005 - 06 - 18

3. Northern Ireland emerges as a **tourist hot spot**: Suddenly, 19th-
century Ireland's most industrial city became a bustling European hot spot.

Daily News, 2008 - 03 - 08

4. Extreme Investing: Inside Colombia — An improbable journey
from crime capital to **investment hot spot**. Can this boom last?

Business Week, 2007 - 05 - 28

5. Not only was Lewis surprised to discover that his buddy wasn't
living in the jungle, but he soon joined the stream of American and
European citizens who are moving here and turning Nicaragua into the latest

retirement and **investment hot spot** in Central America.

The Miami Herald, 2006 – 01 – 29

　　最后,笔者想指出的是,语言是活生生的东西,译者只有洞悉词语的确切用法,方可在翻译时胸有成竹,运用自如。一个类似的例子是"美化"一词的翻译,一般词典中均将其译为 beautify,但也有学者指出beautify 是贬义词,意思是通过装饰掩盖丑陋的东西。按照这个观点,"美化环境"等搭配就不能译为 beautify the environment。但事实如此吗? 否也! 首先,英文词典中的 beautify 并没有加注"贬义"的标签,另外,beautify the environment 这种说法在原版英文资料中也很常见,这足以说明把"美化"译为 beautify 的合理性。

人肉搜索

　　如果你爱他,把他放到人肉引擎上去,你很快就会知道他的一切;如果你恨他,把他放到人肉引擎上去,因为那里是地狱。

　　上面这段话讲的就是如今红遍大江南北的"人肉搜索"。从 2006 年的"踩猫事件"到 2007 年的"钱军打人"事件,再到 2008 年的深圳 11 岁女童遭猥亵事件,各种人肉搜索事件层出不穷。人肉搜索似乎已经发展成了一项系统性的集体行为,以至于在"谷歌"2008 年度热门搜索关键词排行榜上,该词已名列前茅。

　　什么是人肉搜索?目前似乎还没有书面或官方的定义,而"谷歌"的定义则是:"利用现代信息科技,变传统的网络信息搜索为人找人、人问人、人碰人、人挤人、人挨人的关系型网络社区活动,变枯燥乏味的查询过程为……人性化搜索体验。"该词出现之后,网络上出现了各种英文译文:有人译为 human-powered search,有人译为 online manhunt,还有人干脆译为 *renrou* search。

　　以上三种译文均不可取。理由如下:

　　首先,human-powered search(人力搜索)是典型的"假朋友"(false friends),也就是说,表面上看是采用了解释性翻译,但是译文却有其完全不同于字面意义的特定含义。目前来讲,human-powered search 仅在 mahalo(www. mahalo. com)网站上进行,而 Mahalo is a human-powered search engine and a knowledge sharing service, helping people on the Internet quickly find the best possible information on any topic. Members of the public can also earn money by contributing to Mahalo topic pages or by answering questions on the Mahalo Answers system。从这里可以看出，human-powered search 只是发动人力进行搜索，但除此之外还有其他的功能，如公众可以通过撰写话题或回答网站上的问题而赚钱（earn money by contributing to Mahalo topic pages）等。这与国内的人肉搜索还是大有区别的。

其次，an online manhunt（网上追捕）体现了网络在"人肉搜索"中的媒介作用，但是 manhunt 在 *Webster's New World College Dictionary* 中的解释则是"a hunt for fugitive or criminal suspect"，即"网上追捕罪犯"。例如：The FBI on Wednesday said it plans to launch an **online manhunt** for an alleged Boston mob boss, in a novel crime-fighting experiment in partnership with Web portal Terra Lycos. 而人肉搜索在汉语语境中首先搜索的不是罪犯，而是那些做了某件事情的人。这些事情往往是坏事，如南京的周久耕事件；但也可以指好事，如奥运冠军郭文珺寻父事件、武汉最美交警事件等。所以 online 或 cyber manhunt 一词并不适用。

最后，*renrou search* 是一个汉语音译加上意译的译文，这种译文或许可取，因为毕竟"人肉搜索"是一个中国独有的事物，但由于这种音译法往往达不到或只能达到有限的交流目的，在翻译过程中应该谨慎使用。

那么，人肉搜索到底该怎么翻译呢？答案是 human flesh search（engine）。先看网络百科全书 Wikipedia 上"人肉搜索"的条目：Human Flesh Search（Chinese：人肉搜索）is a phenomenon of massive researching using Internet media such as blogs and forums. It is based on massive human collaboration, thus the name。人肉搜索作为中国网民发明的网络新词，新奇而形象，采用直译 human（人）flesh（肉）search（engine）（搜索引擎），既译出人肉搜索的媒介——网络，又体现了人肉搜索销魂蚀骨的破坏力，具有极强的视觉或听觉冲击力。

事实上，该译文国外媒体也广为采用。在历次人肉搜索事件中，国外媒体都有相关报道。例如 2008 年 1 月的"死亡博客"在网上引起了网友对当事人王某进行"口诛笔伐"，他们除了搜索王的个人资料外，还联合上门"讨伐"，这就是"死亡博客"事件。当时，Forbes 网曾有报道：

In Wang's case, his wife posted a series of blog posts expressing her devastation over her husband's infidelity and then lept to her death from their 24th - floor apartment. Almost instantly, an online mob —— **the human flesh search engine** —— enraged at Wang's philandering, exploded into life. Within days, photographs of Wang appeared on numerous Internet forums alongside his phone numbers, address and national ID number.[1]

再看看"辽宁女侮辱地震灾民"事件发生时英国《泰晤士报》的措辞[2]：

Within hours, Ms Gao had become the latest victim of **a human flesh search engine**, where Chinese netizens become cyber-vigilantes and online communities turn into the world's largest lynch mobs. Using the vast human power behind the Chinese web, every detail of Ms Gao's life, from her home and work address in Liaoning province, north east China, to the fact that her parents were divorced, was dug up and published on hundreds of forums and chatrooms.

事实上，尽管"人肉搜索"搜出了大量的贪官污吏和某些人令人不齿的行为，但不可否认的是，使用不当，它便会成为一种网络暴力（online mob）。搜索者往往具有良好的初衷，但往往搜索一经蔓延，便会无法收拾，往往会给当事者造成极大的伤害。例如上文提到的奥运冠军郭文珺寻父事件，到最后不但使得郭文珺及其双方长辈和亲友陷入巨大尴尬，也令家人的那份痛苦再次加剧。后来，郭文珺的母亲和不少网友都通过各种方式表示，希望广大网友停止这种"人肉搜索"。所以，当网民们"发起人肉搜索（call for a human flesh search engine）"或"发动人肉搜索（launch a human flesh search engine）"和锁定"人肉搜索的目标（the target of a human flesh search engine）"时一定要三思而后行，要尊重别人的隐私，避免对当事人造成不必要的伤害。

---

〔1〕 http://www. forbes. com/2008/11/21/human-flesh-search-tech-identity08-cx ＿ cb ＿ 1121obrien. html。

〔2〕 见 http://technology. timesonline. co. uk/tol/news/tech_and_web/article4213681. ece

色　酒

　　关于"色酒"和"香槟酒"的翻译,译界一直有所争论。譬如《新时代汉英大词典》和《新世纪汉英大词典》均将"色酒"译为 wine,champagne。而《新世纪汉英大词典》则把"香槟酒"译为 champagne。但也有人(赫迎红,2007)认为这两种翻译均不准确,前者应该译为"coloured low-alcohol wine(made from grapes or other fruit)",而后者则应该译为 white sparkling wine,因为中文中的"香槟酒"虽然来自 champagne,但它已演变为不限于法国 Champagne 地区的产品,而泛指任何经过两次发酵的、带汽的酒。

　　首先,让我们看看"色酒"的翻译。《现代汉语词典》(第五版)对该词的定义为:用葡萄或其他水果为原料制成的酒,一般带有颜色,酒精含量较低。再看《朗文当代高级英语词典》(2004)对 wine 的定义:(1)an alcoholic drink made from grapes,or a type of this drink. (2)an alcoholic drink made from another fruit or plant。二者实在是完全对应,用 wine 译"色酒"似乎未有不当之处。此外,赫迎红所提供的翻译充其量是解释,而且既然 wine 一个词就已恰当,何必又要啰哩啰嗦? 最后,我们认为,将 champagne 跟在 wine 之后来翻译"色酒"也符合词典翻译中译文之间要相互补充的原则,更何况,"色酒"并非指某种特定的酒,只是指用葡萄或其他水果为原料制成的一种酒,所以 champagne 虽然并非最佳译文,但跟在 wine 的后面对应色酒,并不为错。说不定外国人见了我们的"色酒",第一印象就是 champagne,而非 coloured low-alcohol wine （made from grapes or other fruit）。另外,英文中的"low-alcohol wine"与"色酒"根本没有关系,一般译为"低醇酒",是一种适合老人、妇女、儿童及一些特殊人群如病人、孕妇等饮用的"酒"。

其次,再看把"香槟酒"译为 champagne 是否不当。首先,虽然汉语中的香槟酒语义有所扩大,但其最佳对应词为 champagne 当无疑问。此外,在英文中 champagne 一词的意义也已扩大,可以指和 champagne 同种类的酒,如以下的表述:

Champagne is a sparkling wine produced by inducing the in-bottle secondary fermentation of wine to affect carbonation. It is named after the Champagne region of France. While the term "champagne" is often used by makers of sparkling wine in other parts of the world（and is commonly used by the general public as a generic term for sparkling wine）, many wine enthusiasts maintain it should only be used to refer to the wines made in the Champagne region. When used to refer specifically to wines produced in Champagne, the word may（or may not）be capitalized; when used as a generic term for sparkling wine（or in reference to the color champagne）, it is always spelled in lower case.

这样看来,《新世纪汉英大词典》用 champagne 来译"香槟酒"无论是特指还是泛指均无问题。这也说明了在探讨和评论新词英译时,译者需要深入研究原词和其英文译文的词义,切不可凭感觉来判断。

色 友

我们前边探讨了"驴友"(tourpal)的英译,现在来看看另外一个广为流传的新词:"色友"。看到这个词,读者可不能胡思乱想,这里的"色"可不是情色的"色",而是"色彩"的"色"。"色友"是摄影爱好者之间的称呼,因为有共同的爱好,以摄影结友,并取"摄"之谐音"色",所以戏称为"色友"。"色友"们因为共同的摄影爱好常常走到一起,互相交流学习、共同进步。下面《南湖晚报》2008 年 5 月 27 日的一则关于浙江嘉兴"色友"的报道,会让大家对这个词有一个更为深刻的认识:

"要说拍照,在科技发达的今天,几乎人人都会端着数码相机按下快门,记录生活的点滴。但自从法国摄影家罗伯特·杜瓦诺拍摄的《巴黎市政厅前的吻》以 15.5 万欧元(约合人民币 160 余万元)的天价在巴黎拍卖成功,人们对摄影作品给予了更多艺术价值的肯定。嘉兴就有这么几拨热爱摄影的人,他们聚集在一起,外出摄影采风,相约咖啡馆对作品进行评论、交流意见与摄影器材的信息,称为"色友"。"

有鉴于该词"摄影爱好者"的基本含义,有些地方将"色友"译为 cameraman,还有些地方直接用 photographer 和 lensman。先看 cameraman,该词尽管看起来和摄影有关,但意思并非"摄影爱好者",而是"电影或电视的摄影者":someone who operates a camera for films or televisions。再看 photographer 和 lensman,这两个词确实是摄影者的意思,但二者均为"职业摄影师",请看词典中对这两个词的释义：

Photographer：someone who takes photographs, especially as a professional or as an artist

Lensman：someone who takes photographs professionally

这样看来，photographer 和 lensman 均不可用来翻译"色友"，因为后者在文体上首先是非正式的，甚至常常带有戏虐的味道；其次，"色友"们并非职业摄影者，而是业余摄影爱好者。

那么，"色友"该如何英译呢？答案是 shutterbug。请看词典中 shutterbug 的释义：

Shutterbug：*informal* an enthusiastic amateur photographer

这个释义与"色友"无论在外延、内涵还是文体风格上几乎完全一致：非正式、用于业余摄影爱好。

此外，国内有"色友"自己的组织"色友俱乐部"，会员可以定期聚会，交流经验，相互学习，或相邀外拍。而国外也有类似的 shutterbug club，供"色友"们交流和切磋。下面是一个叫做 The Sherman Shutterbug Club 的"色友"组织，其功能及活动如下：

The Sherman Shutterbug Club is a club for all those interested in photography. Improve your skills, learn from others, share your ideas, concepts, and techniques. Monthly meetings will consist of critiques, hands-on workshops, and photo assignments.

最后，更为有趣的是，除了"色友"，网络上现在又把"色友"和"驴友"放在一起，合称为"色驴"，指那些喜欢摄影的旅行者。请看下面的一则报道：

玩户外的人被叫做"驴友"，爱好摄影的人叫"色友"（摄友），在户外圈子里有那么一批边走边用相机记录下旅程的，常被圈内人开玩笑称为"色驴"。林嵩就是武汉户外圈子里一名小有名气的标准"色驴"。"色驴"都有着专业的装备，出游也比一般的"驴子"辛苦：机身、镜头、三脚架加起来能有十多公斤，好在林嵩以前曾经是田径健将，旅途中经常被其他"色驴"们奉为英雄。

"'色驴'本色"，荆楚网，2008 年 1 月 4 日

那么,"色驴"怎么译呢?结合上面"色友"和"驴友"的译文,不妨译为 shutterbug traveler,该译文基本上表达出了"色驴"的意义,而且其含义也基本可以根据 shutterbug 和 traveler 这两个词的字面意思推知,因此较为可行。

晒 工 资

　　"晒工资"，原来是指网民在网络上匿名把自己的收入公布出来。这种做法不叫"亮工资"、"说工资"，而叫"晒工资"，确实比较准确、形象。"晒"本身就是在阳光下进行，具有公开性，这与当今流行的"阳光操作"、"阳光工程"等词语的比喻意义相吻合。

　　自从北大副教授阿忆于 2006 年 9 月在自己的博客上公布了自己月收入 4786 元的工资条以来，"晒工资"便在网络上蔚然成风。特别是到了春节前夕，"晒工资"已发展为"晒年终奖"、"晒春节加班费"、"晒压岁钱"等，成为使用频率较高的词语之一。

　　虽然从 2006 年 7 月 1 日起，我国开始了新一轮的工资改革，但如何实现公平分配，目前仍然没有大的突破。在这种背景下，网上"晒工资"的盛行，其实是许多人心理焦虑的自然流露和发泄。所以，与其说"晒工资"是展示职场秘密，倒不如说"晒工资"是"晒"出了人们对分配公平的关注，对民生问题的焦虑。当然，在现实生活中，有些人，尤其是那些垄断行业的高收入者，他们"晒工资"的目的纯粹是为了"显摆"。

　　"晒工资"一词虽未为《现代汉语词典》(第五版)所收录，但却同时出现在 2010 年刚刚出版的《汉英词典》(第三版)和《汉英大词典》(第三版)中，足见该词的流行程度。以上两本词典中的译文分别为 make public one's salary 和 show salary、divulge one's salary。另外，*The China Daily* 在 2007 年 1 月 31 日刊登了题为 "'Salary Show'

Hits the Net"的文章,把"晒工资"译为了 salary show。下面是该文中的一段:

China's professionals are detailing their salaries under acquired names on the Net as Spring Festival approaches. Most urban Chinese have got their salaries and year-end bonuses by now, with many of them joining the *Shaigongzi*, or "**Salary Show**", to let anyone interested to know what their after-tax pay packets are.

另外,还有人认为"晒"是英文 share 的英译,据此推断,"晒工资"应该就是 share one's salary online。

那么,"晒工资"到底应该如何翻译呢?在得到答案之前,让我们先看看上面各个译文是否恰当。

先看 make public one's salary。这里译者把"晒"译为了 make public,虽然意思上出入不大,但"晒工资"的"晒"形象尽失,译文干瘪无味。此外,由于"晒工资"是在网络上进行的,所以没有 online 一词,似乎也没有完全表达出"晒工资"的含义。

再看 show salary。这个译文本身语法上有问题,不能说 show salary,最起码应该说 show one's salary,而且也应该加上 online 一词。

此外,再看 divulge one's salary。Divulge 的意思是:to give someone information, especially about something secret,即"泄露秘密"。该词与"晒工资"的"晒"比较契合,因为我们知道,女人的年龄,男人的钱包,那是不能上台面直言的"秘密",这就是为什么在现实生活中,当别人问到你的工资收入时,出于多种原因,自己一般会回答得比较模糊,有的还不真实。但在网上 divulge 你的工资就不同了,因为是匿名,所以不用顾忌什么,数字也比较真实。但是,考虑到"晒工资"是一个网上行为,所以还是建议将该译文稍作修改,加上 online 一词。

再看看 share one's salary online。这个译文放在特定的语境中,的确可以表示"晒工资",即我们共同 share 我们的工资信息。但就单个词的翻译而言,该译文却可能引发歧义,给人感觉是在网上"共享"、"共花"某个人的工资,所以并不恰当。

最后,再看看 *The China Daily* 的译文 salary show。考虑到有些人

"晒工资"就是为了炫耀、显摆,这个译文倒也未尝不可。但由于 show 这个词给人的第一印象就是"秀",是"夸耀",这个译文并没有完全反映出"晒工资"这个现象的真相,因为大多数人"晒工资"并非是为了"秀"自己的工资多高。现实的情况也是,我们通常看到的"晒"在网上的工资往往都不高,有些甚至低得让人伤心。

有鉴于此,我们建议把"晒工资"译为 divulge one's salary online 或 online salary divulging。当然,还可以用 expose、reveal、disclose、lay bare、display 等词来译"晒工资"的"晒",所以"晒工资"还可以译为 expose / reveal / disclose / lay bare / display one's salary online 或 online salary exposure / disclosure / display。下面是笔者找到的用上面这些译文来翻译"晒工资"的实例:

1. This week, our friends at *Parade* magazine published their annual "What People Earn" issue. I'm fascinated by how many diverse and real people are willing to **divulge their salaries online**. We often hear from readers who don't agree with the salary info that we report, which are often national averages. But people want to know what they can earn in their specific professions in their towns.

2. Recently, websites such as sohu. com set up special sections for people to "**divulge their salaries**". The result was that the incomes of almost all industries were exposed.

3. Why do people **expose their salaries online** anonymously? We've learned that it's not polite to ask about how much others earn, but it appears to be that some of us really want to know. Now people may satisfy their curiosity over the Internet as a number of people are **exposing the details of their salaries online** anonymously.

4. Asking a person's earnings is normally considered as rude as asking a woman's age — except on the Internet, where China's professionals **detail their salaries under online pseudonyms**.

"Even Hurun's China Rich List is controversial, so **online salary exposure** shouldn't be taken seriously. The good thing is that it gives us a general idea of where we are," she says.

"**Internet pay-on-display system** attracts grumbles amid cheers",

The People's Daily Online, 2007 - 01 - 31

闪　孕

　　网络时代,什么都流行快速。我们先是有了"网上交友(online dating)",然后就产生了"网恋(cyber love或Internet romance)",进而则出现了"闪电约会(speed dating)"和"闪电恋爱(whirlwind romance)",继而则可能发展为"一夜情(one night stand)",有些头脑发昏者还可能举行"闪婚(flash marriage)",婚后很快鸡飞狗跳,又不得已而"闪离(flash divorce)"。

　　我们姑且不谈这种对待爱情的态度是否可取,或许这也只是网络时代的一个特点而已。而我们这里所说的"闪孕"却完全是另外一回事。2007到2008年的经济危机附带催生了国内的闪孕。根据"百度百科"的定义,所谓闪孕,即突击怀孕、将"生子计划"提前,这是一些白领为躲避经济危机中的裁员风险,突击怀孕,因为根据劳动法规定:女员工在孕期、产期、哺乳期间如果被裁,可以申请劳动仲裁,要求单位经济补偿。这就是职场女性突击怀孕的最大理由。

　　据业内人士估计,2009年3月可能是首批"金融危机宝宝"登记产检的小高峰,而2009年下半年可能是"金融危机宝宝"的出生小高峰。

　　学术界想必也注意到了这个现象,这不,"闪孕"一词已于2010年1月被收入上海译文出版社出版的《汉英大词典》(第三版),英文译文为quick pregnancy。我们一方面赞赏词典编纂人员对语言的敏感性,但另一方面也对该词的英译提出质疑:quick pregnancy是汉语的"闪孕"吗?首先,从该译文的字面上看,quick pregnancy应该是"快速怀孕"的意思,而非"闪孕",后者所表达的是为躲避经济危机中公司裁员而采取的举措。另外,如果一对夫妇刚刚结婚就怀孕,可谓是 quick pregnancy,但这能算是"闪孕"吗? 所以,该词典的译文并不妥当。

事实上,网络上也有人谈论"闪孕"或"闪孕族"的英译,比较典型的是一段来自 *The China Daily* 中的表述,该文不长,摘录如下:

They are female white-collar workers. They didn't have any plan to have a child until the economic crisis struck. Then they decided to get pregnant as quickly as possible.

They are afraid of getting fired. China's labor law stipulates that a company should not fire a pregnant employee unless the company is insolvent. "Get pregnant as soon as possible" became a mantra at the height of the economic crisis. Indeed, so many female employees made this choice that they were collectively dubbed "the rush-to-get-pregnant tribe".

这段文章中共出现"闪孕"的表达两次,一次为动词形式:get pregnant as quickly as possible,另外一次为名词形式:the rush-to-get-pregnant tribe,其中后者明显为"闪孕族"的英译。或许,《汉英词典》(第三版)中的 quick pregnancy 是归纳了上面的表述而得出的一个译文吧。

然而,我们知道,"闪孕"作为一个词典的条目或单个词的英译并不一定等同于上文中的两种表述。原因非常简单,词典条目是脱离语境(decontextualized)的,而文中的表述是有语境来帮助理解的,即 in context。这个道理很容易理解,譬如在 The car can do 80 miles an hour. 这个句子中,do 的意思为"行驶",因为在这个语境中,do 只能这样理解。但 do 作为一个独立的单词,却不能译为"驾驶"。

那么,"闪孕"如何来译呢? 笔者认为,还是套用"闪婚"、"闪离"等英译中的 flash 为好,"闪婚"为 flash marriage,"闪孕"即为 flash pregnancy。当然,如果要更清楚一点,译为 flash pregnancy(to avoid being laid off)可能更为准确,也更能表达"闪孕"一词所出现的背景。之所以采用此译,一方面是考虑到由"闪"这个词所构成的一系列词的对应译法问题,另一方面用 flash 一词表达"闪"中所包含的"迅速"、"快速"之义更为确切。另外,正如我们不提倡闪婚、闪离一样,我们也不提倡"闪孕",因为正如"百度百科"所言,"闪孕"存在各种风险,所以建议年轻父母最好还是以顺其自然的态度对待生育。英文 flash 一词的意思为:happening very quickly or suddenly, and lasting for only a short time,其中则包含有对某种不当行为的规劝和建议。

上 位

    "上位"的原义不难理解,应该就是"上面的位置",但近年来网络新闻,特别是娱乐新闻上频频出现"上位"一词的新用法:走红。例如:

    1. 引用大众的一句顺口溜:女星想出名全靠卖色情,女星要**上位**全靠大牌配。众多女星在黔驴技穷的时候纷纷借机制造绯闻争求**上位**的机会,娱乐圈中众多男星纷纷成为"猎物",等待她们的捕捉。

    2. 小小年纪的她们,成名心切,总幻想着能够一夜**上位**、大红大紫,甚至在摄影师提出性的要求时,她们半推半就、遮遮掩掩,可以说,在一定程度上,她们默许了摄影师的这种行为。

    3. 有一种**上位**,叫一夜成名;有一种成名,叫横空出世。当周杰伦的偶像罗大佑渐渐老去,四大天王日薄西山的时候,周杰伦的"吐字不清"令人耳目一新。

    4.《独立日》不仅将罗兰·艾默里奇送上了神坛,也使"黑马王子"威尔·史密斯极速蹿红、一夜**上位**。

    尽管"上位"一词目前尚未进入汉语及双语词典,但据统计,目前正规出版的期刊杂志上也出现了这种用法。在"中国期刊全文数据库"中搜索,共搜到2001—2007年发表的篇名中带有动词用法的"上位"的文章14篇。这说明越来越多的人开始认可"上位"的动词用法。

    既然"上位"的意思就是"走红",那我们不妨先看看"走红"如何翻译。《汉英词典》(第三版)如下处理"走红":

走红:动词:(1)have good luck; be in luck(2)popular; well-known;

他因为一部电视剧而走红。He became popular because of a TV show.

很明显,上面的第二个义项就是我们这里所讨论的"走红"的意思,但该词典的处理方式让人感到莫名其妙。既然"走红"已经确定为动词,为什么词目译文又是形容词呢?既然词目译文是形容词,为什么例证中又用的是动词短语 become popular?

那么,"上位"抑或"走红"应该如何译呢?become popular / well-known 固然不错,基本上译出该词所表达的意义,但同时,不可否认的是,原文生动的形象在译文中并未有丝毫体现。有鉴于此,不妨将该词较为形象地译为 shoot to fame 或 become a sensation。这里的 shoot 和 sensation 也算是对"上位"和"走红"中所包含的形象的一个补偿了。之所以用这两个表达法,是因为它们在外刊中极为常见,例如:

1. SHE **shot to fame** by stripping for the sexually explicit film *9 Songs* but now American actress Margo Stilley, left, is attracting attention for her choice of attire.

2. Not that Caroline, her elder sister, fared much better in love. She **shot to fame** by stripping off at the Monte Carlo beach club as a teenager and by defying her parents to marry Philippe Junot, a playboy 17 years her senior who sold their honeymoon snapshots to the press.

3. She **became a sensation** by dancing in the nude; within weeks she was the talk of the Parisian Salons.

当然,"上位"一词除了上述译法之外,还可以用 jump to fame、achieve fame、come to fame、claim to fame 等短语来译,例如:

She first **jumped to fame** by sleeping with Luis Miguel when he came to give a series of concerts here in Argentina and giving interviews about it afterwards.

It is a double-sided woman who has **achieved her fame** by sleeping with directors and other powerful men, without a brain, breasts and legs only.

In addition, Kirsten is one of those talentless celebrities who **claimed to fame** by sleeping around with producers to get parts, then by creating rumors about her to keep the parts hot, then by getting paid to do interviews to defend her personal life.

　　而前面提到的"一夜上位",意即"一夜成名"或"一夜蹿红",则可以据此译为 shoot to fame / become a sensation / jump to fame overnight。当然,也可以用 gain / win instant fame 等短语来表达,如:

　　Eva Herzigova is a model and actress. Born in the Czech Republic, she **gained instant fame** by being the initial model used by Victoria's Secret.

剩 女

　　"剩女"一词是教育部 2007 年 8 月所公布的 171 个汉语新词之一，指一部分现代都市女性，她们绝大部分拥有高学历、高收入、高智商，长相也无可挑剔，但因她们择偶要求比较高，导致在婚姻上得不到理想归宿，而变成"剩女"的大龄女青年。日常生活中，我们或称她们为"单身派"，或戏谑地称她们为 3S 女：Single（单身）、Seventies（生于 20 世纪 70 年代）、Stuck（被卡住了——在爱情上停滞不前）。

　　与"剩女"相对应的词则为"剩男"，普遍指代那些年龄在 30—45 岁之间，仍处于单身状态的男士。目前，"剩男"群体的特色在于年龄层次跨度大，所涉及的行业以及各自所处的社会地位也非常广泛。既可以用来指代那些渴望结束单身生活的待娶男士，也可以指代那些只希望享受单身生活的无欲男士。"剩男"群体虽然没有"剩女"群体那么引人注目，却也成为了一种越来越普遍的社会现象。

　　首先看看"剩女"一词怎么译。我们能想到的第一个英文对应词似乎就是 spinster。这个词在英文中确实曾经用来指那些过了适婚或适育年龄却仍然待字闺中的女性，但却常常带有贬义，惹人生怜、招人同情或受人嘲弄。这些女士往往给人感觉冷漠、孤僻、不近人情，是一些人老珠黄、性格古怪、嫁不出去的老处女。尽管后来的女性主义运动使该词的含义有所改善，但这一贬义色彩却很难完全抹去。譬如，根据 *The New Oxford American Dictionary*，"In modern everyday English, **spinster** cannot be used to mean simply 'unmarried woman'; it is now always a derogatory term, referring or alluding to a stereotype of an older woman who is unmarried, childless, prissy, and repressed."

此外,还有些地方将"剩女"译为 old maid,其实这种译法也不妥当,因为 old maid 在英文中的贬义色彩更为浓烈。所以,使用 spinster 和 old maid 这两个词来译那些心高气傲、个人生活丰富多彩的中国式"剩女"并不合适,因为这些"剩女"很多并不孤僻,也不是不想嫁人,只是没有碰到自己所认为的合适人选而不愿屈就而已。她们一旦为丘比特之箭射中,很快就会摆脱"剩女"的尴尬境地,相夫教子,成为贤妻良母。

当然,也有人主张把"剩女"译为 3S woman,这一译文未尝不可,尤其是当其作为戏谑用语的时候,但就翻译而言,该译文似乎更应该看作是一个解释,而非"剩女"一词的英文对应词。此外,还有些地方把"剩女"译为了 left woman 或 surplus woman,但仔细分析之后则会发现问题所在。首先,left woman 意义不明,在不同的语境下具有歧义。其次,surplus woman 为学术用语,譬如,美国学者 Catherine L. Dollard 在 2009 年就曾发表专著 The Surplus Woman,从学术角度探讨了这些终生未婚的女性(unwed woman)的悲惨命运,这与国内的"剩女"大相径庭。

那么,"剩女"究竟应该如何翻译呢? 我们认为,除了所谓的 3S woman,leftover woman / lady 也是一个较为理想的选择,因为该译文不但包含了"剩(leftover)"的概念,也具有调侃、戏弄或自嘲的味道。另外,从翻译学的角度来看,"剩女"这个中国文化特色词,不一定要采用完全归化的英文表达方式,完全可以采用异化的译法,尤其是当这种译法在理解上不构成困难的时候。

其实,leftover woman / lady 这种说法在 The China Daily 这类英文报纸中也能找到,例如:

The social phenomenon of Chinese single women is wonderfully explained in *The Leftover Lady* (Sheng Nu Lang), which is now playing at the Beijing Oriental Pioneer Theater. The story is told from the viewpoint of a fabulous woman, who is 29 years old, but still unmarried.

The China Daily, 2009 - 09 - 05

I am a shengnv, which literally means "**left-over woman**". It used to be a derogatory term, popular only in Shanghai, for unmarried women above 30 years of age. But the number has grown so rapidly in the past decade that we have practically become a cohesive group.

The People's Daily Online, 2009 - 12 - 09

"剩女"的英译解决后,"剩男"就好译了,可以译为 leftover man。有人可能会想到 bachelor 一词,但该词其实并不合适,因为英文中的 bachelor 只是指单身汉,而我们知道,"剩男"是单身汉,但单身汉却不都是"剩男"。

熟　女

　　"熟女"一词目前十分流行,打开网络,关于"熟女"的新闻或报道可真不少,例如:

　　(1) 80后奔三不惧年龄压力 新30岁**熟女**流行中嫩

中国网,2010年1月12日

　　(2)娶"**熟女**"做老婆,跟"**熟女**"做朋友,都是一件赏心乐事。男人还是喜欢拥有真性情的女人,哪怕无缘长相厮守,远远地欣赏着,亦会叫人心情舒畅。

金羊网,2005年10月20日

　　那么,什么是"熟女"呢?"百度百科"认为,"'熟女'来源于日本A片,现在泛指30岁—50岁的成熟女人。但不是所有成熟的女人都是熟女,我们这里要说的熟女不仅仅是性成熟。真正的熟女应该拥有丰富的人生阅历,有内涵,气质优雅,自爱自信,懂得体贴和关怀。"据说,"熟女"必须必备几个条件:经济独立、人格独立;精神独立、心态坚强;举止文明、打扮得体。

　　此外,还有观点认为,"熟女"的历练、智慧、温暖,甚至有历史累积的脂肪所散发出的魅力,让男人无限向往,有人称之为"熟苹果深厚的香味",而不是鲜花肤浅的流香。"熟女"具备以下10个特征:风骚(这是一个绝对的褒义词,与风情、丰韵有关)、母性的力量、女人味、优雅、高贵、独立的美、滚烫的体贴、养内(内心丰富,气质取胜,十分耐读)、最懂性的快乐、最佳红颜知己。"熟女"的要求如此之高,难怪人们惊呼:做

"美女"容易,做"熟女"难。

"熟女"一词比较难译,笔者见到的译文有 mature woman、sophisticated woman、ripe woman、mellow woman、a real peach、easy woman 等等。但这些译文似乎都只反映了"熟女"的一个方面,譬如,"熟女"是 mature,但 mature 的 woman 却不一定是"熟女";a real peach 是指一个人 very sweet;而 easy woman 则是指那些在性关系上较为随便的女性,但这些只是"熟女"的一个特征而已。事实上,似乎很难只用一个词来表达"熟女"的概念,因为从上面的定义中我们可以看出,"熟女"是集 mature、sexy、intelligent、worldly-wise、ripe、independent 等于一身的一个词。但是,从翻译的角度来讲,我们又不能把这些词都堆积在一起,那又似乎纯粹是解释了。

那么,"熟女"难道不可译吗? 这倒也不是,因为不只东方男人欣赏"熟女",西方男人也关注"熟女",为其所倾倒。而在英文中有一个词大致可以表示汉语中的"熟女",它就是 cougar woman! 在讨论为何如此翻译之前,让我们先看看关于 cougar woman 的一段叙述:

Since 2004, the website has dedicated to **cougar women** and the cubs that adore them. The word is not a stigma; it's a sophisticated species of female who knows the pleasure of younger men. She avoids the entanglements of a "relationship," in favor of the freedom of the hunt. She has overcome the taboos related to her sexual identity, embraced her true self, and now lives her life to its fullest. Always one for adventure, she knows what she wants and isn't afraid to get it!

上面这段话中所描述的 cougar woman(有时直接用 cougar)的形象,与我们所谈论的"熟女"何其相似? 她们了解自身的优点、不为情所困;她们拥抱自我,生活充实;她们了解自己的需求,并不遗余力追求之。那么,为什么要用 cougar woman 来表达上述概念呢? Cougar 的原意为"美洲狮",它不但以大型动物为食,也猎取较小的动物,甚至昆虫,这与 cougar women 们常常"猎取"年轻男子较为相似。当然,现实生活中不光有 cougar woman，也有那些"老牛吃嫩草"的"sugar daddy"们[1]。

最后，我们发现，"熟女"尚未退潮，"轻熟女"已悄然登场。所谓"轻熟女"，泛指年龄在 25～35 岁之间的都市精英女性，她们还有一个更绯红温暖的名字，那就是"姐姐"。比如曾经王菲对谢霆锋而言……。"轻"，指的是外貌年轻，甚至还能扮一回粉嫩；"熟"，指的是内心成熟，谈吐优雅，永远得体，从不会着急、慌忙地赶路。不管遇到什么事情，她们都会镇定自若，淡然处之。"轻熟女"在英文中一般用 sexy child woman 来表示，这里的"轻"用"child"来表示，而 woman 则表示已经"成熟"，再加上 sexy 这个词，表明这些女人的魅力所在，较为贴切。

---

[1] Sugar daddy 是一个英文俚语，指那些追求年轻女性的年纪较大的富裕男性。

署 名 权

　　随着社会的进步,人们的维权意识也愈来愈强,这不,前段时间,著名影星章子怡自曝《夜宴》中的露背是由替身完成的,而其"裸替"邵小珊也向导演冯小刚讨要自己在影片中的"署名权"。

　　那么,什么是"署名权"呢? 所谓"署名权",是指作者在自己创作的作品及其复制件上标记姓名的权利,它既包括作者在作品上署真名、艺名、笔名或假名的权利,也包括不署名的权利。"署名权"反映了作者和作品之间的内在联系,表明署名人是一件作品的创作者。

　　《新华新词语词典》和《汉英词典》(第三版)分别将该词译为 right to express the author's name in the works 和 right of signature。按理说,第一种译文也能表达出"署名权"的意思,第二种译文虽让人第一直觉是"签名权",但在一定的语境中也不为错。然而,由于"署名权"为法律术语,所以其译文一定要规范、准确,这也是翻译法律术语的基本原则。

　　"署名权"的规范英译是什么呢? 答案是 right of authorship。下面这段话引自美国州立大学 Binghamton University 研究生院关于研究生和博士生学位论文写作要求的手册,里面就提到了"署名权":

　　To protect **the right of authorship** by copyright, it is only necessary under current law to affix a notice of copyright to the page following the title page. The copyright notice should give the full legal name of the author, centered at the bottom of the page as this sample:

or centered and double-spaced on the page as this sample:

除了"署名权"之外,我们还发现,《新华新词语词典》中对"知情权"和"肖像权"的译法也不准确,这两个词分别被译为 right to inform 和 right of image,而规范的译文则分别为 right to know 和 right of portrait。请看下面引自 *Victoria University of Wellington Law Review* 中的几段话:

1. In the case of *Two Art Models v The Organisers of the Exhibition*, some teachers from the China Central Art Institution held an exhibition of life drawing without the consent of the models. Later, the models sued the organisers for invasion of their **right of portrait**.

2. The understanding of privacy changes with the passage of time and national traditions. China has developed its own concept of **the right to privacy**. During this process many issues have arisen about the elements of privacy or of the right to privacy. Many problems are still unaddressed, such as the conflict between **the right to know** and the right to privacy or the distinction between **the right of reputation** and the right to privacy.

从上面这段话中,我们还可以得知一系列"权"的英译:"隐私权"为 right to privacy,"名誉权"为 right of reputation。此外,"参与权"为 right to participate,"表达权"为 right of expression,"监督权"则为 right of supervision。

双　赢

　　"双赢"、"多赢"、"共赢"是近些年来出现的一系列新词,《人民日报》2006 年 12 月 1 日第九版如此定义这几个词汇:

　　双赢,就是交往的双方都能受益,都为赢家。比如,企业之间、地区之间、国家之间,可以通过资本、科技、人才、信息等方面的交流与合作,实现优势互补,不仅使自身获得发展,同时促进对方的发展。从一定意义上说,人与自然的和谐发展也是双赢,既发展了生产力,又保护了环境、节约了资源。**多赢**,是多个双赢的组合,以双方合作带动多方合作,以多方合作深化双方合作。**共赢**,就是把双赢、多赢扩展到更大的范围,实现不同社会群体之间乃至国家与国家之间的共同发展。

　　下面是《汉英词典》(第三版)和《汉英大词典》(第三版)对这一组词的处理:

　　《汉英词典》(第三版):

　　双赢:win-win:双赢局面:win-win situation (or outcome)

　　多赢:缺

　　共赢:win-win; all-win:各方正加强合作,寻求共赢。All parties are strengthening their cooperation to achieve an all-win result

　　《汉英大词典》(第三版):

　　双赢:win-win; be mutually satisfied; both achieve their purpose; victory for both sides (concerned)

多赢：benefit multilaterally

共赢：win-win；all win；win for all

看到这种处理方式，读者可能会感到迷惑：（1）"双赢"和"共赢"是一回事吗？为什么都译为 win-win？（2）既然"双赢"和"共赢"可以用 win 的不同形式来译，"多赢"难道就不行吗？

要回答这些问题，我们首先要看看上面这些与 win 相关的词都是什么意思。先看 win-win，这个词最具有迷惑性，很容易被理解为"双赢"，因为刚好有两个 win 组合在一起。但 win-win 是否就是"双赢"呢？其实不然，请看下面该词的定义：

win-win：（only before noun）a win-win situation, solution, etc, is one that will end well for everyone involved：It's *a win-win situation all around*.

win-win：*noun* ［countable］：*The agreement is a win-win for everyone*.

Longman Dictionary of Contemporary English

win-win：advantageous or satisfactory to all parties involved ＜a win-win situation＞ ＜a win-win deal＞

Merriam-Webster Unabridged Dictionary

这样看来，win-win 并非"双赢"，而是"共赢"，[1]这从上面两部词典释义中的 everyone 和 all parties 可以看出。下面来自《环球视野》的一个双语对照例子更能充分说明这一点：

国家副主席习近平在接见本会高层访京团时表示：中央全力支持各项有利香港繁荣稳定的举措，特别是香港回归后与内地经济的联系更为密切，期望今后进一步加强合作交流，实现内地和香港互利共赢的前景。

During his meeting with the Chamber's high-level delegation, Vice-President Xi Jinping affirmed that the Central Government will fully support

---

〔1〕 杨全红（2010）先生在"从'双赢'的释义及英译说开去"一文中也认为"真正与英语中 win-win 对等的不是'双赢'而是'共赢'"。

all measures conducive to Hong Kong's stability and prosperity. Based on Hong Kong's closer economic connection with the Motherland since Hong Kong's return to Chinese sovereignty, he looks forward to stronger ties between Hong Kong and the Mainland for the both sides to **achieve a win-win situation**.

另外,"共赢"还可以译为前面所提到的 all-win,例如:

After the end of the Cold War, as China's reform and opening up deepens and China's development keeps speeding up, to seek peace, development, cooperation and **all-win result** has become the consensus of many neighboring countries.

The People's Daily Online, 2005 – 12 – 29

Conversely, if the countries involved are relatively mature and rational and can conduct effective consultation and communication, then it is possible to bring about an **all-win situation** in the course of a share in interests.

The People's Daily Online, 2005 – 03 – 18

"共赢"的问题解决了,那么"多赢"又如何表达呢? 答案是 multi-win 或 multiple win。请看下例:

Online Purchase of GHD- A **Multi-Win** Solution

The Michigan Daily, 2010 – 05 – 05

Move the situation toward a **multiple-win** solution — a win for the other person, for you and for the organization.

It will not be done over night so will need to be a long term programme, and God forbid that it is all radiata pine. It needs to be a variety of species, both production and protection, but first we need some recognition from agriculture that there is a very simple, **multiple win** solution within its grasp.

最后,让我们看看"双赢"应该如何翻译,笔者首先建议使用 double-win 这个词,下面这些来自原版英文的例证足以说明 double-win 就是"双赢":

1. Introducing at the Provident Bank in 1983 while Mahlin was vice president of personnel there, Peak Time Pay is one of the few recent innovations in personnel staffing to have originated outside Congress or the courts. "It is a **double-win** situation for employers and employees alike", explains Mahlin.

Cincinnati Magazine, 1986－07－05

2. Both may enter with the best intentions of reaching a **double win** situation, but usually one walks away feeling he could have done a better job.

3. Along with this **double win** situation, we pick up the extra benefits of cooperation, dedication, sportsmanship, new friendships, and an eagerness to become more adept in both facets of the competition: performing and supporting.

4. It is a **double-win** situation; it gives the older person a way of being valuable and needed, and it also makes an irreplaceable contribution to the child's sense of history and personal continuity.

5. To them this was a **double-win** solution. Win number one — a release mechanism for customer complaints with less hassle that was quickly actionable; and win number two — it was accomplished at less cost.

然而,值得注意的是,double-win 在英文中并不专指"双赢",有时还指"两个胜利(two victories)",例如下文:

The city of New Orleans scored a **double win** over a single weekend; it elected a mayor who could be a unifying force and its NFL team won the Super Bowl. Almost five years after Hurricane Katrina destroyed much of New Orleans, the two events portend better times for a town that has struggled to recover its traditional panache.

"A **double win** for New Orleans", *The Root*, 2010－02－07

其次,"双赢"一词在某些场合下也可省略不译,尤其是当其与"互利"一词连用,构成"互利双赢"时。这时,常见的做法是译"互利",省

"双赢",这样处理的原因估计是译者认为"双赢"和"互利"在语义上相似,没有必要重复。譬如,前面提到的《环球视野》就把"中央全力挺港实现互利双赢"这个标题翻译为了:Central Government In Full Support Of Hong Kong For **Mutual Benefit**。[2]

〔 2 〕 杨全红(2010)先生认为,mutual benefit 是"双赢"的英译。其实我们不妨认为译者在这些语境下其实是把"互利"翻译为了 mutual benefit,而"双赢"则省略未译。

私 房 菜

不知何时开始,人们对酒楼食肆的喧嚣变得有些厌倦了,热爱美食者钻进横街窄巷,寻找美味佳肴,还有那份流失已久的恬淡心情。他们所寻找的就是现在街道上不时可见的"私房菜"。

所谓"私房菜",也叫"私家菜",就是在私密的自家厨房里烹制而成,无所谓菜系,无所谓章法,只要别家没有,只要味道独特即可。一个世纪前,北京曾盛行一句话:"曲界无腔不学谭——谭鑫培,食界无口不夸谭——谭家菜。"这说的就是当时著名的私房菜"谭家菜"。那时,许多头面人物都以能品尝到翰林谭宗浚家的菜为荣,可能这就是私房菜最早的根源吧。

后来,香港、广州、上海、北京等地都出现了一些私房菜馆,虽然数量不一、良莠不齐,却也渐渐成了气候,受到很多人的追捧。的确,"私房"这两个字本身就包含了太多的隐秘,太多的诱惑和太多的期待。

"私房菜"如何翻译呢?众多的汉英词典中只有《汉英词典》(第三版)收录了该词,其译文为 family cuisine。该译文应该说是正确的,譬如,上面提到的享有盛誉的"谭家私房菜"就通常译为 The Tan Family Cuisine。当然,family cuisine 这个词本身还有不同的译法,譬如,在日本通常译为"家庭料理"。

除了 family cuisine 这个说法外,"私房菜"还有没有其他的译文呢?笔者发现,还有以下几个常用的译文可供选择。

1. private kitchen cuisine 或 speakeasy cuisine。这种说法最早起源

于香港,由于香港高额的房租等原因,有些饭店就开始开辟所谓的 private kitchen 或 speakeasy,为客人提供 quality home-made food and drinks,而更重要的则是这些餐馆往往试图营造出一种"家"的氛围。Wikipedia 也收录了 speakeasy 这个词,请看其释义和阐述:

Speakeasy, also termed **private kitchen** in Hong Kong (Chinese:私房菜), is a term in modern Hong Kong referring to an unlicensed, restaurant-like establishment for eating. Some of the perceived problems with running a restaurant in Hong Kong — high rents and the common practice of landlords extracting profits from restaurants through clauses in tenancy agreements — have led to the establishment of this type of eatery.

A typical speakeasy will be based in an ordinary apartment in a block of flats. Customers gain access by ringing the bell before the door is opened from the inside. Inside, the flat will be set out as a simple restaurant. Usually, it provides not only **quality home-made food and drink**, but **a sense of being at home**. Advertising is usually by word of mouth — it's often not possible to have prominent signs outside to advertise the business' presence, as with a normal commercial establishment. Some speakeasies make it compulsory for patrons to phone ahead first to book.

从上面的解释我们可以知道,所谓的 speakeasy 和 private kitchen 应该是"私房菜馆"的意思,而私房菜则为 private kitchen cuisine 或 speakeasy cuisine。譬如下文:

Speakeasy cuisine is guided by word-of-mouth; diners flock to unlicensed restaurants for good food at bargain-basement prices.

另外,也有些地方认为"private kitchen"就是"私房菜"的意思,例如,Virtual China 网站对该词给出如下的释义:

"Private kitchen" = 私房菜 = home-cooked or super-traditional meals that are fixed course depending on the day and the restaurant is usually set in a small apartment upstairs; was all the rage in Hong Kong some years ago.

然而,笔者的调查发现,private kitchen 本身还是没有"菜"的意思,而将该词译为"菜",实属翻译中的变通,例如,新知台由肥妈玛利亚主持的一档综艺饮食节目"肥妈私房菜"的英文就是 Maria's Kitchen,但实际上这里还是指 Maria 在 Kitchen 中做的 dishes,而 kitchen 在这里似乎是一个借喻的用法。

2. private home cuisine:这个译文目前用得很多,譬如 *Shanghai Daily* 等英文媒体都用该译文。下面是摘自 *Shanghai Daily* 中的用例:

Sifangcai or "**private home cuisine**" has become a fad in many large cities around the country. It's a kind of home catering that features traditional family recipes in a setting just like home.

(在如今的大城市里,私房菜已经成为一种时尚了。私房菜馆一般是开在住宅中,以厨师传统秘制手艺为招牌。)

近年来,随着人们生活水平的大幅度提高,人们对饮食更为关注,希望吃得健康,吃得美味。除了上面提到的"私房菜"或"私家菜"外,还出现了一系列的"菜",如"招牌菜"、"特色菜"、"农家菜"、"创新菜"等等。下面再看看这些各色"菜肴"的翻译。

"招牌菜"一般译为 signature dish 或 house special 或 house specialty dishes,但需要注意的是,signature dish 可不能随便使用。一般所谓的 signature dish 都是在那些较为高档的饭馆出现,食者单凭品味,就能知道制作该菜肴的厨师(通常名气较大)的姓名。请看下面 Wikipedia 对该词的释义:

A **signature dish** is a recipe that identifies an individual chef. Ideally it should be unique and allow an informed gastronome to name the chef in a blind tasting. It can be thought of as the culinary equivalent of an artist finding their own style, or an author finding their own voice.

"特色菜"的译文为 chef's specials 或 special cuisine,或有时直接用 special 或 specialty 来译。例如:

Thursday's **special** was steak. 星期四的特色菜是牛排。

What's **special** for tonight? 今晚有什么特色菜?

Today's **special**／Today's **specialties** 今日特色菜

What's today's **special**? 今天的特色菜是什么?

This is Beijing's **special**. 这是北京的特色菜。

"农家菜"的译文则为 farmer's dishes 或 famer's cuisine。而"创新菜"则一般直接译为 innovations，如"红房子的创新菜"便为 the innovations of the Red House Restaurant。

网　恋

　　"网恋"是指通过互联网谈恋爱,也指通过这种途径产生的恋情。"网恋"是在网络流行和普及的背景下出现的一个新词。在现代社会,人们渴望爱情,但是寻求爱情的成本与所承担的风险越来越高。伴随着网络的普及,人们发现虚拟的网络空间可以同时满足他们对爱以及安全感的需求,于是就产生了一种新的恋爱形式——网恋。

　　《新华新词语词典》将"网恋"翻译为 online love affairs。这种译文其实是译者想当然的硬译,并不准确。首先,所谓的"网恋",并非在网上(online)谈恋爱,而是通过网络这个媒介进行恋爱,所以 online 不能使用。其次,牛津词典将 love affair 定义为:a sexual relationship between two people, usually when one or both of them is married to somebody else,实指"风流韵事"、"婚外情"。而汉语中的"网恋"虽也多指青少年等对网络比较熟悉的未婚人群通过网络而产生的恋情,但这二者所指的对象并不完全相同。最后,从牛津词典对该词的释义,我们不难发现,love affair 具有很强的贬义色彩,主要是指婚外情等私通行为,而"网恋"则不具有贬义色彩。在现实生活中,有许多年轻人就是通过网恋获得了梦寐以求的爱情。由此可见,把"网恋"翻译为 online love affairs 是完全错误的。

　　那么,"网恋"到底应该怎么翻译呢? 笔者认为译为 cyber love 或 cyber dating 比较合适。Cyber 是英语中的一个前缀,通常用来表示"网络的、电脑的",如 cyber culture(网络文化)、cyber chat(网络聊天)、

cyber news(网络新闻)、cyber punk(网络科幻小说)、cyber space(电脑空间)、cyber mania(网迷)、cyber resource(网络资源)等。而 love 和 dating 则有"恋爱"、"约会"的意思。合在一起,正好可以表示汉语中的"网恋"一词。

事实上,国内的主流英文媒体如 *The China Daily*, *The People's Daily* 等,一般也都用 cyber love 来译"网恋"。例如,

Sure, if you feel lonely, bored and you've got a computer at hand, **cyber love** may seem like a great means to kill time.

——"Watch out the Cyber Love Trap", *The China Daily*,

2004 – 04 – 30

而用 cyber dating 来表示"网恋"也比较普遍,下面是来自原版英文中的一些例子:

Cyber dating is a boon for those who are too shy to strike up a conversation face-to-face with a stranger or for those who can't easily get out due to physical limitations, illnesses, or other conditions.

Cyber dating is definitely a cheaper and more convenient alternative to meeting people.

最后,笔者发现,西方人有时也把所谓的"网恋"称作"cyber courtship",尽管该表达法是否应该译为汉语"网恋"还要依语境而定,因为"cyber courtship"明显带有"追求"的含义。请看下面的例子:

After 8 weeks of **cyber courtship**, I decided to travel to Malaysia to meet my future life partner.

I joined Match. com and entered the world of **cyber-courtship**.

After 32 months of **cyber courtship**, she's now engaged to this man she's never met.

微　博

　　据香港《明报》报道，日前，广东省党政一把手汪洋、黄华华向网民拜年，称希望网民对民生热点问题"织围脖"，对政府工作不足"拍大砖"。

　　另据《重庆晚报》2010 年 2 月 22 日报道，"中共中央总书记、国家主席、中央军委主席胡锦涛也在人民网'开'微博"了，其'粉丝'一天之内即上升到 8000。"

　　第一则新闻中的"围脖"其实是"微博客"的谐音，也简称为"微博"。微博客在内地流行的时间还不长，主要是年轻人和知识分子发表网路言论的工具。博主可以用三言两语，现场记录，发发感慨，晒晒心情，所以有人将其称为新一代传播媒体。而写微博也被网友戏称为"织围脖"。据说美国总统奥巴马就是国际上最知名的微博网站 Twitter 的忠实拥趸。

　　"微博"的出现，是基于博客(blog)的不足之上的。虽然博客已经流行了很久，但它存在不少不足之处，比如写大段的文章比较困难，小段的又缺少内涵，不容易与博客的主题契合等。"微博"作为一种分享与交流平台则更注重时效性和随意性，更能表达出每时每刻的思想和最新动态，更偏重于梳理自己一段时间内的所见、所闻、所感，因此，它迅速流行起来也就不足为奇了。微博客的魅力主要集中在，第一，群聊功能；第二，跨平台数据交互和互动，挖掘潜力不单停留在文字、图片、视频范畴，隐含有 SNS 交互特性，而中国是移动设备交互最为频繁的国家之一，微博客的出现将更大地提升该块用户使用体验和互动性,而 3G 的普及相信即将带来一场新的跨平台交互风暴。

根据"百度百科",国内比较知名的"微博"有 Follow5、随心微博、新浪微博、大围脖、饭否、品品米、同学网、唠叨(jnettalk)、叽叽网、MySpace 聚友 9911、贫嘴、easytalk。而国外的著名微博,除了 Twitter 之外,还有 jaiku、tumblelog、Thumbcast、Twingr、Sideblog、Yammer、Juick 等。

"微博"更新信息非常简单,用户写起来很轻松,就像平时叽咕两句心情一样。在各种平台上都可以进行更新。这些零散的、及时的信息累积起来,信息量就会非常大。由于它的即时性,微博客的速度可以超过世界上任何一家媒体。未来,我们的世界将会进入一个"人人都是记者"、"人人都是狗仔队"的世界,而且第一手的消息一定是来自"微博"。

说了这么多,那么"微博"的英文是什么呢? 答案就是 microblogging。请看新华社的报道:

Hu Shuli, editor-in-chief of China's leading financial magazine *Caijing*, has resigned, said *Caijing* spokeswoman Zhang Lihui on her **micro-blogging** Monday afternoon.

中国最具影响力的财经类杂志《财经》女发言人张立晖本周一中午在"微博"上透露,该杂志主编胡舒立已经辞职。

上句中的 microblogging 就是我们这里所说的"微博"。事实上,weblog∕blog(博客)自诞生以来,越来越多的用户开始在网上发布 personal online diaries(个人网络日志)。除文字日志外,逐渐衍生出 photo blog(图片博客)、video blog(视频博客)、以及 podcast(播客)。与 mainstream media(主流媒体)不同,最新面世的 micro-blogging(微博)是以短发言为特征的,还常被网友称为"围脖"。这也就是本文刚开始所讲述的汪洋的所谓"围脖"的来源。与此相关,"脖友"则是指"微博用户",可译为 microblogging users。"织围脖"是指写微博和发微博的过程,可译为 to microblog。例如:"现在,人们通过电脑或手机来'织围脖'。"一句就可译为:Now people are microblogging through computers or mobile phones.

蜗　居

随着同名电视剧《蜗居》的热映,"蜗居"这个词迅速传遍了大江南北,也引起了不少有识之士对目前中国房价高企、老百姓住房困难问题的思考。这不,据新华网 2010 年 2 月 27 日报道,最近就连温家宝总理在接受采访时也坦言:"群众的心情我非常理解。**我也知道所谓"蜗居"的滋味**。因为我从小学到离开家的时候,全家五口人只有 9 平方米的住房。"温总理随后表示自己在任内能管好房市。

所谓"蜗居",是比喻狭小的住所。该词来源于著名作家六六 2007 年出版的长篇同名小说《蜗居》,小说围绕住房问题讲述了现代都市青年的情感故事。小说后来被改编成电视连续剧,于 2009 年上映,在国内引起了轰动。

关于"蜗居"的英译大致有如下几种:(1)《蜗居》电视剧上采用的是 A Romance of House 的英文;(2)有些地方直译为 snail's house,因为"蜗居"按照字面理解即"蜗牛的居所";(3)还有些地方译为 dwelling narrowness;(4)另外,还有将该词译为 pigeonhole 的。无独有偶,刚刚出版的《汉英词典》(第三版)也收录了"蜗居"一词,其译文为 humble abode 和 small dwelling。看到这么多译文,笔者不禁产生了疑问:这些译文正确吗?"蜗居"究竟应该如何来译?

首先,A Romance of House 作为电视剧片名,明显是基于剧情的翻译,不能看作"蜗居"一词的真正译文。当然,就该译文本身而言,也算不上佳译,因为 a romance of house 回译成汉语则为"房子的浪漫",与该剧的剧情风马牛不相及。

其次,snail's house 这个直译显然会产生文化误读,因为 snail 一词在英文中并不表示狭小,而是表示"行动缓慢"和"效率低下",例如,英文成语 a snail's pace 意思即为"极慢地"、"慢吞吞地";而另一个成语"snail mail"则是 electronic mail 一词产生之后出现的一个新的表达法,用来指代传统的、传递速度相对较慢的 paper mail、postal mail 或 land mail。此外,在英美文化中,snail 通常被看作是懒惰(laziness)、懒散(sloth)的象征。譬如在犹太教和基督教文化中,snail 常被看作是懒散的表现,是致命的原罪(sin)之一。而在《圣经》"诗篇(Psalms)"中,蜗牛的粘液(snail slime)更被比喻为一种惩罚。把汉语中表示居所狭小的"蜗居"一词按照字面意思译为 snail's house,不但难以唤起英美读者的共鸣,而且极有可能令其产生误解,认为"蜗居"与居所主人的懒惰或不洁有关。

第三,dwelling narrowness 强调的是居所很 narrow,而"蜗居"则强调居所很小,二者并不对等。此外,dwelling narrowness 的重点在 narrowness 这个词上,而"蜗居"则在"居"上,前者是一个抽象名词,而后者则为具体名词,所以,即使 dwelling narrowness 在意义上与"蜗居"对等,也难以将其看作"蜗居"的恰当译文。

第四,humble abode 和 small dwelling 这两种译法首先在文体上与"蜗居"一词不对等。"蜗居"一词在汉语中明显是口语体,有时甚至带有自嘲的意味。而几乎所有的英语词典中都清楚地标明,abode 和 dwelling 为正式文体,有些甚至将这两个词标为法律文体。例如法律中"无固定住所的人"就称作"a person of / with no fixed abode"。另外,humble abode 或 humble dwelling 一般为谦称,常用来翻译汉语中的"寒舍",如"欢迎光临寒舍!"就可以译为"Welcome to my humble dwelling / abode!"(该译例见《朗文当代高级英语辞典》)而"寒舍"在汉语中不但是谦词,即使不仅仅表示谦称,一般也是指简陋的居所,但简陋的居所不一定就是"蜗居"。

最后,pigeonhole 这个译文,乍看上去的确形神兼备,正如该译文的提供者北师大博士后孟凡君先生认为:在英语中,人们通常把小得可怜的房间叫做"pigeonhole",其词义正与"蜗居"相同,故可将"蜗居"一词直接译为"pigeonhole"。然而,这个译文是否正确的关键在于:英文中的 pigeonhole 用来指住房时是否真的是指"小的可怜的房间"。答案其实是否定的。所谓 pigeonhole,原意是指[办公室或墙上的]鸽笼式分类架;信件格;文件格(one of a set of small boxes built into a desk or into a frame on a wall, in which letters or papers can be put)。西方人有时的确用该词来谈论住房情况,但其谈论的重点是类似国人所居住的高层建筑(high-rises),在他们眼中,高层建筑中的每一套公寓房,从楼下看去就像一个个"鸽笼"。而众所周知,国内的这些"鸽笼"并不一定就非常狭小。

那么,"蜗居"一词应如何翻译呢? 笔者认为,这里有一个译"意"和译"形"的问题。如果单从译"意"的角度来看,该词似乎可以简单地译为 tiny apartment / home。该译虽未能译出原词中所包含的形象,但原词"蜗"所包含的"极小"的意义通过 tiny 一词已清楚地表达了出来,因为 tiny 不但有"微型"、"袖珍"(extremely small)的意思,而且往往带有较为强烈的感情色彩,与"蜗居"一词在情感意义(affective meaning)上似乎较为对应。而如果要追求意象上的对等,"蜗居"一词还可译为 a nutshell of a house 或 shoebox apartment。下面就这两个译文一一进行说明:

首先,nutshell 的字面意为"坚果的外壳",在英文中表达住所狭小这个概念时常用到该词。这或许取得是该词"像果壳般大小"的意思吧。譬如 Helen Dagley 的小说 *Told at Last* 中就用到了 a nutshell of a house,与接下来的 mansion(富丽堂皇的大房子)一词构成了对比:

So Clara said, "Now, mamma, that is one of the comforts of not being grand. I can give away an old dress sometimes without being called to an account for it; and another thing, although we do live in **a nutshell of a house** compared to the **mansion** at Hurst Park, yet we can go into any room we like, which is more than Clara can. I look upon those fine servants as being so many ogres and ogresses."

另外,shoebox apartment 用来翻译"蜗居"一词也很形象。原词中的"蜗"这个形象为译文中的 shoebox 这个形象所代替,而原词中的"居",

考虑到中美在居住方面的差异（国人大多住在 apartment 或 flat 中，而英美人的居所则大多为 house），则最好译为 apartment。

当然，shoebox apartment 也是地道的英文表达，例如，一个打算在纽约租房的人曾在网上发帖，询问房租事宜。他的问题如下：

How much is a **shoebox apartment** in NYC, Manhattan? I mean ... Just enough room for a TV and a bed and a bathroom. And I want to rent it by the month. Thanks for the help.

这位先生在这里所描述的房子只能容纳一台电视、一张床、一个洗澡间，与我们所谈论的"蜗居"何其相似啊！

值得一提的是，所谓的"蜗居"在不同国家可能有不同的标准。中国人所谓的"蜗居"在住房宽敞的美国人眼中，的的确确是"蜗牛的居所"，但在国土面积狭小，住房状况极为紧张的日本人眼中，可能还不算太小呢！下面这段话就说明了这种差别：

The biggest expense that most Japanese contend with is the soaring price of real estate, which is made all the more absurd by the total lack of developable land. The term '**shoebox apartment**' has a whole different meaning in Japan, where 100 sq ft is arguably a palace. Indeed, when my Japanese friends first came to the States to stay with my family at our modest—by American standards—house in suburban New Jersey, they seriously thought we were oil moguls.

"Big in Japan：The Myth About Money"

最后，汉语中的"蜗居"一词有时也可用作动词，如：

蚁族生存状况：蜗居在不足 10 平米房内

《西安晚报》，2009 年 12 月 16 日

17 岁少女蜗居在西安公厕内 2 年只出门一次

《环球时报》，2010 年 2 月 11 日

"蜗居"用作动词时似乎可以简单地译为 live in a tiny home 或 confine oneself to a tiny room。例如：

过去，他们一家六口人蜗居在一间仅 10 平方米的陋室。

In the past, the six people of his family lived in a shabby, small home that covered an area of only ten square meters.

这位孤独老人蜗居斗室。

This lonely old man confines himself to a small room.

无效婚姻

"无效婚姻"是指男女两性虽经登记结婚,但由于违反结婚的法定条件而不发生婚姻效力,应当被宣告为无效的婚姻。《中国司法大词典》(2002)从法律效力角度将婚姻分为"有效婚姻"和"无效婚姻"。从法律效力看,无效婚姻又有绝对无效和相对无效之分。绝对无效是指法律有溯及力,婚姻自始无效,不产生夫妻身份及其权利义务关系,子女为非婚生子女;相对无效是指法律无溯及力,婚姻自宣告无效之日起结束,承认以前的夫妻关系,子女为婚生子女。

《新华新词语词典》将"无效婚姻"译为了 invalid marriage。乍看之下,似乎没有什么问题,因为"有效婚姻"所对应的英文术语是 valid marriage。既然如此,"无效婚姻"就应该是 invalid marriage。

然而,invalid marriage 其实是翻译中的一个"假朋友",原因在于它不是规范、标准、统一的法律术语。"无效婚姻"的正确译文应该是 void marriage。*Black's Law Dictionary* (2004)和 *Lectric Law Library's Lexicon* 是这样定义 void marriage 的:

A marriage that is invalid from its inception, that cannot be made valid, and that can be terminated by either party without obtaining a divorce or annulment. For example, **a marriage is void if the parties are too closely related or if either party is already married**.

void marriage:A **void marriage** is one that is void and invalid from its beginning. It is as though the marriage never existed and it requires no formality to terminate it. For instance, an incestuous marriage would likely be considered void.

　　很显然,这里的 void marriage 和中文的"无效婚姻"是一组对应的概念。在这部字典里,我们却找不到 invalid marriage 这样的表述。事实上,我们可以说 a marriage is invalid,但是却不能将 invalid marriage 看作一个法律术语。同样的,我们又查考了《汉英综合大词典》(2001)、《英汉法律大词典》(2004)、《英汉——汉英双向法律词典》(2006)、《英汉法律用语大词典》(2005)和《元照英美法词典》(2003),这些词典中"无效婚姻"的译文均为 void marriage,而非 invalid marriage。由此可见,invalid marriage 是一个未经仔细查证的、想当然的译文。

　　顺便提一下,随着社会的发展以及人们观念的开放,关于婚姻的表达也层出不穷。下面一组热词读者也不妨了解了解:

奉子成婚:shotgun marriage

早婚:early marriage

晚婚:late marriage

"老夫少妻"式婚姻:May-to-December marriage

涉外婚姻:international marriage

无性婚姻:marriage without sex; asexual marriage

新　锐

　　"新锐"一词据说最早起源于美术界 1999 年在北京国际艺苑举办的一场当代艺术展,名曰"新锐的目光"。随后,该词不断被艺术界业内人士复制使用,成为对所谓年轻艺术家、作家等的一种流行称呼。

　　单从字面意思来看,"新锐"是指各个领域中的后起之秀,他们具有打破陈规的勇气和实力,是将来这些领域中的中坚力量。

　　该词出现之后即迅速流行,从词性上而言,既可以用作形容词,也可以用作动词。请看下列引文:

　　1. 就在杂志上市当日,同样的批评声从数位以"80 后"**新锐作家**自诩的人群中发出,他们对韩寒和《独唱团》进行了炮轰。

　　2. 本次入选"2009 中国十大**新锐诗人**"的诗人还有林萧、春树、符国芳、远观、裴福刚、李成恩、林志强、郑小琼、朱长胜。

　　3. 毕竟悦女士是贺卫方教授的门徒,亦是译界**新锐**,她主译或策划引介、组织翻译了一批外国法学、政治学的名著,形成了规模或团队效应,学界反响颇佳。

　　4. 韩寒作为文学界的**新锐**用自己的声音喊出了新一代文人的气魄,这是我们这些整日里胡思乱想于巨大的就业压力之下的迷茫青年无所比拟的。

　　《现代汉语词典》(第五版)目前已收录了该词,以下是它对该词的处理:

　　新锐:(1)形:新奇锐利:～武器 | ～的言论。(2)形:新出现而有锐

气的(人):~诗人 | ~导演。(3)名:指新出现而有锐气的年轻人:棋坛~。

上面的三个义项中,(1)为该词的本义,(2)和(3)则正是我们这里所谈及的"新锐"一词的意义。

目前,该词尚未为现版的汉英词典所收录,笔者在其他出版物上也未见有该词的翻译。但网络上却有少数几个网友尝试着翻译该词,其提供的译文大致有以下三种:new sharp、new prominent、pioneering、top and new。然而,稍作分析,我们即会发现这些译文均不合适,首先,new sharp 和 new prominent 明显属于硬译,不合英文结构,属于汉语式英语;其次,pioneering 是指"开创性的"、"富于开拓精神的",难以体现"新锐"一词所包含的"锐气"。Top and new 这个译法来自"报喜鸟新锐艺术人物大奖"这一比赛的译文,全译为 Saint Angelo Top & New Artistic Figure Prize。这个译文明显基于大赛的语境,是对"新锐"一词的灵活处理,并不能反映该词的核心内容,因为"新锐"不一定是 top,而且上面提到的"锐气"也没有能够体现出来。

那么,"新锐"一词应该如何英译呢?我们认为,这要分该词作为形容词和作为名词两种情况进行讨论。

作为形容词,可以用 aggressive 来译。Aggressive 一词含有"富有进取心"、"饱含冲劲"、"执着不弃"的意思,而这些品质,正是"新锐"一词内涵的核心所在。而且,英文中 aggressive 也常被用作此意,与"新锐"一词的汉语定义较为契合。例如,下面就是美国一位"新锐"画家对 aggressive painter 的看法:

Maybe it's living in the desert that makes me like to paint water so much. New Mexico does have many beautiful lakes and rivers, but I do miss frequent visits to the ocean growing up on the east coast. To paint this large wave painting, it was very physical. At times I felt like a boxer in the ring, at other times I felt like a dancer in a choreographed performance. Once a painting teacher told me I was an "**aggressive painter**". I am taking this as a compliment, as I do gravitate towards abstract expressionist paintings, which was all about physicality and mark making. Nothing like a visit to a museum to see a Jackson Pollock or Cy Twombly in person.

此外，也有观点云："新锐"一词或许来自 2000 年在香港召开的第三届全球华人物理学大会。当时，诺贝尔奖得主杨振宁教授在英文演讲中提到 aggressive 一词，是对"勇敢提出新的看法，敢于挑战学术权威"的总结。Aggressive，在英文里有具有侵略性的、敢做敢为的、锐意进取的含义，可以概括为个人奋斗的威猛作风。

当然，如果只考虑译意，似乎也可以用 up-and-coming 一词来译"新锐"，该词的意思为：(of a person beginning a particular activity or occupation) making good progress and likely to become successful，汉语中通常译为"积极进取的"、"有前途的"、"日渐重要的"，与"新锐"一词所表达的意义基本相符。而"新锐作家"因此也就可以译为 an up-and-coming (young) writer。

作为名词，"新锐"一词完全可以翻译为 an aggressive young (sb)，这里的 sb 可以为 writer、painter、artist 等词所替代。然而，一个更为可取的译文似乎为 up-and-comer，该词的意思为"有进取心的人"、"有前途的人"，大致与汉语中的"新锐"相似。譬如，下面两段引文中的 up-and-comer 大约就可译为"新锐"：

1. From there, Hage acquired a rep as an **up-and-comer in art circles**; both the Canadian Museum of Civilization and the Musée de la civilisation de Québec have acquired his work. Hage credits photography with making him a better writer. "In visual arts, you're encouraged to be more experimental." He tries to bring that attitude to his writing; his prose style, for instance, often displays a dreamy, feverish sensibility.

2. At 38, Williams is the youngest of the candidates for both positions, and he might be the least well known. He also might be the biggest longshot for both jobs. But it is also clear that Williams has emerged as an **up-and-comer in the NBA coaching circuit**, and many feel it's not a matter of whether he becomes an NBA head coach, but when.

信 息 化

　　"信息化"这个概念产生于日本。1963 年,日本学者梅倬忠夫在《信息产业论》一书中描绘了"信息革命"和"信息化社会"的前景,预见到信息科学技术的发展和应用将会引起一场全面的社会变革,并将人类社会推入"信息化社会"(谢阳群,1996)。1967 年,日本政府的一个科学、技术、经济研究小组在研究经济发展问题时,依照"工业化"的概念,正式提出了"信息化"的概念,并从经济学角度下了一个定义:"信息化是向信息产业高度发达且在产业结构中占优势地位的社会——信息社会——前进的动态过程,它反映了由可触摸的物质产品起主导作用向难以捉摸的信息产品起主导作用的根本性转变。"

　　在中国大陆,信息化一词的广泛使用是在实行改革开放、确立现代化目标这一大背景下发生的。在中共中央办公厅、国务院办公厅印发的《2006—2020 年国家信息化发展战略》中,我们可以发现中国大陆对"信息化"这个概念较为正式的界定:信息化是充分利用信息技术,开发利用信息资源,促进信息交流和知识共享,提高经济增长质量,推动经济社会发展转型的历史进程。

　　虽然有关信息化的研究在西方学者那里早就开始了,但根据一些学者的意见,"信息化"一词至少在几年前在西方(英文)世界还没有普遍公认的对等概念,也没有现成的英文对应词,它主要在中国、日本、韩国、俄罗斯大量使用。由于不是兴于英语文化圈,这个单词的英文翻译也不统一。

　　目前,国内关于"信息化"的英译也争论颇多,譬如,外交部翻译王弄笙先生(2002)在批判了 informationization 这个译文后,提议把该词译为 to promote IT for national economic and social development。这一观点也得到了金其斌先生(2003)的赞同,他认为:"'化'字频繁出现在汉语中,不能一概借用英语中的后缀'-ize'。'信息化'译成'informationalize'则属'硬译',使人不知所云。王弄笙先生译作'to promote IT for national economic and social development',意义通畅。建议采用王译。"

　　首先,让我们看看王弄笙先生的译文 to promote IT for national economic and social development。的确,这个译法有一定的道理,譬如,在一篇讲述中国第九个和第十个五年计划的文章中就有如下表述:

Measures should be taken to stabilize and strengthen agriculture as the foundation of the economy, accelerate industrial reform, reorganization, upgrading and optimization, vigorously develop the service industry, **promote IT for national economic and social development**, and continue to reinforce the infrastructure.

　　但这个译文存在一个致命的弱点,那就是它的实用性太差,难以运用到我们日常频繁所见的各种"信息化"的表述中。譬如,农业信息化、军队信息化、上海市经济和信息化委员会、信息化建设、《上海信息化》杂志社等等。看来要翻译上述例子中的"信息化",译者需要另辟蹊径。

　　"信息化"到底应该如何翻译? Informationization 或 informatization 是否是硬译? 事实上,从上面对"信息化"和其渊源的谈论中,我们已经知道该词其实是一个舶来品,所以,我们需要做的只是找到它的最初表述而已。

　　根据"维基百科","信息化"这一概念出现后,Simon Nora 和 Alain Minc 在他们发表的报告"L' Informatisation de la société: Rapport à M. le Président de la République"之中创造了术语 Informatisation(原义为:计算机化协会:给法国总统的报告)。1980 年,这份报告被译成了英文,即"The Computerization of Society: A Report to the President of France (SAOUG)"。然而,Minc 在其 1987 年所发表的一篇文章中则倾向于采用"informatisation"或"informationization",而不是"computerization"(计

算机化)。

这样看来,"信息化"这个外来词的最初翻译就是 informatisation 和 informationization,这两个译文并非所谓的硬译。其他例证还有:

Rogers, Everett M. 2000. **Informatization**, globalization, and privatization in the new millennium. *The Asian Journal of Communication*, *Volume 10*, *Number 2*: pp. 71 - 92.

Flor, *Alexander G. 1993*. The **informatization** of agriculture. *The Asian Journal of Communication*. Volume 3, Number 2: pp. 94 - 103.

当然,如果"信息化"用 informatisation 或 informationization 来译的话,很多实际的翻译问题就可迎刃而解了。譬如,

"农业信息化"就可以译为 the informatization of agriculture。

"军队信息化"就可以译为 military informatization/informationization。

"上海市经济和信息化委员会"就可以译为 Shanghai Municipal Commission of Economy and Informatization。

"信息化建设"就可以译为 informatization construction。

形象大使

　　"形象大使",又称"形象代言人",指"以个人形象及影响力为某个领域、单位或产品等进行推介宣传的人,多为有一定知名度的公众人物",例如,企业形象大使、公益活动形象大使等。但也有观点认为,"形象大使"和"形象代言人"有所区别,前者适合比较正式的场合,像政治场合,往往代表企业、地区、国家推广公益性活动,后者是指请一些社会名人来为商品进行广告宣传,利用知名人物(多是演艺界或者体育界的明星)的号召力和影响力来扩大商品的知名度,从而最终达到提高销量、获得更大效益的目的。这种说法有一定的道理,但在日常使用中,这两个词似乎并无区别,例如,姚明、朗朗、成龙等既可以叫世博会的"形象大使",也可以叫"形象代言人"。请看下面报道:

　　"郎朗"蜡像特地从香港来到上海,为世博助兴。3 位**世博会形象代言人**郎朗、姚明、成龙蜡像至此齐聚上海新世界杜莎夫人蜡像馆。从明天起至 5 月 31 日,凭世博会门票,可半价参观上海新世界杜莎夫人蜡像馆。

《中国青年报》,2010 年 4 月 28 日

　　昨晚 10 点不到,**世博会形象大使**成龙带着近 10 人的创作团队慕名夜访世博园浦西片区,匆匆参观了太空家园馆、石油馆、国家电网馆、可口可乐馆和日本产业馆后,成龙感慨道,"世博园的夜景效果震撼极了。"

《东方早报》,2010 年 5 月 14 日

目前,各汉英词典均把"形象大使"和"形象代言人"翻译为 image representative。这个译文看似忠实,其实有"假朋友"之嫌。笔者查遍英文资料,发现只有国内的不太知名的英文媒体使用该译文,而英美网站上出现的 image representative 中,representative 一般为形容词,相当于 an image which is representative of sth。因此,image representative 这个译文并非"形象大使"的正确译法。

"形象大使"怎么译呢? 杨力(2009)认为,英文中的 ambassador 本来就含有"形象大使"的意思,所以,用 ambassador 来翻译"形象大使"要比用 image representative 恰当得多。为了证明他的观点,他引用了 *Webster's Third New International Dictionary* 和 *The New Oxford Dictionary of English* 这两本词典给 ambassador 的定义。杨立的观点显而易见是没有问题的,这也从另外一角度推翻了另外一个常为国内媒体所采用的译文 image ambassador,因为既然 ambassador 已有"形象大使"的意思,就没有必要再画蛇添足增加 image 了。下面是一些媒体采用 image ambassador 的报道:

Tibetan girl selected tourism **image ambassador** for Tibet

The People's Daily Online, 2009 - 09 - 20

Obama half-brother named Chinese "**image ambassador**"

The People's Daily Online, 2009 - 12 - 15

然而,我们发现,"形象大使"或"形象代言人"除了用 ambassador 一词来译之外,还可用 (product) spokesperson、brand ambassador、(product / brand) endorser 甚至 endorsement 等词来译。下列引文可以佐证:

1. Using a **health product endorser** is a must if you are trying to create a solid market for your health products. It's all the more effective if the person you have in mind is a celebrity or a famous sportsperson. People will immediately latch on to the message that would come out of such a campaign — that using the concerned health product will make them as fit or as glamorous or as successful as the **health product spokesperson.**

2. Effective **brand ambassadors** are those who are interested in the

product they are promoting, who can easily connect with the product. "During the live brand experience they become the identity of the brand, because they are the only human interface between the brand personality and the consumer. A **brand ambassador** needs to be carefully trained and properly matched to the brand and the target audience to ensure that the live brand experience will be a success.

3. McDonalds Signs Yao Ming As **Global Spokesman**

4. Yao Ming became McDonalds' **global brand ambassador**(全球品牌代言人).

5. China's basketball star Yao Ming became the replacer of Los Angeles Lakers' guard Kobe Bryant for **endorsement** with the McDonald's Restaurants.

型　男

　　"型男"、"索女"是近几年在网络、报纸等媒体上较为流行的一对新词,它们有时独用,有时共现,如:

　　(1)今天,纽曼新品 M521 已经到货,其小巧的身躯、超炫的外型吸引了众多**型男索女**。

　　(2)**型男**陈坤接受重庆晨报专访,解读时尚生活(《重庆晨报》2009年 11 月 30 日)

　　(3)30 岁的林嘉欣依旧小姑独处——典型的"**索女**"。但是在电影《爱情呼叫转移 2:爱情左右》中,她扮演的女主角聂冰却有幸与 12 个**型男**谈起了恋爱。(《新闻晨报》2008 年 12 月 1 日)

　　"型男"、"索女"这对词首先在香港、广州等粤语地区使用,属于粤方言词汇,但最新出版的《汉语新词词典》(王均熙,2006)已将其网罗其中,可见其生命力之强盛。

　　"型男"、"索女"是什么意思呢? 先看"型男",《汉语新词词典》(2003)对其的释义为"有型的男子",这大概是从"型"的引申义"楷模"而来吧。众所周知,那些时尚、英俊、潇洒的男子是普通男人追求、效仿的"楷模"。张沛(2006)指出:"香港人首先将这个意义(时尚、潮流)上的"style"翻译为汉语的"型",并将它的派生词"stylish"(即 has style)翻译成为汉语的"有型",指男性相貌、身材和气质具有吸引力。"事实上,在粤方言中,"型"既是一个词,也是一个词素,表示人英俊、潇洒(郑定欧,1997),例如,"有型"(时尚、有派头、造型独特)、"型款"(款式、样式)、"型仔"(指人英俊、潇洒)、"有型有款"(指装扮得体,很有风度)等。

"索女"常与"型男"成对出现,单独使用的情况较少。《汉语新词词典》(2003)对其的释义为"个性冷傲独特,我行我素的女子"。但从这个释义中,我们难以睹其渊源。"索女"的来源是什么呢?张沛(同上)提出了两种看法:"在粤语中,'索'有'吸(液体)'的意思。网络上流传一种说法:那些骨感的苗条女生让人忍不住流口水,只得用力吸回去。她们因此被称为'索女'。也有人认为'索'是麻将中的条子,引申为苗条。'索女'即苗条的女郎。"罗荣华(2009)等则认为:"'索'在粤语中的本义是'大绳子',粤语区的人们在口语中常常使用本义,即呼'绳子'为'索'。我们知道,绳子的外形是长条形,表面呈现波浪式的曲线,这种外形的特点与女人的苗条身材有相似之处。在相似原则的支配下,便产生隐喻引申,即由工具(绳子)认知域投射到人体(苗条的身材)认知域。因此,像绳索一样修长且有波浪式曲线身材的女人,就称作'索女'"。

罗荣华等(同上)还指出:"索女"在后来的使用中,也被人们进一步丰富了其内涵,不仅指身材苗条的女人,还指时尚、打扮入时的女人,或敢于尝试新鲜事物,对传统有更多反叛的女人,或有冷傲、独特个性的女人。例如:

(1)美女我是没希望了,才女太花工夫,**索女**我会扮啊!(《南方都市报》,2004年3月4日)

(2)可说到底了,如何成为**索女**的标准关键还看处世态度,酷辣服装不过是载体,有些人哪怕不这么穿仍然非常之"索"。王菲是,张曼玉也是,共同点都在性格独特,个性里有不在乎与冷傲的成分,"人言可畏"四个字碰到她们就像皮球被弹回来。(《新民晚报》,2005年9月2日)

通过以上的追根溯源,我们可以得出如下结论:"型男"的英文应该是stylish guy,而"索女"则应该翻译为slim girl,或照顾到该词词义的泛化,笼统译为stylish girl。

值得一提的是,现代汉语中还出现了大量与"男"、"女"二词连用的新词,譬如"打女"(martial lady:动作影片中身手不凡的女演员)、"没女"（woman with nothing：指相貌平平、没有学历也没有钱的女人）、"超女"（super girl）、"俊男"（handsome guy）、"靓女"（pretty girl）、"酷男"（cool guy）、"浪女"（dissipated girl）。

休 渔

根据《现代汉语词典》(第五版),"休渔"一词的意思是"为保护渔业资源,在一定的时期和范围内停止捕鱼"。《辞书研究》2009 年第 5 期"新词语新说"一栏中刊登了周邦友先生的短文"小议'休渔'的英译",文中以《新华新词语词典》对该词的释义为基础,列举了几本汉英词典中该词的英译,最后得出的结论是:"休渔"在英语中是有现成说法的,在英语里,既不采用上述译文中的动词"suspend",也不选用构词成分"－off",而是使用形容词"close"和"closed"。前者为英式英语,后者为美式英语。"休渔期"应译为 close season 或 closed season。

事实上,周先生的讨论有点跑题,因为他在结论中只说 suspend 和"－off"不能用来翻译"休渔",但却没有告诉读者"休渔"到底应该如何翻译,而他提供的 close season 和 closed season 其实不是"休渔"的译文,而是"休渔期"的译文。

那么,"休渔"到底应该怎么译呢?笔者认为,译者首先应该从该词的词性入手,为该词"定性",然后讨论现有译文是否正确,最后再归纳出该词的确切译法。下面按照这个程序一一进行讨论。

首先,根据《现代汉语词典》(第五版)及该词的实际用法,"休渔"一词应为动词。例如:

1. 从 5 月 13 开始,我市应休渔船陆续回港**休渔**。

2. 南海海域实行伏季**休渔**制度。

所以,"休渔"一词最好译为英文的动宾词组,以便与原词在词性上相互照应。在此基础上,也可以提供该词在其他语境中可以使用的译文。

其次,现有汉英词典中的译文"suspend fishing"就是"休渔"的正确译文,具体请看下列来自原版英文的例子:

In 1992, Canada, which had waited too long to restrict the catch in its 500-year-old cod fishery off the coast of Newfoundland, was forced to **suspend fishing** there entirely, putting some 40,000 fishers and fish processors out of work.

To **suspend fishing** in any fishery is a very difficult decision to take as we are aware that such a decision will have an impact on the livelihoods of many people and families in the industry.

According to *the Belfast Telegraph*, **the suspension of fishing** for a period of time would help to assist salmon to spawn more easily.

另外,"休渔"一词还可译为动宾结构 to close fishing 或其名词结构 fishing closure。例如:

High water temperatures and low flows prompted Montana Fish, Wildlife & Parks officials to **close fishing** from 2 p.m. to midnight on the Yellowstone River from the Yellowstone National Park boundary near Gardiner in Region 3 to the Huntley diversion downstream of Billings in Region 5.

In its lawsuit, CCA is challenging the right of federal managers to use an interim rule to **close fishing** for all 12 species of Gulf grouper to protect one species.

Begin the seasonal **fishing closure** on the San Poil Arm of Lake Roosevelt one month earlier. **Fishing** for all game fish from the outlet of French Johns Lake on the San Poil Arm upstream **will be closed** beginning January 1,2005.

最后,英语中还有 to ban/prohibit fishing(fishing ban/prohibition)以及 fishing moratorium 的说法,有时候翻译为"禁渔",但事实上,汉语中的"禁渔"就是"休渔",如《现代汉语词典》(第五版)对"禁渔"的释义就是"为了保护渔业资源,在一定时期或一定水域内禁止捕捞",与"休渔"的释义毫无二致。

　　值得一提的是,周邦友先生在文中所提到的 close / closed season 也不能单独译为"休渔期",因为 close / closed season 是一个多义词,即可以指"禁捕期",也可以指"禁猎期",当然也可以指"禁渔期"。所以"休渔期"一词比较确切的英文说法为 close / closed season for fishing。

学 区 房

　　"学区房"算得上中国楼市中的一朵奇葩。众所皆知,国内房价十年来一路上行,堪比神舟飞船,但其间难免也有缓冲,而"学区房"则不然,犹如嫦娥奔月,别人跌伊在涨,别人涨伊在飞。一所著名中小学的周边,总会布满房地产中介,门口黑板上总是猖狂地写着"学区笋盘,今日必走"。可以说,如果房市是肥皂泡,学区房就是金钟罩。

　　何谓"学区房"呢? 其实就是指重点中小学附近的房产。这里需要注意的是"重点中小学",这是"学区房"产生的一个重要基础,"一般中小学"附近的房子可不叫"学区房"。要搞清楚"学区房"这个概念,首先要看看"学区"的概念。所谓"学区",《现代汉语词典》(第五版)的释义为"为了便于学生上学和对学校的业务领导,根据中小学分布情况划分的管理区"。划分学区本来也无可厚非,但偏偏国内中小学实行的是就近免试入学,也就是说,你要不进入"学区"这个金钟罩,就意味着名牌中小学与你无缘。而要破这个罩也容易,掏钱买房,买所谓的"学区房"。多少父母为了下一代,咬咬牙闭闭眼就这么上了,少说也是上百万的投入,你说送孩子读书容易吗? 教育"减负"哪能减得下来?

　　"学区房"的出现折射出我国现行教育体制的弊端,主要体现在一个城市教育资源的分配非常不均衡,造成一些所谓的"好"的优质中小学校。该词同时也体现出了教育的不公平性,也就是说,不是所有的义务教育阶段的孩子都能享受到优质教育的权利。

　　The China Daily "翻译点津"栏目中将"学区房"译为 elite school

property。该译文虽注意到了"重点学校"这个概念,但首先,该译文使用 elite 这个词翻译"重点"并不恰当,该词人为划分学生阶层,给读者的感觉好像重点学校的学生都是"精英分子",这与汉语事实不符,因为汉语中的重点学校只不过是教学质量好一些而已。另外,这个译文具有歧义,school property 给人感觉好像是"学校的资产或房产"。

那么,"学区房"怎么译呢?或许我们首先应该参看"学区"的译法。《汉英词典》(第三版)和《汉英大词典》(第三版)均把"学区"一词译为 school district。或许正是由于这个原因吧,很多地方都把"学区房"译为 school district house／housing。这个译法如何呢?笔者以为并非佳译,因为它表意模糊,难以清楚表述"学区房"所包含的具体内容,因为学区有好坏,有些学区可能并没有重点的学校等等。

有鉴于此,笔者建议将上面第二种译文稍做调整,变为 house／apartment in a good school district。此译文虽然有些啰嗦,但却清楚无误地说明了"学区房"的内涵。注意,good 一词的运用较为清楚地把"学区"分成了三六九等,也部分解释了为什么学生家长们对"学区房"会如此趋之若鹜。

其实,和中国一样,西方国家也有所谓的"学区房",孩子父母在购房时也会考虑是否是"学区房"。当然,由于西方国家教育机会相对比较公平,父母们在寻找"学区房"时,不但考虑的是教学质量,而且还考虑交通、学校的课外活动等其他方面。下面是 ehow[1] 上的一篇短文的节选,或许能部分说明 house／apartment in a good school district 这个译文的合理性以及中西方家庭在购买"学区房"时考虑问题的差异。

How to Buy a House in a Good School District

When buying a home, there is more to consider than the house itself. If you have children, one of the most important considerations will be the school district they will attend. If you have found a house you would like to make an offer on, it's a good idea to do a quick investigation of the school

---

[1] http://www.ehow.com/how_2126660_buy－house－good－school－district.html。

district to make sure it is a good one.

Instructions

1. Determine what the schooling options in the neighborhood are. Determine if there is a private school close enough to the house to be an option.

2. Consider the distance of the schools from the house.

3. Set up a visit with the school. Ask to speak with the principal and some of the teachers. Get a copy of the curriculum and the student handbook to look over after the meeting.

4. Ask questions. Ask what the average class size is, how the school district ranks on standardized tests, what the graduation percentage is, and what the per-pupil expenditure is. Also ask about the extracurricular activities.

5. Talk to other parents in the area. Find out what the reputation of the school district is and how involved the parents are in the school.

6. Attend a Parent-Teacher Association meeting. This is a good opportunity to see what problems the school district might have and how the association deals with them.

当然,如果不考虑国内"学区房"的特殊性,我们有时也可以简单将该词译为 apartment in the vicinity of a key primary or elementary school。譬如,*Shanghaiist* 就采用了这一译文(当然,如上所言,笔者并不赞同使用 elite 一词):

Many parents will pay a higher price for an **apartment in the vicinity of an elite school** to ensure their child receives a better education.

眼　缘

"眼缘"涉及"缘",是一个比较玄乎的概念,基本的意思应该是人与人(通常是异性,但也可能是同性)或人与物之间首次见面即为对方的气质、相貌或神韵所吸引。例如:

1. **眼缘**者,熟也。有**眼缘**的人自来熟一样的亲和亲切,话匣子打开像黄河之水天上来一样的壮观。当然,生活当中要碰到有**眼缘**的人实属难事,因为有**眼缘**的人是可遇不可求的。

2. 实际上,相亲是一种很讲**眼缘**的约会。一见钟情的秘诀在于你必须跟她是一号人。如果你是牛,她是马,你的条件再好,跟她也是风马牛不相及;无论你夸她还是踩她,都属于白费力气。

3. 这套房子,于我,有**眼缘**。第一眼看上就很喜欢,从各个角度说,它都不算一套称心如意的好房,我指在大众眼里。但我喜欢就行了,反正房子是我住。

之所以说"眼缘"玄乎,是因为用科学难以将这种感觉讲得清楚。因此,有人说这可能与基因有关,但物体难道也有基因吗?"百度百科"甚至将"眼缘"分得更为细致:"眼缘有一眼缘和终身眼缘。一眼缘指短暂的认同愉悦,而终身眼缘指那种'相看两不厌,只有敬亭山'那种百看不厌、不关岁月的、真正的眼缘。"

"眼缘"这个词用英语怎么表达呢? 或许我们很快会想到 love at first sight 这个英文成语,但仔细想想,就会发现有"眼缘"可不一定就有 love,正如当年宝黛初见时,宝玉不也说过"这位妹妹好像曾经在哪里见过"么,至于 love 不 love,那是后面的事情。

有鉴于此,我们或许可以把这个说不清道不明的"眼缘"译为 affinity／attraction／like at first sight。Attraction 和 like 这两个词大家都知道是什么,这里就看看 affinity 是否适合译"眼缘"的"缘分"。Affinity 的意思是:a strong feeling that you like and understand someone because you share the same ideas or interests,即"情投意合",这是"眼缘"产生的一个必要条件。事实上,英美人碰到这种感觉时也常常用 affinity 来表述,例如:

Love is a culmination of shared experiences and regularly being in contact with each other so you can develop a bond and grow to care for and respect that person. I do believe in **"affinity" at first sight**. Where you have a sense that you've met the person before or you have a very strong feeling of comfort or safety or attraction that compels you to want to keep interacting with them. I also believe there is lust at first sight, but it is usually fleeting.

而 attraction 和 like 也常作此用,尽管可能存在"度"上的差异。例如下面两例:

1. So my experience with kelvin may not have been love at first sight, but it was definitely **like at first sight** — that grew into more over time. And I believe God set us up for that.

2. I always have an **attraction at first sight** with someone I'm going to get involved with, but I don't think of it as "love".

3. Is there such a thing as love at first sight? Not really. This doesn't mean two people don't guess well and find they connect with someone immediately. However, their love has to get far beyond "**first sight attraction**" to last.

当然,以上译文均是"眼缘"作为名词时的英译文,而在实际的翻译实践中,译者大可不必拘泥于此,完全可以用动词 attract、like 等加上 at first sight 来译,也可以用 feel an attraction to、feel an affinity to 等短语来英译"眼缘"。

最后,需要指出的是,"眼缘"是一个特殊的汉语表达,以上译文回译为汉语时,既可作"眼缘"解,也可不作此解,但汉语"眼缘"所表达的含义却可以通过这些译文较为准确地传递到英文中去。

艳　遇

　　"艳遇"，是一个令女人心动，令男人冲动的词汇。"艳遇"，顾名思义就是一场美艳的偶遇。"艳遇"又表示某人在特定的场合遇到了他/她所中意的人，发生了一段奇怪的感情。"艳遇"之所以动人，就是因为它的短暂，就像一段美妙的插曲，虽然如昙花一现，却明艳动人；如烟花一样短暂，却璀璨无比。

　　近些年来，该词的使用十分频繁，媒体上经常报道所谓的"艳遇之都"、"艳遇指数"、"上海十大艳遇地标"、"艳遇高发地"、"艳遇情缘"等等。

　　《汉英词典》(第三版)收录了"艳遇"一词，并将其标注为动词，翻译为 encounter with a beautiful woman。然而，我们很容易就会发现，这个译文存在不少问题。第一，"艳遇"一词确实可作为动词，但更常见的则是作为名词，如"邂逅一场艳遇"、"在这样一个繁华如锦的城市，说不定就会有一场艳遇"等。第二，"艳遇"可不一定是男人的专利，在这样一个"食色性也"的年代，女性们也不甘寂寞，渴望和寻求"艳遇"，例如，"单身女十一出游艳遇全攻略"、"也有女人来丽江，就是为了寻找艳遇，于是遇上花心的男人，被他们泡上一回！也不知道到底是谁泡谁了？其实女人和男人一样的需要这些！"所以把"艳遇"翻译为 encounter with a woman 是不合适的。第三，谁也没有规定，"艳遇"的对象必须是"美女"，"艳遇"难道不能发生在"帅哥"身上？发生在相貌普通的男女之间吗？所以译文中的 beautiful 一词，纯属多余。

那么,"艳遇"一词该如何翻译呢? 答案是 romantic encounter。这个译文既揭示了"艳遇"的内涵,又避免了"性别歧视"。请看下面 romantic encounter 的用法实例:

1. As many as 38 per cent of Londoners have had a fling or a **romantic encounter** with a non-English speaking person while on holiday.

2. Kevin struggles with his sexual identity, yearning for a **romantic encounter** with a handsome boy at school.

3. Psychologists at the University of Nottingham in the U. K. asked students to imagine a **romantic encounter** with an attractive member of the opposite sex or a casual conversation with someone older.

4. Now he must learn how to cope with the unfamiliar world of grown ups, including getting a job and having his first **romantic encounter** with a woman.

5. Looking for that perfect secluded spot for a **romantic encounter** with the one you love? How about a private dinner or lunch cruise on Lady Bird Lake.

以上是"艳遇"作为名词的译法,当然,"艳遇"作为动词时,也可以用 romantic encounter 来译,无非是在前面加上动词 have 等而已。当然,英译动词"艳遇"时,也可以用 encounter romance。例如:

1. He had always lived a very regular life, enlivened only by philosophical debate; now, at the height of his fame, he **encountered romance**.

2. At Kirkcaldy, where he was teaching, he **encountered romance** in the person of Margaret Gordon, a pupil of much higher social standing than his own.

3. About this time the handsome six-footer of fine physique **encountered romance** and lost his heart to a highland lass, Bandara Menike of Harispattuwa whom he married in 1847.

蚁　族

2010 年 1 月 23 日，对外经贸大学副教授、"大学毕业生低收入聚居群体"调研课题主持人廉思所撰写的《蚁族》一书被国内 30 余家媒体评为"2009 华语传媒年度图书"。此前的 19 日，"蚁族"刚刚入选国内语言文字专家评选出的"2009 年十大流行语"。1 月 12 日，"蚁族"现象当选凤凰网推选出的影响时代的 2009 年度十大沸点事件。

2009 年 9 月，在总结了大学毕业生低收入聚居群体与蚂蚁的三个共同点（高智商、弱小、群居）后，廉思新造了"蚁族"这个崭新的汉语单词。短短 3 个月，这个沉重、形象而饱含感情色彩的词汇，一跃成为年度十大热词。一个庞大的、难以统计的城市沉默群体，由此浮出水面——他们远低于城市普通人群的月收入、窘迫的生存环境、无处安放的青春，让无数父母揪心不已。

根据廉思的定义，所谓"蚁族"，是指"大学毕业生低收入聚居群体"。这些受过高等教育，却从事着保险推销、电子器材销售、广告营销、餐饮服务等临时性工作的大学毕业生们，主要居住在城乡接合部或近郊农村；绝大多数没有"三险"和劳动合同；月均收入低于 2000 元；年龄集中在 22 岁至 29 岁之间。他们中有九成人是童年时曾被称为家中"小太阳"、"小皇帝"的"80 后"。目前，"蚁族"被认为是继三大弱势群体（农民、农民工、下岗职工）之后的第四大弱势群体，目前隐约已与"啃老族"和"月光族"在 80 后中形成三"族"鼎立之势。

"蚁族"一词出现后，也迅速引起了国外媒体的关注，请看下列例证：

China's "ant tribe" poses policy challenge for Beijing

They sleep in boxy rooms crammed into dingy low-rises and spend hours commuting to work on crowded buses as part of a trend of poorer white-collar workers being forced to the fringes of China's wealthiest cities.

Some say these struggling college graduates who swarm out of their cramped accommodations and head to work in the urban sprawl each morning are reminiscent of worker insects in a colony. Not surprisingly, they are often referred to as China's **ant tribe**.

Reuters, 2010 - 02 - 18

China's growing postgrad "ant tribes"

A recent Chinese university graduate embraces the **ant tribe** lifestyle.

If you are a Chinese university graduate born in the 1980s, working an unstable job that pays less than RMB 2,000 per month, living in a shared RMB 350 apartment and spending over two hours a day travelling to and from work, then you're officially an "ant". Welcome to the **ant tribe**.

"**Ant Tribe**," a recently published anthropology book that's making waves, describes China's post - 80s generation: university graduates from rural China who dream of a better life in big cities but struggle with low-paying jobs and poor living standards.

CNN, 2009 - 11 - 27

China's Ant Tribe: millions of unemployed college grads

Despite China's fast-growing economy, many Chinese college grads are struggling to find jobs or scraping by on meager salaries. Beijing worries that this new group — the "**Ant Tribe**" — could pose a threat to political stability.

The Christian Science Monitor, 2009 - 12 - 21

从上面的报道我们看出，"蚁族"一词通常被外媒译为 ant tribe，这是一个地地道道的直译,但该译却完全符合"蚁族"一词创造者廉思的初衷,因为在《蚁族》一书中,作者就是在对比了蚂蚁和处于这一阶层的年轻人的相似点后才提出"蚁族"这个概念的。作者甚至根据该群体所处地域的不同,分别冠之以**京蚁**(北京)、**沪蚁**(上海)、**江蚁**(武汉)、**秦蚁**(西安)、**穗蚁**(广州)等称呼。

异性合租

俗话说，"男女搭配，干活不累，住着有味"。异性合租，这个让老一辈人感到匪夷所思的事情，在如今的都市生活中成了一些拼客男女的新时尚。所谓"异性合租"，是指男女同租一套房子，各项成本开销 AA 制的一种租房形式。这种现象在国外非常常见，但在中国城市最近几年才开始流行。

由于城市生活成本的提高，异性合租在现代都市中将越来越多，因为这种租房方式至少可以节约租金。另外，有些人也认为这种方式可以帮助合租双方养成相互忍让、相互帮助的习惯，有利于未来与异性的正常相处。然而，不可否认的是，由于是异性之间的合租，有时也会出现一些诸如性骚扰之类的问题。尽管我们提醒女性合租者要有自我保护意识，但严格来说，这些问题不是"异性合租"这种方式所固有的，问题的产生与许多其他因素有关，不能一味赖在租房方式上面。

"异性合租"应该如何翻译呢？我们可以试译为 rent a flat／(an) apartment with a person of the opposite sex，或在语义清楚的情况下译为 share a flat／(an) apartment with someone of the opposite sex。这里需要注意的是 flat 或者 apartment 的使用，切忌译为 house 或 room。首先，国内外住房情况有别。在英美等发达国家，人们住的一般是 house，而 house 一般最少两层，带有院子、车库等配套设施，国外 flat 的数量很少，主要供那些大学刚毕业，没有经济能力买房的年轻人作为过渡之用；而在国内则主要是 flat 或 apartment，国内的 house 要不就是农村自建的大房子,要不就是城市有钱人的别墅了。异性合租者一般租用的都是 flat 或 apartment。其次,异性合租不是男女同室 share a room,这样就不叫合租,而叫同居(cohabitation)了。所以英译该词时,选词一定要谨慎。

事实上,异性合租虽然在西方由来已久,但是合租者,尤其是女性合租者,常常也感到忧心忡忡,怕择伴不当,受到伤害。下面这段摘自 *Daily Mail*（London, England）2000 年 3 月 13 日的报道就讲述了这个问题:

Quite why the balance seems so difficult to achieve today is not easy to fathom. Both sexes have freedom and choice. But it is a double-edged sword.

People may be financially independent and secure, but emotionally immature.

Young people often **share a flat with someone of the opposite sex**, who becomes a surrogate partner.

Each has a traditional role, but there is no sex. That part of their lives is usually volatile.

A FRIEND in this position nearly always chooses unsuitable men-serial womanisers or married men — so ensuring the relationship could never work.

此外,在英文报纸 *The China Today* 中也有一篇关于异性合租的文章,题为:Let's Be Lodgers! —— Urban China's New Wave of Platonic Cohabitation[1]。在这篇文章中,出现了"异性合租"在不同语境下的译文,值得我们借鉴。以下 8 个段落均摘自该文:

1. "I am a man of integrity with a university education, and have recently begun renting a fully furnished apartment in Chaoyang District. I would like to share it with a tidy, outgoing woman of a similar educational background." The average Chinese person would read this as a Lonely Hearts ad. The advertiser is, however, genuinely **seeking a housemate**,

---

[1] http://www.chinatoday.com.cn/English/e2004/e200403/p28.htm。

nothing more, **of the opposite sex.**

2. Those that strongly advocate **man / woman apartment shares** have gone so far as to come up with a slogan: "Let's be lodgers!"

3. A few years ago, a single man and woman sharing accommodation would be construed as cohabitation, in the sense of what used to be called "living in sin". Today, people looking to **share their abode with someone of the opposite gender** use the term according to its etymology, i. e. co: together + habitation: dwelling = shared dwelling, period.

4. According to research, most **mixed lodgers** are single, between the ages of 22 and 30. They are generally newly graduated, on modest incomes and consequently find a monthly rent of one or two thousand yuan beyond their means.

5. Controversy has reigned ever since **mixed gender lodging** began to catch on in big cities.

6. Other advocates of **mixed gender apartment shares** have similar views. Women commonly agree that lodging with a man brings a feeling of security, and men appreciate going back to a home with a pleasantly feminine touch. As the old Chinese saying goes: Things become easier when a man and woman pair up.

7. **Sharing an apartment with a person of the opposite sex** is not illegal, but many people oppose it.

8. When recalling how quickly the controversy in the 1930s caused by Chinese men and women using the same swimming pool died down, **men and women sharing apartments** may soon become as commonplace in China as in the West.

音乐电视

音乐电视，顾名思义，是由音乐和画面构成的。音乐配以画面，使原本只是听觉艺术的音乐，变为视觉和听觉相结合的一种新的艺术形式。音乐与画面相互融洽、相互交错、相辅相成，令人陶醉。一首成功的音乐电视作品必定是这二者有机、和谐、契合的结晶。

2003 年商务出版社出版发行的《新华新词语词典》把"音乐电视"译为了 MTV／music television。2000 年世界知识出版社出版发行了杨晓鲁先生的专著《音乐电视（MTV）编导艺术》，直接把 MTV 用在了书名之中。而在 2010 年年初出版的《汉英词典》（第三版）以及 2009 年年底出版的《汉英大词典》（第三版），均沿用了《新华新词语词典》中的译文。

音乐电视是否就是 MTV 呢？这要从 MTV 和音乐电视的起源谈起。

1981 年，美国有线电视网开办了一个新栏目 Music Television（简称 MTV），内容都是通俗歌曲。由于节目制作精巧，歌曲都是经过精选的优秀歌曲，因此观众人数直线上升，很快就达到数千万。之后，英、法、日、澳大利亚等国家的电视台也相继开始制作、播放类似节目，并为 MTV 的制作定型，即用最好的歌曲配以最精美的画面，使原本只是听觉艺术的歌曲，变为视觉和听觉相结合的一种崭新的艺术样式。随后 MTV 发展成专门的音乐电视频道。

MTV 这种音乐形式于 20 世纪 90 年代传入中国，称作"音乐电视"，这一方面是从英文的直译，另一方面可能也因为当时的视频载体只有电视一种。但不论何种原因，该词很快成为了普通老百姓口中一个时髦的词语。然而，到了 90 年代中期，有关人士认为"MTV"有侵权的嫌疑，因为这是国外电视台开办的音乐栏目/频道。同时，让这种电视的表现形式更加专业化的呼声也越来越高，加之目前视频的载体已不仅仅是电视，还可以是单独发行的影碟、手机或网络等，如果还用"音乐电视（MTV）"不仅范畴狭窄，而且有点词不达义了。

这时，MV（Music Video）应运而生，并逐渐取代了 MTV，成为"音乐电视"的代名词。北京广播学院文艺系副教授、音乐教研室主任、中国音乐家协会会员曾田力在一次访谈中就曾谈到这两个概念的区别[1]。以下是她的说法：

【崔磊】曾老师，您好！请问 MTV 与 MV 有什么区别？

【曾田力】MTV 指音乐电视台，是一个音乐频道，MV 指音乐录像带。

【绿色小精灵】能解释得再详细些吗？

【网络主持人：罗石曼】这里存在着一个概念上的误解，可以请诗翌再解释一下。

【栏目主创：施翌】最初的时候我们把 MTV（music television）理解成音乐电视，其实这样的理解是不正确的。MTV 是一个专门播放音乐电视的频道，就像我们经常看到的 Channel V 是一样的。而 MV（music video）是指音乐电视，可以说在 MTV 里我们可以看到 MV。

当然，目前的"音乐电视（MV）"与 MTV 已经大相径庭了。除了上面访谈中谈到的区别外，我们还可以进行如下区别：

MTV 重在音乐，影像不过是点缀而已，完全配合音乐而来。比如歌手推出自己的 MTV，主要是宣传歌曲。

MV 重在影像，音乐只是点缀而已，是配合影像内容的。比如你很喜欢某部影片中的一个角色，就把关于他/她的一些情节剪辑做成一段影像，再配合影像内容配上一首歌或一段音乐。还有一种 MV，也可以

---

〔1〕 田力，关于中国音乐电视的民族特色，http://www.cctv.com/tvguide/tvcomment/special/
　　　C11876/20040924/102456_3.shtml。

没有歌,它的内容不是视频剪辑,而是你自己拍摄的,可以是风景,也可以是自编自导的短剧等。这种 MV 在大学里是很流行的,还经常有比赛。

下面 Wikipedia 中的一段引文,可以帮助读者更好地理解这两个概念:

A **music video** or **song video** is a short video or film that accompanies a piece of music or song. Modern music videos are primarily made and used as a marketing device intended to promote the sale of music recordings. Although the origins of music videos date back much further, they came into prominence in the 1980s, when **MTV** based their format around the medium. Prior to the 80s, these works were described by various terms including "illustrated song", "filmed insert", "promotional (promo) film", "promotional clip" or "film clip".

综上所述,"音乐电视"的英文表达不是 MTV,而是 MV。另外,根据 Wikepedia,"音乐电视"还可以译为 song video。

本文是"也评《新华新词语词典》的英译"一文中的一部分,载
《双语词典新论》(四川人民出版社,2007),有改动

印 象 分

　　什么是"印象分"？就是通过给别人留下好的印象而得到的加分。这个词在日常生活中使用得极为广泛,例如:

　　1. 山东人才网人力资源师刘谦表示,应聘者在面试时一定要处理好一些细节问题,尽量多争取一些"印象分"。

　　2. 到底不愧是"王者之师"！中国体操队从上到下,无论是领队、教练,还是"金牌选手",个个都是亲切随和,有问必答。实力是底气,自信是前提。看着杨威、程菲等人不厌其烦地为追星族签名,笑容可掬地与"粉丝团"合影,在感动之余,相信他们的所作所为无疑为中国和中国体育得到了很好的"印象分"。

　　3. 俄罗斯花游有着自己的先天优势。队员漂亮、身材好、腿长,所以在出水水位和出水高度上非常占便宜。她们表现力强,擅长表演节奏快的节目,发挥稳定,失误少,在裁判心目中一直有很高的印象分。

　　尽管如此,现有的汉语和汉英词典均只收录了"印象",而无"印象分",而 Shanghai Daily's Blog-Buzzword & Talk Shanghai [1] 则将该词译为了 image point,并给出了如下英文解释: The popular expression is meant to be the sketchy assessment by others of a person's overall quality through contact in a short time, rather than insightful judgment after long observation. 这个解释没有问题,但这个译文却不甚妥当。首先,image

---

〔1〕 http://www.shanghaidaily.com/buzzword/default.asp? page = 7

point 为地理专业词汇,意思为"像点",并非"印象分";其次,image 往往表现的是"形象",而非"印象"。或许影响"印象分"的有"形象"的因素,但除此之外,肯定还有其他方面的因素。

其实,英文中就有"印象分"的说法,那就是 brownie / Brownie points。下面看看 Wikipedia 对该词的定义:

Brownie points in modern (21st century) usage are a hypothetical social currency, which can be accrued by doing good deeds or earning favour in the eyes of another, often one's superior.

为什么用 brownie 这个词呢?原来该词的原义为自家做的小饼干,由于小学生常常带此类小饼干或水果给老师(其实这是二十年前美国社会的刻板印象而已),故 brownie point 原义为"做讨老师喜欢的事",而现在则引申为"印象分"。当然,Wikipedia 认为 brownie points 这个词的来源不明,并给出了其他几种对该词词源的猜测。下面请看一些使用 brownie point 的例证:

1. I thought I might **get some brownie points** by helping to organize the party.

2. All that is required is a perfect blend of some chivalry and intelligence and you are all set to **gain some brownie points**.

3. You'll **earn brownie points** by addressing a Chinese national with his proper designation, instead of the common Mister or Miss.

以上这些例子不但告诉我们"印象分"应该如何翻译,而且告诉我们"得印象分"的不同译法,值得参考。

为了进一步阐明 brownie points 的确就是"印象分",下面再引一篇题为"Easy Ways to Earn Brownie Points With Your Professor"的小短文,该文章就是教学生如何在教授面前获得"印象分"。

Easy Ways to Earn Brownie Points With Your Professor

July 20th, 2010

by Laura Milligan

Whether you're one face in 300 in an introductory course at a large university, trying to boost your grade and level of participation in a small seminar class, or are trying to connect with your professor in an online course, **racking up extra brownie points** is a worthwhile endeavor. The last thing you want to do is to come across as a brown noser — you're in college now, and your professors probably have less patience for insincerity and obnoxious flattering than your high school teachers did. Plus, they have less time to deal with you, and may have a very weak impression of you already, the basis of which could be as simple as the one time you were late to class or that time you accidentally sent to them an e-mail meant for your best friend. Whatever your motives are, **earning brownie points** in college is actually very easy.

The most straightforward way you can get on your professor's good side is to do all — or at least some — of the extra work he or she recommends. Head to blackboard and do the supplemental readings, and make sure to post on the message board. You don't have to write a whole paper on the subject, but submit a question or two-sentence response to the piece, proving that you read it and cared enough about the class to discuss it. Respond to other students' threads too, to show your interest in collaborating over the material. Besides supplemental reading, show up for optional review sessions or movie showings that the professor has organized after class. Attend guest speaker events, and try to sit near your professor if other students in the class are all going together.

In class, professors love energetic participation, so try to write down one question to ask during each class. Pay attention to the lecture and discussion, though, because if your question is already addressed before you have time to ask it, you'll frustrate the professor and other students, revealing your inattention. Also make it to your professor's office to visit during his or her set hours, just to say hi or to ask how you can raise your grade in the class. This one-on-one time is crucial to boosting your professor's view of you, and can make all the difference in letters of recommendation, letting an absence slide, or giving you that extra point on an exam.

原 生 态

　　说起"原生态"这个词,很多人会联想起青年歌手阿宝那未经雕凿、浑厚雄健又婉转动人的歌声,他所采用的唱法被称为原生态唱法。事实上,原生态这个词现在的使用频率很高,除了大家所熟悉的原生态唱法,还有诸如原生态民居、原生态歌手、原生态文化、原生态食品等说法,甚至还有什么原生态户外运动、原生态旅游、原生态艺术等等的表述,不一而足。

　　那么,到底什么是原生态呢?"百度百科"对这个新生的文化名词的定义如下:没有被特殊雕琢,存在于民间原始的、散发着乡土气息的表演形态,它包含原生态唱法、原生态舞蹈、原生态歌手、原生态大写意山水画等新说法。

　　据称,"原生态"一词最早出现在对张艺谋《印象·刘三姐》的评价上。张艺谋以桂林的真山真水为舞台,让当地的农民尽情欢歌漫舞,模糊的原生态艺术表演就这样被人们所发现。杨丽萍和她的《云南印象》则把原生态表演发扬光大——云南当地人用他们日常生活中的舞蹈以原始性的风姿,挤进了电视和荧屏,和千家万户见面了。从那时起,原生态才正式发芽了。而央视"春晚"阿宝的出现,算真正使"原生态"有了正式的名分。原来被一些所谓的专家所不齿的"下里巴人"散发出了强大的魅力!纯朴的吟诵以一种朴实艺术的新形态走向了舞台,逐渐被人们所接受。而在"第十二届 CCTV 全国青年歌手电视大奖赛"中,原生态唱法又被给予了和美声、通俗、民族唱法并列的位置,真正地列入了艺术的行列。也许,这株新型的野花将成为一门艺术领域的新星,从此将走入大家的音乐,走进千家万户。

关于"原生态"一词,现版的各种单语和双语词典均未收录,但网络上关于该词的翻译的争论却颇多,有译作 original 的,也有译作 primitive 的,甚至还有些地方使用了 untutored 等词。笔者认为,这些译法都有道理,但需要注意的是,原生态这个词根据其搭配的不同,应该有不同的译法。下面一一说明:

1. 在原生态唱法、原生态音乐之类的搭配中,原生态可以译为 primitive、untutored 等词。请看下列例证:

Today, music schools have incorporated pop music into their curricula. However, singing styles, from Western opera to Chinese opera (once known as "Chinese folk"), have not changed much in the past three decades. Some new styles are emerging, such as "**primitive singing**", usually by ethnic minority groups without academic training. Some call these "real Chinese folk songs", but even as a group, they have yet to match the commercial success of Jay Chou.

"The way we were during past 30 years",

The China Daily, 2008 - 12 - 08

American Negro was chiefly imported. If in this area it is found that no single type of singing technique predominates but that there is a blend of many types, complications will arise. Also the question is still open as to how much of the freedom found in American or African Negro singing, felt to be characteristically Negro by the investigators, is general to **primitive singing** or **untutored singing**, and how much of it is a distinctly Negro cultural trait.

George Herzog, University of Chicago

2. 在原生态食品这样的搭配中可以使用 natural、organic、ecological 等词,即 natural/organic/ecological food。很明显,这里如果使用 primitive 则有点不伦不类。请看下面 Wikipedia 的相关定义:

Natural foods are often assumed to be foods that are minimally processed and do not contain any hormones, antibiotics, sweeteners, food colors, or flavorings that were not originally in the food. The terms are often misused on labels and in advertisements. The term "organic (foods)" has similar implications and has an established legal definition in many countries and an international standard.

Organic foods are foods that are produced using methods that do not involve modern synthetic inputs such as synthetic pesticides and chemical fertilizers, do not contain genetically modified organisms, and are not processed using irradiation, industrial solvents, or chemical food additives.

Organic or ecological foods are produced according to certain production standards, meaning they are grown without the use of conventional pesticides, artificial fertilizers, human waste, or sewage sludge.

3. 在原生态旅游、原生态舞蹈这样的搭配中,"原生态"一词最好译为 primitive/original ecological 或 primitive/original eco-,因为这里的"生态"是实指,而非虚指。原生态旅游应该译为 primitive/original eco-tourism,而原生态舞蹈也可以译为 primitive/original eco-dancing。例如:

It's a national sacrifice that has paid off: Costa Rica is the **original eco-tourism** success story, the home of innovations like zip-line tours through the rainforest canopy, and a world leader with 25 per cent of its land protected from development.

"Eco-tourism leaves print in Costa Rica", Canada. com

Highlights from the Maya Joy Dancers production of an **original eco-dance-play**, "Awakening Earth," performed in Pine, Arizona, in the summer of 2010.

Arizona Video Production

最后,值得注意的是,还有把原生态译为 indigenous 或 aboriginal 的,譬如把原生态旅游译为 aboriginal tourism,把原生态唱法译为 indigenous singing。其实,经过考察,我们发现这两种译法均有问题,因为这两个词均指的是"原住民的"或"当地土著民的",所以 aboriginal tourism 的意思是游览土著民的聚居地,而 indigenous singing 则是指土著或原住民的歌唱,这与我们所说的原生态旅游或原生态唱法其实风马牛不相及。

愿　景

　　"愿景"一词自 2005 年国民党主席连战造访大陆并与胡锦涛主席发表联合公报之日起，便开始逐渐流行。《现代汉语词典》(第五版)的编者们反应迅速，在词典出版前夕，争分夺秒地把该词收入了词典。更有甚者，2009 年高考天津语文作文题目就是这两个字"愿景"。当然，这可能难倒了一大批对该词仍感陌生的考生。

　　2009 年 1 月出版的吴光华先生主编的新版《汉英大词典》也不甘落后，收录了该词，并提供了其英文译文：perspective view。然而，细细考察后，我们发现这个译文并不准确。

　　那么，"愿景"应该怎么翻译呢？回答这个问题之前，让我们先考察一下该词的来源和意义，然后再探讨其英文译文。

　　"愿景"一词，过去比较少见，在《现代汉语词典》前四版中也查不到这个词汇。然而，该词在海外和我国的港、澳、台地区却使用得极为普遍。2003 年，厦门大学嘉庚学院兴办之初，校董事会从新加坡聘请了一位早年毕业于厦大的学者担任院长。他就职后就写了一篇名为《学院的战略目标和愿景》的文章，放在学院的主页。2005 年，连战、宋楚瑜访问大陆后，"愿景"一词在大陆的使用才多了起来，甚至被写进了国共两党会谈公报："共同谋求两岸关系和平稳定发展的机会，互信互助，再造和平双赢的新局面，为中华民族实现光明灿烂的愿景。"2005 年以后，"愿景"一词使用频繁，新版《现代汉语词典》遂将"愿景"一词收入，释义为"所向往的前景"。

　　"愿景"与"愿望"是近义词,在某些语境中甚至有替代"愿望"的趋势。该词与其他词语的组合与"愿望"也类似,如"个人愿景"、"共同愿景"、"美好愿景"等。"愿景"与"愿望"的不同之处就是"愿景"在某些语言环境中意思的侧重点是前景、未来景象。如"公司愿景"、"企业愿景"、"学校愿景"等,强调公司、企业、学校发展的战略方向和前景,而"愿望"则没有这层意思,不能作此用。

　　现在,让我们看看 perspective view 在英文中是什么意思。*Business Dictionary* 对该词如此定义:Drawing that shows the exterior view of an object or an assembly, without any parts removed. With cutaway (sectional) views it shows parts normally hidden from the observer. Also called perspective drawing. 根据这个定义,我们可以知道,所谓的 perspective view 其实是"透视图"的意思,和"愿景"并无丝毫关联。例如下面两个例子中的 perspective view 均为"透视图"的意思:

　　Try to find a location that gives you the **perspective view** of the scene that you like.

　　This is a **perspective view** of the design for a cast iron bridge, consisting of a single arch 600 feet in span and calculated to supply the place of the present London Bridge.

　　而所谓的"愿景",其实来源于英文的 vision 一词,所以理所当然应该回译为 vision。譬如"企业愿景"可以译为 corporate vision,"公司愿景"可译为 company vision,"愿景描述"可译为 vision statement,"品牌愿景"可译为 brand vision,"可行愿景"可译为 viable vision,"使命和愿景"可译为 Vision and Mission 等等。

月 光 族

　　现代城市生活的成本愈来愈高,而另一方面,不少年轻人也刻意追求一种超前消费的生活方式,这样就产生了所谓的"月光族"。该词指那些将每月收入都用光的一族人。同时,也用来形容赚钱不多,每月收入仅可以维持本月基本开销的一类人。"月光族"是相对于努力攒点钱的储蓄族而言的。他们的口号:挣多少花多少。

　　一般认为,"月光族"是一个中性词,没有绝对的褒贬义之分。"月光"们通常有知识、有头脑、有能力,花钱不仅表达对物质生活的狂爱,更是他们赚钱的动力。老一辈信奉"会赚不如会省",对他们的行为痛心疾首;而他们的格言是"能花才更能赚",花光用光自得其乐。当然,现实生活中还有那些无奈而成为"月光"的人,譬如在房价高企、物价飙升的大城市,很多白领,尽管不愿"月光",也被迫"月光"。他们甚至调侃道:"工资就像大姨妈,一个月来一次,一周就没了!"

　　现实中的"月光族"一般都是年轻一代,往往是参加工作不久,积蓄不多。他们喜欢追逐新潮,扮靓买靓衫,只要吃得开心,穿得漂亮。想买就买,根本不在乎钱财。然而,令人心酸的是,由于近两年物价狂涨,很多本应依靠退休金安度晚年的退休老人们,也被迫成为"月光族"的一员。例如,搜狐网 2010 年 9 月 15 日就登载了题为"物价攀升,受苦的何止'退休族'"的报道,该报道开篇有云:

　　当提到"月光族"时,人们往往与小年轻联系到一起,然而,在不断攀升的物价指数背后,"月光族"这个称号已经不单是年轻一代独享的专利了,一群年龄在 55—65 岁之间的企业退休族们也不得不无奈地分享着这一称号。

关于"月光族"的英译,除了《辞书研究》2006 年第 2 期"新词新义荟萃"栏目中纯粹为解释的英译 young people relying on their parents 外,目前常见的还有 moonlite 和 moonlight clan 两种。譬如,前者可见于"互动百科",甚至有人认为:This concocted Chinese term is the moniker(绰号) for people who always spend all their salaries or earnings before the end of the month. The first Chinese character in the term means "month" or "moon," and the second "leaving nothing behind" or "light."

然而,如果我们调查一下这个译文,就会发现两个问题:第一,该译法来历不明,不知道为什么要把 light 改写为 lite;第二,英文中确实存在 moonlite 这个词,但却不是"月光族"的意思,而是 Moon Lightweight Interior and Telecoms Experiment(MoonLITE)的缩写,意思是:a proposed British space mission to explore the Moon and develop techniques for future space exploration(英国的一项太空探测工程)。所以,用 moonlite 来译"月光族"并不恰当。

用 moonlight clan 来译"月光族"使用的频率很高,如商务印书馆出版发行的《汉语世界》2006 年第 1 期中就用了该译文;另外,*Shanghai Star* 2005 年 5 月 26 日也刊登了题为"China's 'Moonlight Clan' Indulges in Shopping Spree"的报道。当然,该译文也出现在诸如 *The China Daily*、*The People's Daily Online* 等国内的英文媒体之中。此外,专收一般词典没有收录的英语俚语、行话及新词的 *The Double-Tongued Dictionary* 也将 moonlight clan 一词收录入典,并采用了下面的引语:

She and her overspending friends are creating a phenomenon now being discussed widely in the Chinese media. They have been dubbed "fu weng" (a coined Chinese word for "people in debt", pronounced as the Chinese word for a person of wealth), or **"the moonlight clan"** (**a Chinese pun meaning people who spend all their money by the end of each month**).

至此,"月光族"译为 moonlight clan 似乎已成定局。这样翻译的原因也似乎显而易见："月光族"中的"月光"是一个双关语(pun)，译者采用异化的方式，旨在保留原词的形象。双关语本就难译，有些甚至不可译，译者如此处理，也可以理解。

然而，该译文也有一些内在的不足。其一，汉语中的"月光族"既可指一群人，也可指单个人，譬如我们经常听到"我是月光族"这样的说法，因此，从这个意义上而言，moonlight clan 只注重了作为"一群人"的"月光族"，而忽略了作为"个体"的"月光族"。在翻译实践中我们将不得不进行增补，采用"I'm a member of the moonlight clan."这样的表述。其二，英文中的 clan 一词为"宗族"、"氏族"的意思，即"同姓家族(a large group of families that often share the same name)"，所以，"月光族"的"族"译为 clan，似乎并不合适，而用 group 似乎才能更好地表达原词的意义。其三，moonlight clan 这个表述在英文中容易引起误解，因为，moonlight 在英文中不但是一个名词，指"月亮的光线"，同时也是一个动词，非常形象地指代那些"乘着月光，在外面赚外快的人(to have a second job in addition to your main job, especially without the knowledge of the government tax department)"。当该词与 clan 连用时，读者的第一印象就是指那些兼职赚外快的人。

这样看来，moonlight clan 翻译"月光族"只能算是差强人意。但考虑到这么多的媒体和词典已收录该译法以及约定俗成的力量，我们权且承认"月光族"一词可以如此来译，但如果可以稍做改动，将译文变为 moonlight group，或许更为理想。

另外，笔者认为，在翻译实践中，为了理解的方便，我们也可把"月光族"采用归化的方法译为"spend-all group"或"all-salary spender"及"spend-all"。"spend-all group"明显是指这个族群，而"all-salary spender"及"spend-all"则指这个族群中的个体。先看"all-salary spender"，这个译法是基于英文中 big spender、top spender 这样的说法之上的，属于生造词(coinage)，但这个生造词似乎更为简洁、易懂，而且英文中的 salary 一词也通常指"月工资"，而"all"则是"completely"的意思。Spend-all 则是地道的英文词汇，虽然缺少了"月"这个意象，但在特定的语境中翻译作为个体的"月光族"则更为地道，请看下列原汁原味的英文表述：

I am a **spend-all** so I asked my boss to pay me some money before the end of the month.

So, again, you and I are both lawyer's clerks, but we wear our rue with a difference, for you are a save-all while I am **a spend-all**.

月　嫂

随着 2010 年的到来，80 后这个群体也到了一个而立之年的关口。他们中的一部分已结婚生子，为人父母。缺乏育婴经验的他们，给"月嫂"市场带来了一片繁荣。天津市月嫂市场有八成左右的雇主都是 80 后，有职业证书的专职月嫂更是到了"一嫂难求"的境况。

"月"是"月子"的简称。一般来说，妇女生下孩子后往往需要调养一个半月左右的时间，这段时间通常被称为"月子"。而"月嫂"就是指在产妇的月子期间，来到家里照顾产妇和孩子的女性服务人员。

月嫂是专业护理产妇与新生儿的一种新兴职业。相对于普通保姆，"月嫂"属于高级家政人员，她们每月拿着比普通保姆多几倍的薪金，肩负一个新生命与一位母亲是否安全健康的重任，有的还要料理一个家庭的生活起居。通常情况下，"月嫂"的工作集保姆、护士、厨师、保育员的工作性质于一身，对婴幼儿进行系统专业的育儿早期教育、以及科学喂养使其可以健康成长的幼儿教育人才，这大大提升了"月嫂"的服务层面，使其最终成为新兴服务行业中的高级蓝领。

"月嫂"一词如何译为英文呢？先看《汉英词典》（第三版）中的译文：maid attending the confinement; women employed to look after a lying-in woman and her baby。很明显，这两个译文均不可用。原因如下：第一，该译文与其说是翻译，不如说是解释，而解释性的译文在很多语境下无法直接使用；第二，maid 一词通常指"未婚少女"或"一个大家庭中的女仆（female servant in a large house）"，这两个义项与我们通常所说的

"月嫂"并不契合;第三,第二个译文似乎还有逻辑表述上的问题,最好使用单数 woman,而非 women,这不仅和第一个译文中的单数 maid 相照应,而且与后面的 a lying-in woman 逻辑上相一致。

其实,月嫂一词大致有以下 3 种译法可供参考:

1. confinement nurse

2. monthy nurse

3. maternity matron

首先看 confinement nurse / lady。Nurse 一词在英文中本来就有"保育员"的意思,而 confinement 则为"产期",二者合为一体,即可表示"月子期间照顾婴儿或产妇"的意思。譬如,在英文中就有 confinement nurse service 的表达。而下面这段话[1]更是说明了该译文的合法性。

CONFINEMENT NURSE is a visiting nurse who will come live with you the first month. The purpose of the nurse is to teach new parents how to take care of their newborn and to help the new mother. The nurse lives in a spare bedroom. They extract mother's milk during the day and the baby sleeps with nurse, perhaps allowing the mother to get a good night's rest. The term comes from the idea that a newborn mother and baby are confined to the house for the first month.

再看 monthly nurse。这个表述看似直白,其实也是地道的英语。譬如在一段英国人写的文字中,就有如下的表达:

I discovered that my Great Grandmother was a **monthly nurse**. Her job was to attend women during the first month after childbirth, aka '**Confinement Nurse**'. Sometimes also listed as Subsidiary Medical Services (S. M. S.).

上面这段话不但说明了 monthly nurse 用来表述"月嫂"这一概念的正确性,而且还佐证了 confinement nurse 这个译文的合法性。

最后再看看 maternity matron 这个译文。如果说 monthly nurse 和 confinement nurse 只是译出了"月嫂"的含义的话,那么,maternity matron

---

〔1〕 参见:http://www. hps. com/ ~ tpg/singapore/index. php? file = vol18

则不但"意似"而且"形似",体现出了"嫂"的含义,因为 matron 一词在英文中的意思即是 an older married woman(年龄较大的已婚女性),这与国内大部分月嫂的状况也较为相近:已婚、已育,因而具有照顾婴儿和产妇的经验。此外,maternity matron 这种说法也多次出现在诸如 *Shanghai Daily* 这样的国内著名英文报刊以及诸如 *shanghaiist*(www. shanghaiist. com)这样在上海最富盛名的英文博客之中,例如:

This group of women in Guangxi Province's Nanning have just completed their state-sponsored training and received their certification as trained **maternity matrons**, who according to our favorite English-Chinese dictionary, are maids — usually married women who already have their own kids — that are hired to take care of mothers and their newborns ("Chinese women traditionally are confined indoors for a month after delivering a baby on the grounds that they are particularly susceptible to various gynecological diseases in this period."). Apparently, even the recruiting companies have all come waiting like vultures at the certification ceremony, and are paying as much as RMB2,800 per month for a **mid-level maternity matron** and RMB4,800 for a **senior-level maternity matron**. That's more than some white collar workers get!

Jobs to Die for in China[2]

---

〔2〕参见:http://shanghaiist. com/2007/08/28/jobs_to_die_for. php。

宅 男

　　最近几年,"宅男宅女"是继抗压能力较低的"草莓族"及储蓄为零的"月光族"之后,又一个被网络热炒的现代族群。通俗地讲,所谓的"宅男"和"宅女",就是指那一类整天大门不出二门不迈类型的人。这一解释从字面上理解也是合理的,因为"宅"即是家的意思。在互联网迅猛发展的今天,随之而来的是依靠网络生存的这一类人,他们的普遍特征就是不喜外出,讨厌应酬,向往自由与无拘无束。

　　新近出版的吴光华教授主编的《汉英大词典》(第三版)中已经收录了该词,并给出了其英文对应词:宅男:otaku、宅女:otaku girl。经过细致的调研,笔者认为,这两个译文均不可取。下面就这两个词的英译进行论述:

第一,Otaku 与"宅男"、"宅女"的区别

1. 所指不同

　　Otaku 是一个日语词,中文翻成"御宅族",是指迷恋某种品牌、商品,对其他事物漠不关心的人,这与汉语中的"宅男"在意义上并不对等。正如 *The China Daily* "翻译点津"栏目中所言:"在日语中的确有otaku 这个词,而且与'宅'字有关,不过不是'宅男',而是'御宅'(おたく)。'御宅'在日语中有几种含义,本来是第二人称单数对对方的尊称,相当于'您'或是'府上'的意思,后来被日本年轻人转意用来指沉迷于某种兴趣爱好中而不可自拔的个人或群体,比如沉溺于动漫、电玩游戏,整天处于幻想世界中,欠缺正常社交生活经验的一族就是'御宅'。

在日本，otaku 成为形容"动漫迷"的专有名词，衍生的名词还包括"同人志"，就是御宅族，简单说是对某样事物有狂热追求的人，一般指对动漫的狂热。

汉语中的"宅男"、"宅女"与日本的 otaku 是不同的。中国的"宅男"、"宅女"并不是指那些迷恋动漫，而不愿出门，"宅"在家里的人。群邑智库（GroupM Knowledge Center）2008 年 6 月份发布了一份涵盖了当前中国 30 个城市中人群的，题为"聚焦'宅世代'——中国宅男宅女研究报告"的报告[1]，报告指出，中国的宅男之女之所以"宅"在家中，主要原因在于：

（1）喜欢呆在家里，享受独处、安静的时光；

（2）与外出相比，家中更有吸引力，因为在外开销大，不愿意经常出去玩，而且现代的信息科技使他们在家也能得到放松或精神上的满足；

（3）独生子女们已经习惯了独处的生活方式，习惯于安静地自娱自乐。独处的生活方式造就了他们更为自我的性格，且不习惯于和外人交流。

（4）缓解工作和社会压力。有不少社会学专家也曾对"宅人"进行过研究，在专家们看来，宅人们"宅"的最主要原因是生存压力太大。所以，"下班之后足不出户"对他们而言是一种缓解压力、恢复体力的最好方式。

这样看来，otaku 与国内的"宅男"、"宅女"完全不同，尽管当初创造这两个汉语词汇的人可能是从日本的 otaku 一族中得到了灵感。

2. 语体色彩不同

Otaku 在日本人的心目中其实是一个贬义词。笔者最近就 otaku 一词咨询了自己所任教的国际班里一位日本籍的学生，她的第一反应就是该词指那些酷爱动漫，而不愿出门的年轻人。并说一般日本人对 otaku 的生活态度和方式都不赞成。这个观点在 *Urban Dictionary* 中也可找到证据。下面是摘自该词典中关于 otaku 的一些描述：

Otaku is extremely negative in meaning as it is used to refer to

---

〔1〕http://www.groupmchina.com/images/upload/file/zhaishidai.pdf

someone who stays at home all the time and doesn't have a life (no social life, no love life, etc.)

Usually an otaku person has nothing better to do with their life, so they pass the time by watching anime, playing videogames, and surfing the Internet (otaku is also used to refer to a nerd/hacker/programmer).

Generally speaking, calling someone an otaku in Japan is an insult, implying that their social skills have atrophied or never even developed, due to their manic involvement in their chosen fandom.

由此可见,在日语中,otaku 完全是个贬义词。在日本,如果某个人被称为 otaku,这个人会认为这是对自己的一个侮辱(insult)。

而在汉语中,"宅"这个词并不含有贬义色彩,因此,与"宅"相关的"宅男"、"宅女"在一般意义上也不是贬义词。事实上,青年人选择"宅男"、"宅女"的生活不啻于选择一种节约生活成本的生活方式。例如:

(1)的确,"宅"在家中过春节,省了诸多交通、送礼开支,省去了挤车的一身臭汗,省下了难得的假期时光。对于平日辛劳奔波的"上班族"而言,这些好处都是实实在在的。

"乌鲁木齐:'上班族'流行'宅'在家里过春节",

新华网,2010 年 2 月 16 日

(2)来厦创业的台胞汪杰说,厦门"宅男宅女们"越来越多,"宅经济"已然成为流行趋势,他自主开发的"商圈宅配购"的网络宅配送系统,就是想顺应当下"宅经济"的呼唤。

"社区商家瞄上宅男宅女,创新商业模式",

《厦门商报》,2009 年 2 月 26 日

第二,英美人对 otaku 一词的看法

"宅男"、"宅女"的翻译是否能用日语词 otaku 来翻译,还得看看英美人对 otaku 一词的看法,看看他们是否知道和认可这个词。关于这个问题,*Urban Dictionary* 中恰好有所提及。请看下面该词典中的几段描述:

In American culture, "Otaku" means "One who is obsessed with Japanese culture, entertainment, etc."

In the Western culture, people confuse otaku to be something positive like "Guru". If you think about it, it's not really good to be called a guru if it means you are a total loser who can't socialize with other people except through the Internet.

This is a high-context word, in the American dialect, given the type of people using the word and the context of the discussion, this OTAKU could mean expert or geek, complemetary or derogatory.

从上面的引述可以发现,英美人常把 otaku 一词误解为"专家"或者"怪人",这与汉语中的"宅男"、"宅女"也没有任何共通之处。此外,当笔者把该词让一个美国朋友看后,他的回答为:Personally, I'm surprised to see people suggesting 'otaku' and 'hikikomori' as English words. I've never heard those words used in English, only in Japanese. We might have suitable words already in our vocabulary. For example, a recluse is anyone who doesn't go out, avoids social situations, that type of thing. If any native English speaker can tell me that otaku is in common use in our language, please dispel my ignorance. 这就说明,对英语为母语的人而言, otaku(以及提到的另外一个日语词 hikikomori)在英语中即使存在,也极不常用。这与"宅男"、"宅女"在汉语中遍地开花,路人皆知的状况构成了较大的反差。

第三,《汉英大词典》(第三版)英译的谬误

事实上,单从翻译学的观点来分析,otaku 这个译文也经不起推敲。Otaku 是一个地地道道的日语单词,如何能直接用作英文单词,来表达汉语中的一个文化局限词呢? 这正如我们不能把某个汉字直接用在英语中当作英语单词一样。当然,汉语中的一些表形意味强烈的词则除外,如"工"、"大"等词。

另外,"宅女"用 otaku girl 来翻译更是匪夷所思。首先,据笔者上面提到的日本籍学生所言,在日语中不管是男性还是女性的"宅人"都叫做 otaku,根本没有 otaku girl 的说法。事实上,当我们站在日本人的角度来看待 otaku girl 这个日语加英语构成的译文时,可能会感到不伦不类,这就像我们中国人开玩笑可以把"宅男"译为"宅 man",把"宅女"译

为"宅 woman"一样。当然,除了为了搞笑之外,这种"译文"是没有任何意义的。

最后,需要指出的是,《汉英大词典》(第三版)把"宅女"译为 otaku girl 也不符合国人对"宅女"的理解,因为在汉语语境中,"宅女"不仅指未婚的 girls,也可以指迫于生活压力而不愿外出消费的已婚女子。例如:

过年不出门? 越来越多的年轻人选择"宅居"在家,通过网络拜年祝福、微博交流、视频唠嗑等方式过大年,这种与中国传统春节过年风俗截然不同的方式,受到了年轻人的大力追捧,甚至一些小夫妻成了"**双宅夫妻**"——两人除了吃饭睡觉看电视打游戏,春节就没干别的了。由此,也引发观念上的一场碰撞:春节也玩"宅",是不是对传统节日的"忘本"?

"年轻人追捧'宅居'在家里过年",

《现代快报》,2010 年 2 月 16 日

第四,"宅男"、"宅女"的英译

从上面的讨论我们可以得出以下结论:首先,《汉英大词典》(第三版)中关于"宅男"、"宅女"的英译是不妥当的;其次,日语中的 otaku 和汉语中的"宅人"的所指并不相同;第三,otaku 一词在英语中并不流行,英美人对其往往产生误解。那么,"宅男"、"宅女"到底应该如何翻译呢?

事实情况是,中国有"宅男"、"宅女",英美国家也有。我们只需要找出英美国家人对自己国家"宅男"、"宅女"的称呼即可解决汉语中"宅男"、"宅女"的英译。经过调查,我们发现,在英语中,如果形容一个人很"宅",英美人通常用形容词 indoorsy 来表达,而英美人通常把自己国家的"宅男"用 indoorsman 或 indoorsy person 来称呼。例如,在美剧 *Big Bang Theory* 中就有下列表述:

Jimmy is a very **indoorsy person** because he hates camping.

"What better than playing games and enjoying the luxury of your house?" says an **indoorsman.**

"Sean, an avid **indoorsman**, is highly regarded for his skill at video games and computer programming."

另外，请看 *Urban Dictionary* 对 indoorsman 的定义：a person who spends considerable time in indoor pursuits, such as computing, sleeping and watching sports on television. 这一定义与我们对"宅男"的理解基本相符。

依此类推，"宅女"则应该译为 indoorswoman。

事实上，indoorsman 这个词在英语中已经非常热门流行，有些商家甚至将该词配上有趣的漫画，印制为 T 恤等商品。例如，有一款印着 Avid Indoorsman 字样的 T 恤，搭配的漫画是一个坐在电视机前的沙发上，拿着遥控器、戴着眼睛、身材略胖的秃头男，不知身为"宅男"一族的男士们收到这样的一份礼物，会不会感到哭笑不得？此外，在热门影音分享网站 You Tube 上，有些"宅男"甚至不惜牺牲形象现身说法，在家自拍各式"跟伟大宅男一起"（With the Great Indoorsman）系列爆笑短片，引发热烈回响。其中一个短片片名为 The Great Indoorsman Goes Outdoors，片中的"伟大宅男"打扮成一身登山造型，背着背包在自己家里的楼梯上从一楼辛苦地爬上二楼。

原载《东方翻译》2011 年第 2 期

植入式广告

　　虎年春晚已圆满落幕,亿万观众议论最多、最不满意的恐怕就是春晚节目中过多的"植入式广告"了。而在加入植入式广告的小品中,又以赵本山的小品《捐助》最为赤裸、直白。一时间,"植入式广告"成了街头巷尾的话题,本来就对广告相当排斥的亿万观众突然发现植入式广告更令大家感到不适,但又不得不极其被动地接受。事实上,植入式广告本身并没有什么过错,而且在广告行业还算得上一个崭新的发明创造,但在实践中,如果广告"植入"不恰当、不协调,往往会产生适得其反的效果。

　　什么是植入式广告呢? 事实上,植入式广告属于隐性广告(recessive advertisement),也是软广告(blind advertising)的重要分支之一。其大量运用始于 20 世纪 80 年代,这种广告形式把产品或品牌(包括其代表性的视觉符号),甚至服务内容策略性地融入到电影、电视剧或电视节目的内容中,通过场景的呈现,让观众留下对产品及品牌的深刻印象,继而达到营销的目的。目前,植入式广告不仅运用于电影、电视,而且被"植入"各种媒介,包括报纸、杂志、网络游戏、手机短信、文学作品以及各类活动平台中。

　　既然植入式广告如此流行,那就有必要了解其确切的英语表达方式。目前我们见到的该词的译文有: implantation advertising、implantable advertisement、commercial insert、product placement 和 embedded marketing。那么,究竟那些译文才是正确的呢? 下面我们一一进行剖析:

首先，implantation advertising 和 implantable advertisement 这两个译文显然没有从植入式广告的含义出发，而是把"植入"和"广告"的英文简单地进行了相加，是纯粹的中式英语。这从对该译文的 *Google* 搜索结果中也可以证明，搜索显示，第一种译文有 55 条，而第二种译文仅有 13 条，且绝大多数是中国的网站。考虑到植入式广告并非中国本土的产物，而是来源于西方，因此，这两种译法肯定不是"植入式广告"的正确表达方式。

其次，commercial insert 的意思是"插播广告"，即打断正常电视或电台节目的播放而插入，强迫观众观看或收听的广告（A commercial insert is a form of advertisement presented between major radio or television programs.），与"植入式广告"明显是两码事，并非其正确译法。

接下来再看一下 product placement 和 embedded marketing。Wikipedia 对该词表述如下：**Product placement**, or **embedded marketing**, is a form of advertisement, where branded goods or services are placed in a context usually devoid of ads, such as movies, the story line of television shows, or news programs. The product placement is often not disclosed at the time that the good or service is featured.

对比上面"植入式广告"的汉语释义，我们不难看出，product placement 和 embedded marketing（嵌入式营销）正是我们所讨论的"植入式广告"。

值得一提的是，目前植入式广告又衍生出了其他形式，如直接将广告而非产品本身放置到情节之中（advertisement placement）和为综艺节目提供奖品赞助（promotional consideration）等等。看来，观众要逃离植入式广告并非易事，我们只能期望这些广告能"植入"地更为艺术，更为巧妙，不要给观众造成不适的感觉。

钟 点 房

　　"钟点房",顾名思义就是按"钟点",一般是小时,收取费用的宾馆的房间。"钟点房"最初是为那些因办事时间未到,需要找一个舒适的地方休息片刻的客人所准备的,但现在却出现了宾馆为高考生所准备的"高考钟点房",不良商人为大学情侣所推出的"校园钟点房"、"情侣钟点房"等等,后者严重影响了学校的教学秩序和社会风气,也增加了校园不安全因素,譬如,近几年来,全国各地已相继发生了数起大学生在钟点房内被杀被抢的案件。

　　"钟点房"一词尚未见于《现代汉语词典》(第五版)及诸汉英词典。笔者见到的译文主要有 love hotel、hour room、hourly room、clock room。然而,这些译文中除了 hourly room 之外,其他都有问题。Love hotel 是源于日语的一个词,指那些专门为情侣的性生活提供短暂场所的宾馆(A love hotel(ラブホテル)is a type of short-stay hotel found in Japan operated primarily for the purpose of allowing couples privacy to have sexual intercourse.),一般设施齐全,装修华丽而暧昧。这不但与一般意义上的"钟点房"不同,也与"校园钟点房"和"情侣钟点房"在外延和内涵上不同。Hour room 则是一个典型的汉语式英语,我们常见到的是24-hour room service,但这不是"钟点房",而是"24 小时客房服务"。而clock room 在英文中只有一个意思:放有 clock 的 room,所以估计该词用来翻译"钟点房"是纯粹的误译,译者可能把 cloak room 误认为了 clock room,而前者的意思则为"衣帽间"。

那么,"钟点房"如何翻译呢? 答案有二:

第一,hourly room。下面是美国纽约 Brooklyn 的一家 hotel 为其"钟点房"所发布的广告,可以证明用 hourly room 来译"钟点房"是完全正确的:

Hourly room rates:

- $25／hour, $60 block of three hours

Room includes equipment for daily use, and Wi-Fi as well.

Close to many rock clubs and bars.

Make your life and work easy. Rent this space and enjoy all the great scene Brooklyn has to offer!

Go to www. roughmagicstudios. com for availability.

第二,hourly rate hotel room。英文中有一种非常流行的提供"钟点房"的"钟点宾馆",叫 hourly rate hotel,所以"钟点房"便可以译为 hourly rate hotel room。当然,这里的 hotel 有时也可省略不译。Rate 在英文中有费用的意思,如宾馆的房价就是 room rates,按小时付的房钱就是 hourly rates。下面这篇短文题为"The Big Apple Sleeps, or Not, in Short Stay Lodging"是摘自 *New York Magazine* 中的两段话,讲述什么是 hourly rate hotel 以及纽约最著名的三家 hourly rate hotels: Liberty Hotel、Kew Motor Inn、Airway Inn。

As the "city that never sleeps", it's not surprising that New York City is a place that has plenty of **hourly rate hotels**.

Hourly rate hotels are places where people go for various reasons, some as innocent as a place to stay during a layover between flights, and other reasons that are, well, not so innocent. With three major airports nearby, many do actually need a place to stay for a few hours to catch a nap.

了解了"钟点房"的英译后,我们还可以推导出不少与"钟点"相关的其他新词的英译。如"钟点工"则可译为 hourly worker,如 Wikipedia 对该词的定义为:An hourly worker or hourly employee is an employee paid an hourly wage for their services, as opposed to a fixed salary;"钟点

票"（由入口站发出的普通感应币，停车费由停车时间决定，持此币在收款台前付款，之后在出站处收回此币）可译为 hourly ticket；"钟点费"可根据不同语境译为 hourly rate、hourly billing、hourly pay；而"钟点课程"（指按小时收费的课程）则可译为 hourly classes。

撞　衫

　　所谓"撞衫",通常是指两个明星在出席同一场合时穿了套相同或者非常相似的衣服。由于明星们都是讲究个性的,都希望自己能够在众人的眼光中显得与众不同,所以"撞衫"会让明星们显得非常尴尬,特别是当发现自己穿该套衣服居然没有对方好看时,那更会有一种无地自容的感觉。然而,尽管该词主要用于明星,但在实际应用中,显然已不局限于明星,可以泛指在同一场合中着装相同或相似的人。例如,新加坡《联合晚报》2010年5月23日题为"希拉莉游中国馆与　海宝'撞衫'"的报道就说:"参观期间,身穿蓝色外套的希拉莉邂逅蓝色的世博吉祥物"海宝"人偶时很高兴,主动合影留念,一点也不介意跟海宝'撞衫'"。

　　"撞衫"可以根据其意义简单翻译为 wear an identical / the same clothes / dress with sb. at a public occasion,尽管这个译文明显显得平淡,未能把汉语中"撞"字所体现的"动态美"表现出来。当然,在具体的语境中,该译文也可以简单进行调整,如"At the award-giving party, the two actresses happened to be dressed in the same style and color."就可以翻译为"在颁奖晚会上,这两位女演员撞衫了。"

　　此外,《中国日报》中国"特色词汇"栏目中采用了 clothing clashing 的译法,并给出了下面的解释:

This Chinese term means two or more people appear in a gathering or a public place accidentally wearing identical clothing. So, all fashion-minded ladies would try their very best to avoid zhuangshan or "**clothing**

clashing. " For them, **clothing clashing** is a disaster or an embarrassment, to say the least.

受此影响,目前很多地方都将"撞衫"翻译为 clothing clashing。除此译文之外,笔者发现,"撞衫"一词还可译为 outfit clash。然而,王逢鑫教授在《环球时报》2010 年 8 月 18 日的"翻译点津"栏目中撰文指出,"撞衫"一词不可用 clash 来译,因为"to clash 的意思是 to look ugly when put together,即'不协调'、'不搭配'。没有'撞衫'的意思。"他还特地举出下面这个汉英对译的例子来说明自己的观点:

影星很忌讳穿衣服不搭配。

Outfit clashes are taboo to movie stars.

王教授的观点有一定的道理,因为 clash 一词作动词用时意思的确是"[颜色或花样]不搭配、不协调(if two colors or patterns clash, they look very bad together)"。例如:That purple tie clashes with your red shirt.(那条紫色领带与你的红衬衫不相配。)

然而,clothing clashing 和 outfit clash 中的 clashing 和 clash 是否就不能译为"撞",而要译为"不搭配"、"不协调"呢? 其实也不尽然,因为当你的衣服和别人的衣服 clash 的时候,肯定不会牵扯到"不搭配"、"不协调"的问题,你自己的衣服怎么会和别人的衣服不搭配、不协调呢? 其实,只有你自己所穿的衣服才有可能会上下或颜色或式样不搭配、不协调。譬如在"That purple tie clashes with your red shirt."这个例子中,也是讲这个人身上的领带与他所穿的红色衬衣不协调、不搭配,而非是讲他的领带和别人穿的衣服不协调、不搭配。所以,我们认为,汉语中的"撞衫"完全可以译为 clothing clashing 和 outfit clash。下列摘自原版英文的例证也可以佐证笔者的观点:

1. Everyone wants to have her wedding dress only for herself; she does not expect to wear the same with others. **Clothing clashing** is really bad experience for any girls, especially for the brides.

2. Avoid **clothing clashing** and not wear the same dress to take part in contiguous parties. It seems a little rigor to have this requirement, but compared with the embarrassment of wearing the same dress with another

lady in the party, I think try to wear different dress in different parties can be reasonable and acceptable.

3. **Outfit clash** at fashions on the field

IT'S every woman's nightmare to be caught in the very same outfit at a very public outing.

So just imagine the embarrassment of Channel 9's Elise Mooney when it happened to her while presenting fashions on the field at Guineas Day at Caulfield racecourse.

One of the finalists was wearing the same black and white dress from Ink of Chadstone as Mooney presented her on stage.

The crowd burst into hoots of laughter as Mooney cracked up.

The A Current Affair reporter took it all in good spirit and had a good laugh over the incident in the Pegasus Club marquee.

But by then she was wearing a coat over the dress.

——*Herald Sun*, 2007 – 10 – 15

最后，值得一提的是，只要译者能够区分清楚比较的对象，clash 的动词形式完全可以用来翻译"撞衫"。这里仍然以王逢鑫教授文中的例子为例。王教授认为，"这位女演员走红地毯时发现与另一位影星撞衫了。"这句话翻译为"When this actress was walking on the red carpet, she found her outfit clashed with another film star."属于误译。但笔者认为，这个英文译文并没有错误，因为比较的对象是完全不同的两个人，所以 clash 在这个地方不可能是"不搭配"、"不协调"的意思，只能是"撞衫"的意思。而如果把这个英文句子变为"The actress found her dress clashed with her shoes（in color/style）."，比较的是一个人身上的不同服饰，这才是"不搭配"、"不协调"。

综上所述，汉语"撞衫"一词既可以注重传意，译为 wear an identical/the same clothes/dress with sb. at a public occasion，也可以形神兼顾，译为 clothing clashing 和 outfit clash。

走 光

　　"走光"一词近来颇为流行,有美女不小心走光的,也有明星故意走光的。网上更是有不少所谓的"走光图"。至于如何才算"走光",似乎还有不少争议。譬如,有人说,穿透视装不穿内衣,就是走光;有人说,只要不露点都不算走光;又有人说,故意性感不叫走光,无意间露了才叫走光。但大致而言,较轻的"走光"应该是指不小心露出内衣,而较为严重的"走光"则指露出不该露的身体隐私部位。

　　目前该词的英译尚未见诸各汉英词典,但网络上却热衷于讨论其英文表达。譬如,有人望文生义将该词译为"go(走)light(光)",也有人直译为"accidental exposure of some intimate parts of human body",更有人直截了当地译为"accidental nudity"。

　　以上三种译文,"go light"为死译,不值一评。"accidental exposure of some intimate parts of human body"倒确实有走光的意思,但却只是解释。而"accidental nudity"不但译文生硬,而且"nudity"词不达意,与"走光"其实大相径庭,因为"nudity"的英文意思为"the state of being without clothes(裸体)"。

　　那么,"走光"如何用英文来表达呢? 答案是"wardrobe malfunction"。首先,我们来看看 *Macmillan English Dictionary for Advanced Learners* 对这个短语的定义:the accidental exposure of an intimate part of the body because of a problem with an article of clothing(由于衣服关系不小心暴露出部分身体隐私部位)。与我们的"走光"不谋而合! 其次,英文中的

"wardrobe malfunction"甚至比汉语中的"走光"一词更新,因为它是歌手贾斯汀·廷伯雷克(Justin Timberlake)在 2004 年第 38 届橄榄球超级碗大赛(Super Bowl)后所生造的一个委婉表达。在这次大赛中,实力派天后珍妮·杰克逊(Janet Jackson)和人气偶像贾斯汀·廷伯雷克受邀为本次盛会带来了表演节目,当时两人正在台上演唱贾斯汀的热门畅销单曲"Rock Your Body",孰不知表演进行到一半时,贾斯汀在做出一个姿态亲昵的单手罩住杰克逊胸部的动作后,后者紧身皮装的右胸部部分竟然突然破裂,导致这位流行乐天后的右边胸部整个呈现于亿万电视观众面前,场面一时颇为尴尬。赛后,贾斯汀·廷伯雷克就走光事件对公众致歉:"I am sorry that anyone was offended by the **wardrobe malfunction** during the halftime performance of the Super Bowl. It was not intentional and is regrettable.

——"Statement from Justin Timberlake," *PR Newswire*, 2004 - 02 - 01

该表达一经出现,即迅速流行,以至于 US Global Language Monitor 将其列为"2004 年对英语语言最具影响的好莱坞词或短语(Hollywood's Top Word or Phrase for Impact on the English Language in 2004)"。该词之所以如此流行,大概是因为它用一种正式的、准技术性(quasi-technical)的短语表达出了这样一种戏剧性的场面。

当然,汉语中的"走光"似乎可以作动词也可以作名词,而英语中与"wardrobe malfunction"构成的搭配则有:have / suffer a wardrobe malfunction; a slight wardrobe malfunction; celebrity wardrobe malfunction,例如:

That's all right. I just had a wardrobe malfunction, but I'm fixing that up.

—"Weather Report," *The Early Show*, 2004 - 02 - 02

She suffered a slight, slight wardrobe malfunction when her hot pink bra peeked out from her top.

celebrity wardrobe malfunction pictures

主要参考文献

Ben Hu, *Exchanging a Leopard Cat for a Prince*：*Famous Trials by Lord Bao*, Beijing：Foreign Languages Press, 1997.

Chun Yan, *Lord Bao Interrogates the Stone*, Beijing：Dolphin Books, 1997.

Macmillan English Dictionary for Advanced Learners, Beijing：Foreign Language Teaching and Research Press, 2002.

Thompson, Della, *The Concise Oxford Dictionary* (ninth edition), Beijing：Foreign Language Teaching and Research Press, 2000.

Westmacott, Charles, *Slang Dictionary*, Totowa, N. J：Rowan and Littlefield, 1869.

崔山佳,"按揭"是外来词吗?,《辞书研究》,2010(4)。

程超凡,《英汉—汉英双向法律词典》,北京:法律出版社,2006。

邓巨,以语境化实现翻译的忠实原则——农家乐翻译论,《西南民族大学学报》,2009(3)。

赫迎红,双语词典编纂的借鉴与创新——以《新时代汉英大词典》和《新世纪汉英大词典》为例,《辞书研究》,2007(5)。

何俊,"留守儿童"英译辨,《湖南城市学院学报》,2008(6)。

惠宇,《新世纪汉英大词典》,北京:外语教学与研究出版社,2003。

霍恩比,《牛津高阶英汉双解词典》(第六版),北京:商务印书馆,2004。

江平,《中国司法大词典》,北京:人民法院出版社,2002。

金其斌,谈一些汉语新词语的英译问题——评《新华新词语词典》部分词条的译文,《中国翻译》,2003(6)。

《朗文当代高级英语辞典》,北京:商务印书馆,2000。

《朗文当代高级英语词典》(英英·英汉双解),北京:外语教学与研究出版社,2004。

亢世勇,《新词语大词典》,上海:上海辞书出版社,2003。

李宗锷、潘慧,《英汉法律大词典》,香港:商务印书馆(香港)有限公司,2004。

刘谨,新词新义荟萃:负翁,《辞书研究》,2006(2)。

刘谨,新词新义荟萃:啃老族,《辞书研究》,2006(2)。

刘谨,新词新义荟萃:月光族,《辞书研究》,2006(2)。

陆谷孙,《英汉大词典补编》,上海:上海译文出版社,1999。

陆谷孙,《英汉大词典》(第二版),上海:上海译文出版社,2007。

罗荣华,说"型男"道"索女",《现代语文》(语言研究),2009(36)。

马季,《相声艺术漫谈》,广州:广东人民出版社,1980。

《麦克米伦高阶英语词典》,北京:外语教学与研究出版社,2002。

《牛津大学英语词典》,上海:上海译文出版社,2005。

齐奥尔格·西美尔,时尚心理的社会学研究,载刘小枫译《金钱、性别、现代生活风格》,上海:学林出版社,2000。

秦海,"形象工程"和"面子工程",《杂文选刊(上旬版)》,2008(8)。

曲伟、韩明安,《当代汉语新词词典》,北京:中国大百科全书出版社,2004。

商务印书馆辞书研究中心,《新华新词语词典》,北京:商务印书馆,2003。

邵景安、刘秀华,城市病及大城市发展对策,《湖南农业大学学报》(社会科学版),2002(3)。

宋雷,《英汉法律用语大词典》,北京:法律出版社,2005。

孙万彪,《中级翻译教程》(第二版),上海:上海外语教育出版社,2003。

陶炼,新词新义荟萃:关键先生,《辞书研究》,2006(2)。

王均熙,《汉语新词词典》,上海:汉语大词典出版社,2006。

王弄笙,"汉英翻译中的 CHINGLISH",《中国翻译》,2002(2)。

《韦氏新大学词典》(第九版),北京:世界图书出版公司北京公司,1995。

魏令查,流行新词语解读:房奴,《汉语世界》,2006(1)。

魏令查,流行新词语解读:月光族,《汉语世界》,2006(1)。

吴光华,《汉英综合大词典》,大连:大连理工大学出版社,2001。

吴光华,《汉英大词典》(第三版),上海:上海译文出版社,2010。

吴景荣、程镇球,《新时代汉英大词典》,北京:商务印书馆,2000。

吴思,《潜规则:中国历史中的真实游戏》,昆明:云南人民出版社,2001。

吴思,《血酬定律》,北京:语文出版社,2009。

谢阳群,信息化的兴起与内涵,《图书情报工作》,1996(2)。

薛波,《元照英美法词典》,北京:法律出版社,2003。

杨力,小议"形象大使"的译名,《辞书研究》,2009(6)。

杨全红,《汉英词语翻译探微》,上海:汉语大词典出版社,2003。

杨全红,从"双赢"的释义及英译说开去,《东方翻译》,2010(3)。

杨晓鲁,《音乐电视(MTV)编导艺术》,北京:世界知识出版社,2000。

姚小平,《汉英词典》(第三版),北京:外语教学与研究出版社,2010。

叶敬忠、詹姆斯·莫瑞,《关注留守儿童》,北京:社会科学文献出版社,2005。

张健,汉语新词翻译中出现的失误,《北京第二外语学院学报》,2003(2)。

张沛,"型男索女"一箩筐,《咬文嚼字》,2006(4)。

张世银,城市病防范与治理,《中国外资》,2008(8)。

赵诚,"弔诡"、"公职",《词库建设通讯》,1997(12)。

赵刚,试论汉英词典中配套词的处理,载《双语词典研究》,上海:上海外语教育出
　　版社,2005。

赵刚,小议"宅男"、"宅女"的英译,《东方翻译》,2011(2)。

赵刚,"城市病"英译探究,《中国科技术语》,2011(1)。

赵刚,评〈新华新词语词典〉中法律词目的英译——兼谈对双语辞书编纂者的要
　　求,载《面向翻译的术语研究论文集》,南京:南京大学出版社,2011。

赵刚,新词语新说:白骨精,《辞书研究》,2009(1)。

赵刚,新词语新说:"人治"和"法治"怎么译?,《辞书研究》,2008(6)。

赵刚,新词语新说:倒按揭及其英译,《辞书研究》,2008(2)。

赵刚,新词语新说:潜规则,《辞书研究》,2007(5)。

赵刚,新词语新说:关键先生,《辞书研究》,2007(4)。

赵刚,新词语新说:走光,《辞书研究》,2007(3)。

赵刚,也评《新华新词语词典》的英译,载《双语词典新论》,成都:四川人民出版
　　社,2007

赵刚,探微求是,有的放矢——就一些新词的翻译问题与金其斌先生商榷,《上海
　　翻译》,2005年双语词典学专刊。

赵刚,因特网与汉英词典的编撰,《西安外国语学院学报》,2005(1)。

郑定欧,《香港粤语词典》,南京:江苏教育出版社,1997。

中国社会科学院语言研究所词典编纂室,《现代汉语词典》(2002 增补本),北京:
　　商务印书馆,2002。

中国社会科学院语言研究所词典编纂室,《现代汉语词典》(第五版),北京:商务
　　印书馆,2005。

周邦友,"充电"的英译,《辞书研究》,2008(1)。

周邦友,小议'休渔'的英译,《辞书研究》,2009(5)。

图书在版编目（CIP）数据

曲径通幽——汉语新词英译析辨百例/赵刚,陈翔著.
—上海：上海三联书店,2012.3
ISBN 978-7-5426-3762-8

Ⅰ.①曲…　Ⅱ.①赵…②陈…　Ⅲ.①英语—翻译—
文集　Ⅳ.①H315.9-53

中国版本图书馆 CIP 数据核字（2012）第 022745 号

.

曲径通幽——汉语新词英译析辨百例

著　　者／赵　刚　陈　翔

责任编辑／王笑红
装帧设计／豫　苏
监　　制／李　敏
责任校对／张大伟　殷亚平

出版发行／上海三联书店
　　　　　（201199）中国上海都市路 4855 号 2 座 10 楼
邮购电话／24175971
印　　刷／上海叶大印务发展有限公司

版　　次／2012 年 3 月第 1 版
印　　次／2012 年 3 月第 1 次印刷
开　　本／890×1240　1/32
字　　数／260 千字
印　　张／10
书　　号／ISBN 978-7-5426-3762-8/H·19
定　　价／38.00 元